Zoomigurumi
Favorites

COMPILED WITH CARE BY
Amigurumi.com

Copyright © 2022 Meteoor BV (BE0550756201)

Zoomigurumi Favorites
The 30 Best-Loved Amigurumi Patterns

Fourth print run, April 2024

First published, April 2022 by
Meteoor BV, Antwerp, Belgium
www.meteoorbooks.com
hello@meteoorbooks.com

Pictures by Sophie Peirsman (sophiepeirsman.be) and
Joost de Wolf (JdW fotografie)
Printed and bound by Grafistar

ISBN 978-949164-341-5
D/2022/13.531/1

A catalogue record for this book is available from the Royal
Library of Belgium.

HI!

Welcome to the wonderful world of amigurumi crochet! This best-of book collects the 30 most loved designs from the popular Zoomigurumi series into one. With this collection, we hope to inspire everyone who has a soft spot for cute crafts and cuddly animals to give it a try. You'll be surprised to find how easy it is to make them all.

In this book you'll meet 30 fan favorites from designers all over the world. There's plenty to choose from, and if you're feeling a bit playful, you can adjust the yarn color, facial expressions and accessories to make your amigurumi friend truly yours.

Is this your first time making amigurumi or do you want to refresh your stitch knowledge? The clear illustrations and handy video tutorials at the beginning of the book will help you master the stitches and techniques in no time. Projects cover a variety of skill levels, from beginner-friendly to suitable for advanced crocheters, and are accompanied by easy-to-follow instructions. Surprise your friends and family with handmade gifts, or simply make them for yourself.

Have you made a design and do you want to share your cute crochetwork and passion for amigurumi with your fellow crochet fans? We'd love to see your photos on www.amigurumi.com/3800 or on Instagram with #zoomigurumifavorites.

We wish you a lot of fun crocheting!

In this book you will find

Stitches
& info

BASIC STITCHES

If this is your first time making amigurumi, you might find it useful to have a tutorial at hand. With the stitches explained on the following pages you can make all of the amigurumi in this book. We suggest you practice the basic stitches before you start making one of the designs. This will help you to read the patterns and abbreviations more comfortably, without having to browse back to these pages.

STITCH TUTORIAL VIDEOS

With each stitch explanation we have included a URL and QR code that will take you to our online stitch tutorial video, showing the technique step by step. Simply follow the link or scan the QR code with your smartphone. Phones with iOS will scan the QR code automatically in camera mode. For phones with Android you may need to activate QR code scanning or install a separate QR Reader app.

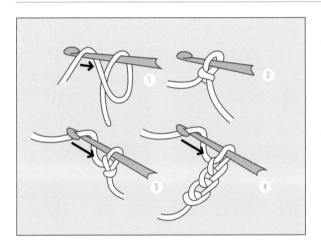

CHAIN *(abbreviation: ch)*

This stitch is the basis for many crochet patterns. If you're working in rows, your first row will be a series of chain stitches. Use the hook to draw the yarn through the loop (1) and pull the loop until tight (2). Wrap the yarn over the hook from back to front. Pull the hook, carrying the yarn, through the loop already on your hook (3). You have now completed one chain stitch. Repeat these steps as indicated in the pattern to create a foundation chain (4).

Scan or visit
www.stitch.show/ch
for the video tutorial

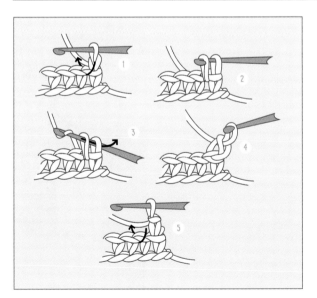

SINGLE CROCHET *(abbreviation: sc)*

Single crochet is the stitch that will be most frequently used in this book. Insert the hook into the next stitch (1) and wrap the yarn over the hook. Draw the yarn through the stitch (2). You will see that there are now two loops on the hook. Wrap the yarn over the hook again and pull it through both loops at once (3). You have now completed one single crochet (4). Insert the hook into the next stitch to continue (5).

Scan or visit
www.stitch.show/sc
for the video tutorial

Scan or visit www.stitch. show/slst for the video tutorial

SLIP STITCH *(abbreviation: slst)*

A slip stitch is used to move across one or more stitches at once or to finish a piece. Insert your hook into the next stitch (1). Wrap the yarn over the hook and pull it through both loops at once (2).

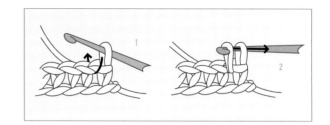

HALF DOUBLE CROCHET *(abbreviation: hdc)*

(When starting a new row of half double crochet, work two chain stitches to gain height.) Bring your yarn over the hook from back to front before placing the hook in the stitch (1). Wrap the yarn over the hook and draw the yarn through the stitch. You now have three loops on the hook (2). Wrap the yarn over the hook again and pull it through all three loops on the hook (3). You have completed your first half double crochet. To continue, bring your yarn over the hook and insert it in the next stitch (4).

Scan or visit www.stitch. show/hdc for the video tutorial

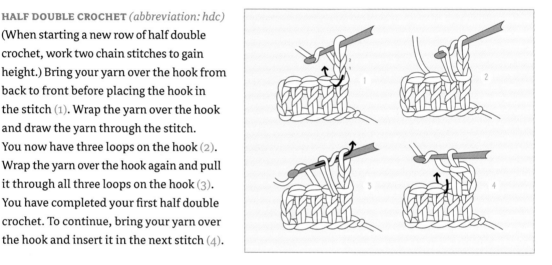

DOUBLE CROCHET *(abbreviation: dc)*

(When starting a new row of double crochet, work three chain stitches to gain height.) Bring your yarn over the hook from back to front before placing the hook in the stitch (1). Wrap the yarn over the hook and draw the yarn through the stitch. You now have three loops on the hook (2). Wrap the yarn over the hook again and pull it through the first two loops on the hook (3). You now have two loops on the hook. Wrap the yarn over the hook one last time and pull it through both loops on the hook (4). You have now completed one double crochet. To continue, bring your yarn over the hook and insert it in the next stitch (5).

Scan or visit www.stitch.show/dc for the video tutorial

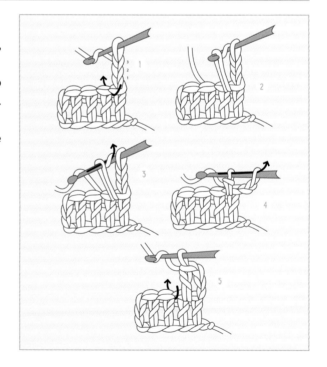

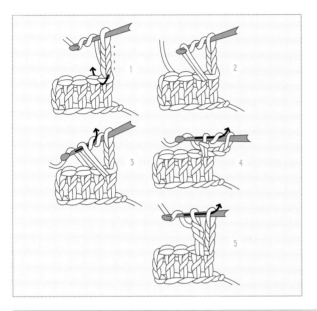

TRIPLE CROCHET *(abbreviation: tr)*

(When starting a new row of triple crochet, work four chain stitches to gain height.) Bring your yarn over the hook twice before placing the hook in the stitch (1). Wrap the yarn over the hook and draw the yarn through the stitch (2). Wrap the yarn over the hook again and pull it through the first two loops on the hook (3). Repeat this last step twice (4, 5). You have now completed one triple crochet. To continue, bring your yarn over the hook twice and insert it in the next stitch.

Scan or visit www.stitch.show/tr for the video tutorial

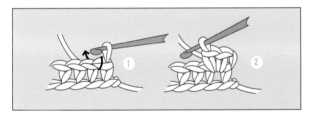

INCREASE *(abbreviation: inc)*

To increase you make two single crochet stitches in the next stitch.

Scan or visit www.stitch.show/inc for the video tutorial

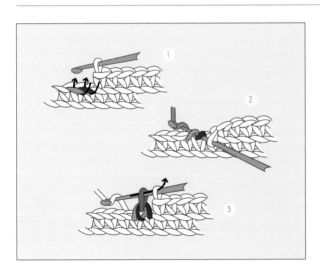

INVISIBLE DECREASE *(abbreviation: dec)*

The invisible decrease is a method which will make your decrease stitch look much like the other stitches in the row, resulting in a smooth and even crochet fabric. Insert the hook in the front loop of your first stitch. Now immediately insert your hook in the front loop of the second stitch (1). You now have three loops on your hook. Wrap the yarn over the hook and pull it through the first two loops on the hook (2). Wrap the yarn over the hook again and pull it through the remaining two loops on the hook (3). You have now completed one invisible decrease.

Scan or visit www.stitch.show/dec for the video tutorial

**INVISIBLY DECREASE 3 STITCHES
AT ONCE** *(abbreviation: sc3tog)*

Scan or visit
www.stitch.show/
sc3tog
for the video tutorial
↓

Insert the hook under the front loop only of
the next three stitches (1). This gives you four
loops on the hook (2). Wrap the yarn over the
hook and pull it through the first three loops
on the hook. Wrap the yarn over the hook
again and pull it through the remaining
two loops on the hook (3). You have now
completed one sc3tog.

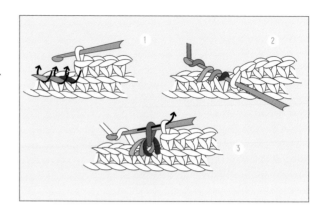

CROCHET AROUND A FOUNDATION CHAIN

Some pieces start with an oval instead of
a circle. You make an oval by crocheting
around a foundation chain. Crochet a
foundation chain with as many chains as
mentioned in the pattern. Skip the first chain
on the hook (1) and work a sc stitch in the
next chain stitch (2, 3). Work your crochet
stitches into each chain across as mentioned
in the pattern. The last stitch before turning
is usually an increase stitch (4). Now, turn
your work upside down to work into the
underside of the chain stitches. You'll notice
that only one loop is available, simply insert
your crochet hook in this loop (5). Work
your stitches into each chain across. When
finished, your last stitch should be next to
the first stitch you made (6). You can now
continue working in spirals.

Scan or visit
www.stitch.show/
oval
for the video
tutorial
↓

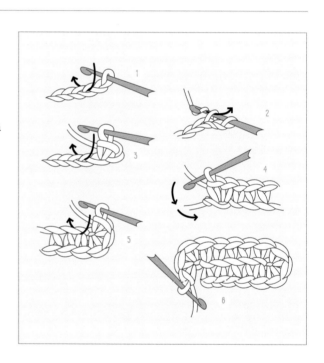

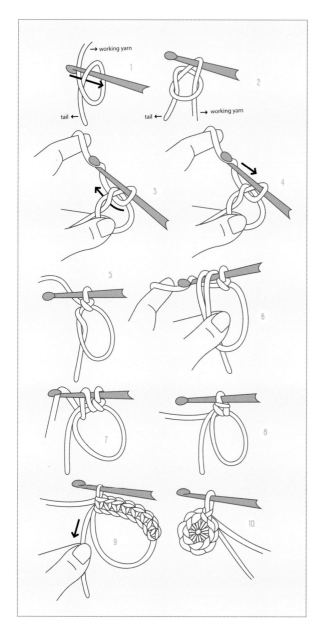

MAGIC RING

A magic ring is the ideal way to start crocheting in the round. You start by crocheting over an adjustable loop and finally pull the loop tight when you have finished the required number of stitches. The advantage of this method is that there's no hole left in the middle of your starting round.

Start with the yarn crossed to form a circle (1). Draw up a loop with your hook, but don't pull it tight (2). Hold the circle with your index finger and thumb and wrap the working yarn over your middle finger (3). Make one chain stitch by wrapping the yarn over the hook and pulling it through the loop on the hook (4, 5). Now insert your hook into the loop and underneath the tail. Wrap the yarn over the hook and draw up a loop (6). Wrap the yarn over the hook again (7) and pull it through both loops on the hook. You have now completed your first single crochet stitch (8). Continue to crochet (repeating step 6, 7, 8) until you have the required number of stitches as mentioned in the pattern. Now grab the yarn tail and pull to draw the center of the ring tightly closed (9, 10). You can now begin your second round by crocheting into the first single crochet stitch of the magic ring. You can use a stitch marker to remember where you started.

If you don't want to use this technique, you can start each piece using the following technique: ch 2, x sc into the second chain from the hook – where x is the number of sc stitches you would make in your magic ring.

Scan or visit
www.stitch.show/
magicring
for the video tutorial

CROCHET INTO A RING

Scan or visit
www.stitch.show/
ring
for the video
tutorial
↓

When you want a center ring that is open, you start with a series of chain stitches and close with a slip stitch in the first chain to make a ring (1). Insert your hook into the center of the ring, instead of into the chain stitch (2) and complete the stitch in the usual way. Follow the pattern instructions to determine how many stitches to work into the ring.

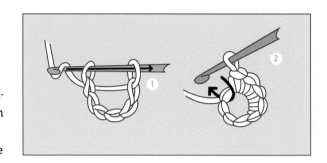

FRONT LOOPS ONLY *(abbreviation: FLO)* **AND BACK LOOPS ONLY** *(abbreviation: BLO)*

Scan or visit
www.stitch.show/
FLO-BLO
for the video tutorial
↓

When making a crochet stitch, you end up with two loops at the top of the stitch, a front loop towards you (1) and a back loop (2). When asked to crochet FLO or BLO, you make the same stitch but leave one loop untouched.

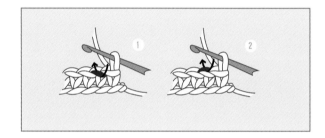

BACK POST OR FRONT POST SINGLE CROCHET *(abbreviation: BPsc, FPsc)*

Scan or visit
www.stitch.show/
BP-FP
for the video tutorial
↓

To make a back post or front post single crochet, insert the hook from right to left around the vertical post of the next stitch according to the picture. Wrap the yarn over the hook and draw up a loop. Finish the single crochet stitch as usual.

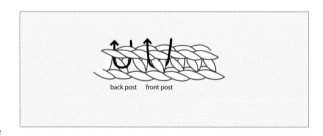

back post   front post

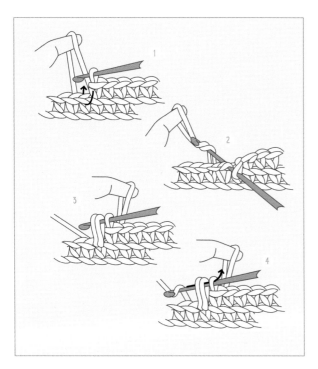

LOOP STITCH

Loop 1: Wrap a loop of yarn around your index finger (1). Insert your hook in the next stitch, grab both strands of the loop and draw them through the stitch (2). Make sure you draw this loop out to approx. 1.5" / 4 cm. You now have three loops on your hook (3). Now wrap your yarn around your hook and pull it through all three loops on your hook (4).

Loop 2: Make two loops as described above in the next stitch.

Scan or visit www.stitch.show/loop for the video tutorial

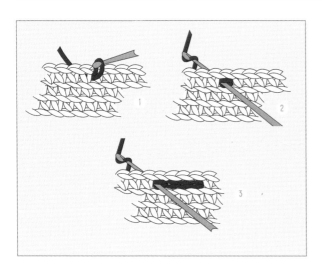

SURFACE SLIP STITCH

The surface slip stitch is an embellishment of slip stitches worked on top of the fabric of your crochetwork. Insert the hook from the right side to the wrong side where you want your line of slip stitches to start, now wrap the yarn over the hook and draw it through the stitch (1). Insert the hook in the next stitch, wrap the yarn over the hook (2) and pull it through the stitch and the loop on the hook. This is the start of your line of surface slip stitches. Repeat this to the end of your crochetwork or in any shape you like (3).

Scan or visit www.stitch.show/ surfaceslst for the video tutorial

SURFACE SINGLE CROCHET

Scan or visit
www.stitch.show/
surfacesc
for the video
tutorial

Use a slip knot to tie the yarn onto the crochet hook. Insert the hook around the back horizontal bar of the stitch you're working over (1). Wrap the yarn over the hook, pull that loop through (2). Wrap the yarn over the tip of the hook again (3) and carefully pull it through both loops on the hook.

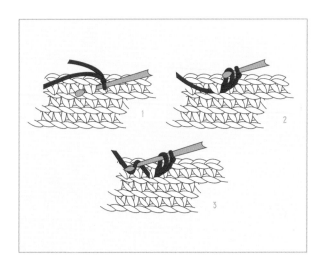

FRENCH KNOT

The French knot is a sewing stitch. Insert a threaded embroidery needle from the back to the front through the stitch where you want the knot to show. Keep the tip of the needle flat against your crochetwork and wrap the yarn around your needle twice (1). Carefully pull the needle through these loops so that you end up with a double knot. Insert the needle in the crochet stitch next to the knot (2) – not in the same stitch, this will make the knot disappear – and fasten the yarn at the back.

Scan or visit
www.stitch.show/
frenchknot
for the video tutorial

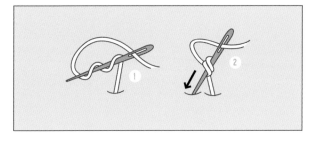

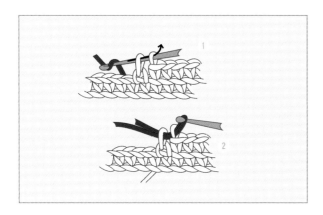

INVISIBLE COLOR CHANGE

When you want to switch from one color to the next, you work to within two stitches before a color change. Make the next stitch as usual, but don't pull the final loop through (1). Instead, wrap the new color of yarn around your hook and pull it through the remaining loops (2). To make a neat color change, you can make the first stitch in the new color a slip stitch instead of a single crochet. Don't pull the slip stitch too tight or it will be difficult to crochet into in the next round. Tie the loose tails in a knot and leave them on the inside.

Scan or visit
www.stitch.show/
colorchange
for the video tutorial

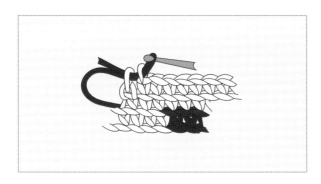

JACQUARD

When working jacquard, you work with two colors and leave the yarn you don't use on the back (inside) of the work. When it's time to use it again, you pick up the yarn and carry it across the back (inside) of your work before making the next color change. Take into account that a color change always starts a stitch before. The strands that remain inside your crochet-work between color changes must be loose enough so that the fabric doesn't pucker.

Scan or visit
www.stitch.show/
jacquard
for the video tutorial

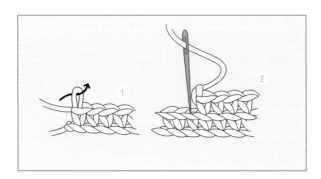

FASTENING OFF

When you've finished crocheting, cut the yarn a couple of inches / cm from your last stitch. Pull the yarn through the last loop until it's all the way through (1). You now have a finished knot. Thread the long tail through a tapestry needle and insert your tapestry needle through the back loop of the next stitch (2). This way the finishing knot will remain invisible in your finished piece. You can use this piece of yarn to continue sewing the pieces together.

Scan or visit
www.stitch.show/
fastenoff
for the video tutorial

JOINING ALL PARTS

First, pin the parts you want to sew to one another, so you can evaluate the result and adjust if necessary. If possible, use the leftover yarn tail from when you fastened off, or use a new length of the same yarn color of one of the pieces that you want to join.

When the different pieces are open: position the piece on the body and sew all around it, going through the front stitches of both the extremity and the body.

When the opening of the different pieces is sewn closed before attaching them to the body: line up the stitches of one side with the other side and sew through the front loop of one side and the back loop of the other side. Use the same color of yarn as the pieces you want to join together.

Always make sure the pieces are securely attached so that they can't be pulled off. Make small, neat stitches and try to make them show as little as possible.

SKILL LEVEL

easy (✳), intermediate (✳ ✳), advanced (✳ ✳ ✳) Every pattern is marked with a skill level to indicate how easy they are to make. If this is your first time making amigurumi, it's best to start with an easy pattern and work up to the intermediate and advanced ones.

PATTERN STRUCTURE

Unless mentioned, the patterns in this book are worked in **continuous spirals**, not in joined rounds.

Crocheting in spirals can be confusing since there's no clear indication of where a new round begins and the previous one ends. To keep track of the rounds, you can mark the end of a round with a stitch marker or safety pin. After crocheting the next round, you should end up right above your stitch marker. Move your stitch marker at the end of each round to keep track of where you are.

At the beginning of each line you will find 'Rnd + a number' to indicate which round you are in. If a round is repeated, you'll read 'Rnd 9 – 12', for example. You

then repeat this round four times, crocheting the stitches in round 9, 10, 11 and 12.

Some parts in this book are worked in **joined rounds**, not continuous spirals. In this case, this is clearly mentioned before you start. You'll see that these rounds are closed with a slip stitch in the first stitch of the round, followed by a chain. The first stitch of the next round is made in the same stitch where you crocheted the last slip stitch.

Occasionally it happens that we crochet in **rows**, going back and forth instead of working around a piece. When we switch to rows, it will be indicated with 'Row + a number'.

At the end of each line you will find the number of stitches you should have indicated between square brackets, for example [9]. When in doubt, take a moment to check your stitch count.

When parts of the instructions repeat throughout the round, we place them between rounded brackets, followed by the number of times this part should be worked. We do this to shorten the pattern and make it less cluttered.

AMIGURUMI GALLERY

With each pattern, we have included a URL and QR code that will take you to that character's dedicated online gallery. Share your finished amigurumi, find inspiration in the color and yarn choices of your fellow crocheters and enjoy the fun of crocheting. Simply follow the link or scan the QR code with your mobile phone. Phones with iOS will scan the QR code automatically in camera mode. For phones with Android you may need to activate QR code scanning or install a separate QR Reader app.

Scan or visit **www.amigurumi.com/3800/** to share pictures of the creations you made with patterns from this book or find inspiration in characters made by others.

BASIC MATERIALS

YARN

For every pattern in this book we've listed the materials used to create that design, including the yarn type used by the designer. Don't feel tied to the choices of yarn weight though: any weight of cotton, acrylic or wool can be used as a substitute, provided you use the right crochet hook accordingly.

The patterns don't give the yarn quantity. The amounts are rather small and will vary according to how loosely or tightly you crochet. You could use some of the remnants from other projects or start with a new ball of yarn. One or two balls per color is usually enough.

CROCHET HOOKS

Not only yarn, but hooks as well come in different sorts and sizes. Bigger hooks make bigger stitches than smaller ones. It is important to match the right hook size with the right weight of yarn. In the table on this page you find the standard hook size recommended for each yarn weight. For amigurumi, however, you generally use a hook two or three sizes smaller than what is recommended for your yarn and in this table. The crochet fabric should be quite tight, without any gaps through which the stuffing can escape. Using a smaller hook makes it easier to achieve this.

Hooks are usually made from aluminum or steel.

Metal hooks tend to slip between the stitches more easily. Preferably choose a crochet hook with a rubber or ergonomic handle.

STITCH MARKER

A stitch marker is a small metal or plastic clip. It's a simple tool to mark your starting point and give you the assurance that you've made the right number of stitches in each round. Mark the last stitch of the round with your stitch marker and move it with each round.

STUFFING

For the filling, polyester fiberfill is advised. You can purchase this at any craft shop. It is inexpensive, washable and non-allergenic. Be careful not to over-stuff your amigurumi as the stuffing might stretch the fabric and show through.

FACIAL FEATURES

For some patterns safety eyes are used. These are widely available in craft shops. Be careful when you apply safety eyes: once you put the washer on, you won't be able to pull it off again, so make sure that the post is where you want it to be before attaching the washer.

If you're crocheting for children under the age of three, it is advised to embroider the facial features for safety. For embroidery, a tapestry needle with a rounded tip is used.

NUMBER (SYMBOL)	1	2	3	4	5	6
CATEGORY NAME	super fine	fine	light	medium	heavy	very heavy
UK YARN TYPE	3 ply	4 ply	double knitting (DK)	aran	chunky	super chunky
US YARN TYPE	fingering	sport	light worsted	worsted	bulky	extra bulky
RECOMMENDED HOOK IN US SIZE *	B-1 to E-4	E-4 to 7	7 to I-9	I-9 to K-10 1/2	K-10 1/2 to M-13	M-13 and larger
RECOMMENDED HOOK IN METRIC SIZE *	2.25 to 3.5mm	3.5 to 4.5mm	4.5 to 5.5mm	5.5 to 6.5mm	6.5 to 9mm	9 mm and larger

* Do note: for amigurumi you generally use a hook two or three sizes smaller than what is recommended for your yarn and in this table.

Patterns

KAI
THE
KOALA

by Lemon Yarn Creations
(Andreia Ferreira)

SKILL LEVEL: ★ ★

SIZE: 4"/ 10 cm tall when made with the indicated yarn.

MATERIALS:
– Light worsted weight yarn in light gray, dark gray, light green, pink (leftover)
– Chunky weight fluffy yarn in white (the pattern also includes an option for ears made with regular light worsted weight yarn)
– B-1 / 2.5 mm crochet hook
– US-7 / 4.5 mm crochet hook
– Black embroidery thread
– Sewing needle
– Yarn needle
– Stitch markers
– Fiberfill for stuffing

AMIGURUMI GALLERY

Scan or visit
www.amigurumi.com/3404
to share pictures and find inspiration.

NOTE: Use a B-1 / 2.5 mm crochet hook, unless the pattern states differently.

HEAD *(in light gray yarn)*

Starting at the top of the head.

Rnd 1: start 6 sc in a magic ring [6]

Rnd 2: inc in all 6 st [12]

Rnd 3: (sc in next st, inc in next st) repeat 6 times [18]

Rnd 4: (sc in next 2 st, inc in next st) repeat 6 times [24]

Rnd 5: (sc in next 3 st, inc in next st) repeat 6 times [30]

Rnd 6: (sc in next 4 st, inc in next st) repeat 6 times [36]

Rnd 7: (sc in next 5 st, inc in next st) repeat 6 times [42]

Rnd 8: (sc in next 6 st, inc in next st) repeat 6 times [48]

Rnd 9: (sc in next 7 st, inc in next st) repeat 6 times [54]

Rnd 10: (sc in next 8 st, inc in next st) repeat 6 times [60]

Rnd 11 – 16: sc in all 60 st [60]

Rnd 17: (sc in next 9 st, inc in next st) repeat 6 times [66]

Rnd 18: sc in all 66 st [66]

 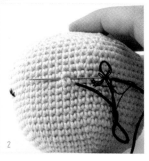  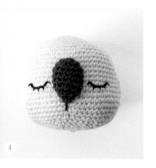

Rnd 19: sc in next 18 st, (inc in next st, sc in next st) repeat 3 times, sc in next 16 st, (sc in next st, inc in next st) repeat 3 times, sc in next 20 st [72]

Rnd 20 – 21: sc in all 72 st [72]

Rnd 22: (sc in next 10 st, dec) repeat 6 times [66]

Rnd 23: (sc in next 9 st, dec) repeat 6 times [60]

Rnd 24: (sc in next 8 st, dec) repeat 6 times [54]

Rnd 25: (sc in next 7 st, dec) repeat 6 times [48]

Rnd 26: (sc in next 6 st, dec) repeat 6 times [42]

Stuff the head with fiberfill and continue stuffing as you go.

Rnd 27: (sc in next 5 st, dec) repeat 6 times [36]

Rnd 28: (sc in next 4 st, dec) repeat 6 times [30]

Rnd 29: (sc in next 3 st, dec) repeat 6 times [24]

Rnd 30: (sc in next 2 st, dec) repeat 6 times [18]

Rnd 31: (sc in next st, dec) repeat 6 times [12]

Rnd 32: dec 6 times [6]

Fasten off, leaving a yarn tail. Using your yarn needle, weave the yarn tail through the front loop of each remaining stitch and pull it tight to close. Weave in the yarn end.

Use black embroidery thread and a sewing needle to embroider the eyes with backstitches on round 17. The eyes are 5 stitches wide and start on the alignment of the inner increase of round 19 (pictures 1-2). After embroidering the eyes, wrap the thread around each stitch to make a thicker line. Tie the loose ends together and hide them inside the head (picture 3). To add the bottom lashes, separate your thread, using only half the number of strands, and sew a small line through each of the stitches of the eyes on round 18, making 5 lashes in total.

NOSE *(in dark gray yarn)*

Rnd 1: start 6 sc in a magic ring [6]

Rnd 2: inc in all 6 st [12]

Rnd 3 – 6: sc in all 12 st [12]

Rnd 7: (sc in next 2 st, dec) repeat 3 times [9]

Rnd 8: (sc in next, dec) repeat 3 times [6]

Fasten off, leaving a long tail for sewing. The nose doesn't need to be stuffed. Using your yarn needle, weave the yarn tail through the front loop of each remaining stitch and pull it tight to close. Sew the nose between the eyes, between rounds 13 and 20. For the mouth, embroider a line across 2 rounds, below the nose (picture 4).

CHEEK *(make 2, in pink yarn)*

Rnd 1: start 5 sc in a magic ring [5]

Rnd 2: inc in all 5 st [10]

Rnd 3: (sc in next st, inc in next st) repeat 5 times [15]
Fasten off, leaving a long tail for sewing. Sew the cheeks next to the eyes, between rounds 18 and 22. They should cover the increase of round 19 of the head.

EAR – OPTION 1 *(make 2, in fluffy white yarn, with a US-7 / 4.5 mm hook)*

Rnd 1: start 6 sc in a magic ring, ch 1, turn [6]
Continue crocheting in rows.

Row 2: inc in all 6 st, ch 1, turn [12]

Row 3: sc in all 12 st [12]
Fasten off, leaving a long tail for sewing. The ears don't need to be stuffed. Sew the ears to the sides of the head, between rounds 6 and 18, at 3 stitches from the cheeks.

EAR – OPTION 2 *(make 2, in light gray yarn)*

Rnd 1: start 6 sc in a magic ring [6]

Rnd 2: inc in all 6 st [12]

Rnd 3: (sc in next st, inc in next st) repeat 6 times [18]

Rnd 4: (sc in next 2 st, inc in next st) repeat 6 times [24]

Rnd 5: (sc in next 3 st, inc in next st) repeat 6 times [30]

Rnd 6 – 10: sc in all 30 st [30]
Fasten off, leaving a long tail for sewing. The ears don't need to be stuffed. Flatten the ears and sew them to the sides of the head, between rounds 6 and 18, at 3 stitches from the cheeks.

BODY *(in light gray yarn)*

Rnd 1: start 6 sc in a magic ring [6]

Rnd 2: inc in all 6 st [12]

Rnd 3: (sc in next st, inc in next st) repeat 6 times [18]

Rnd 4: (sc in next 2 st, inc in next st) repeat 6 times [24]

Rnd 5: (sc in next 3 st, inc in next st) repeat 6 times [30]

Rnd 6: (sc in next 4 st, inc in next st) repeat 6 times [36]

Rnd 7: (sc in next 5 st, inc in next st) repeat 6 times [42]

Rnd 8: (sc in next 6 st, inc in next st) repeat 6 times [48]

Rnd 9: (sc in next 7 st, inc in next st) repeat 6 times [54]

Rnd 10 – 15: sc in all 54 st [54]

Rnd 16: (dec, sc in next 2 st) repeat 3 times, sc in next 42 st [51]

Rnd 17: sc in all 51 st [51]

Rnd 18: (sc in next 15 st, dec) repeat 3 times [48]

Rnd 19: sc in all 48 st [48]

Rnd 20: (sc in next 6 st, dec) repeat 6 times [42]

Rnd 21 – 22: sc in all 42 st [42]

Rnd 23: (sc in next 5 st, dec) repeat 6 times [36]

Rnd 24 – 25: sc in all 36 st [36]
Stuff the body with fiberfill up to this point.

Rnd 26: (sc in next 4 st, dec) repeat 6 times [30]

Rnd 27 – 28: sc in all 30 st [30]

Rnd 29: (sc in next 3 st, dec) repeat 6 times [24]
Flatten the opening of the body and work the next round through both layers to close.

Rnd 30: sc in next 12 st [12] (pictures 5-6)
Fasten off, leaving a long tail for sewing. Pin the last round of the body to the bottom of the head over round 29, aligned with the nose. Sew from one side of round 29 of the head to the opposite side (picture 7). Continue

sewing the next body rounds to the head in the same manner until you reach round 22 of the body. This gives the koala a sleeping position (picture 8).

ARM *(make 2, in light gray yarn)*
Rnd 1: start 6 sc in a magic ring [6]
Rnd 2: inc in all 6 st [12]
Rnd 3 – 14: sc in all 12 st [12]
Stuff the arm lightly with fiberfill. Flatten the opening of the arm and work the next round through both layers to close.
Rnd 15: sc in next 6 st [6] (picture 9)
Fasten off, leaving a long tail for sewing. Sew the last round of the arms to the sides of the body, to round 19. Make a few stitches where the arms touch the head to keep them in place (picture 10).

LEG *(make 2, in light gray yarn)*
Rnd 1: start 6 sc in a magic ring [6]
Rnd 2: inc in all 6 st [12]
Rnd 3: (sc in next 3 st, inc in next st) repeat 3 times [15]
Rnd 4 – 7: sc in all 15 st [15]
Stuff the leg with fiberfill up to this point.
Rnd 8: inc in next 3 st, sc in next 12 st [18]
Rnd 9: (sc in next st, inc in next st) repeat 3 times, sc in next 12 st [21]
Rnd 10 – 12: sc in all 21 st [21]
Rnd 13: (sc in next 5 st, dec) repeat 3 times [18]
Rnd 14: (sc in next 4 st, dec) repeat 3 times [15]
Rnd 15: (sc in next 3 st, dec) repeat 3 times [12]
Rnd 16: dec 6 times [6]
Fasten off, leaving a long tail for sewing. Using your yarn needle, weave the yarn tail through the front

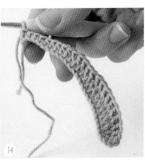

loop of each remaining stitch and pull it tight to close. Flatten the unstuffed part and sew the legs to the sides of the body between rounds 8 and 16, with the feet at the same height as the arms (pictures 11-12).

LEAF BLANKET *(in light green yarn)*
Ch 27. Crochet around both sides of the foundation chain.
Rnd 1: start in 4th ch from hook, tr in next 10 st (picture 13), dc in next 5 st, hdc in next 5 st, sc in next 4 st (picture 14). Continue on the other side of the foundation chain (picture 15), sc in next 4 st, hdc in next 5 st, dc in next 5 st, tr in next 10 st, ch 3, slst back into the foundation chain [48]
Rnd 2: hdc in the 3 unworked ch of the foundation ch (picture 16), 3 dc in next st, dc in next 12 st, hdc in next 6 st, sc in next 4 st, slst in next st, ch 1, slst in next st, sc in next 4 st, hdc in next 6 st, dc in next 12 st, 3 dc in next st, hdc in the 3 unworked ch [58]
Stem: slst in same st, ch 4, start in second ch from hook, slst in next 3 st, slst in next st on the leaf.
Fasten off, leaving a long tail for sewing if you'd like to attach the blanket to the back of the koala, or weave in the yarn end if you'd like to leave it as a separate piece.

CARLOS THE HUMMING-BIRD

by YOUnique Crafts (Noah McLeroy)

SKILL LEVEL: ✦ ✦

SIZE: 5" /13 cm tall when made with the indicated yarn.

MATERIALS:

– Worsted weight yarn in green, petrol blue, blue, gray and black (leftover)
– Safety eyes (12 mm)
– E-4 / 3.5 mm crochet hook
– Yarn needle
– Fiberfill for stuffing
– Pipe cleaners
– Stitch marker
– Scissors

AMIGURUMI GALLERY

Scan or visit
www.amigurumi.com/1403
to share pictures and find inspiration.

HEAD *(in green yarn)*

Rnd 1: start 6 sc in a magic ring [6]

Rnd 2: inc in all 6 st [12]

Rnd 3: (sc in next st, inc in next st) repeat 6 times [18]

Rnd 4: (sc in next 2 st, inc in next st) repeat 6 times [24]

Rnd 5: (sc in next 3 st, inc in next st) repeat 6 times [30]

Rnd 6: (sc in next 4 st, inc in next st) repeat 6 times [36]

Rnd 7: (sc in next 5 st, inc in next st) repeat 6 times [42]

Rnd 8: (sc in next 6 st, inc in next st) repeat 6 times [48]

Rnd 9: (sc in next 7 st, inc in next st) repeat 6 times [54]

Rnd 10 – 13: sc in all 54 st [54]

Rnd 14: (sc in next 8 st, inc in next st) repeat 6 times [60]
Mark stitches 22 and 40 of round 17, as a guide to place the safety eyes later.

Rnd 15 – 19: sc in all 60 st [60]

Rnd 20: (dec, sc in next 8 st) repeat 6 times [54]

Rnd 21: (dec, sc in next 7 st) repeat 6 times [48]

Rnd 22: (dec, sc in next 6 st) repeat 6 times [42]

Rnd 23: (dec, sc in next 5 st) repeat 6 times [36]

Rnd 24: (dec, sc in next 4 st) repeat 6 times [30]
Insert the safety eyes in the marked stitches. Stuff the head with fiberfill and continue stuffing as you go.
Rnd 25: (dec, sc in next 3 st) repeat 6 times [24]
Rnd 26: (dec, sc in next 2 st) repeat 6 times [18]
Rnd 27: (dec, sc in next st) repeat 6 times [12]
Rnd 28: dec 6 times [6]
Fasten off and weave in the yarn ends.

FACE SHAPING (optional)
With a strand of green yarn, insert your yarn needle in round 27 of the head and bring it back out next to

the inside of the right eye (picture 1). Wrap the yarn around the back of the eye (picture 2) and insert your needle back into the same stitch it came out of. Bring your needle back out in round 27, one stitch away from where your yarn entered into the head. Pull on both strands and tie them together (picture 3). Repeat these steps for the left eye and weave in all yarn ends.

BODY *(start in green yarn)*
NOTE: For Carlos' body, you continually switch between 2 colors of yarn. Handling of the yarns may be a little complicated. We recommend to use the jacquard technique (tutorial page 17, picture 4).

Rnd 1: start 6 sc in a magic ring [6]
Rnd 2: inc in all 6 st [12]
Rnd 3: (sc in next st, inc in next st) repeat 6 times [18]
Rnd 4: (sc in next 2 st, inc in next st) repeat 6 times [24]
Rnd 5: (sc in next 3 st, inc in next st) repeat 6 times [30]
Rnd 6: (sc in next 4 st, inc in next st) repeat 6 times [36]
Work the next rounds with color changes. The color change is indicated in italics before each part.
Rnd 7: *(green)* (sc in next 5 st, inc in next st) repeat 5 times, sc in next 2 st, *(petrol blue)* sc in next 3 st, inc in next st [42]
Rnd 8: sc in next 3 st, *(green)* (sc in next 3 st, inc in next st, sc in next 3 st) repeat 4 times, sc in next 3 st, inc in next st, *(petrol blue)* sc in next 6 st, inc in next st [48]
Rnd 9: sc in next 5 st, *(green)* sc in next 33 st, *(petrol blue)* sc in next 10 st [48]

Rnd 10: sc in next 8 st, *(green)* sc in next 30 st, *(petrol blue)* sc in next 10 st [48]

Rnd 11: sc in next 6 st, dec, sc in next st, *(green)* (sc in next 5 st, dec, sc in next st) repeat 3 times, sc in next 4 st, *(petrol blue)* sc in next st, dec, sc in next 6 st, dec [42]

Rnd 12: sc in next 9 st, *(green)* sc in next 24 st, *(petrol blue)* sc in next 9 st [42]

Rnd 13: sc in next 9 st, *(green)* sc in next 25 st, *(petrol blue)* sc in next 8 st [42]

Rnd 14: sc in next 5 st, dec, sc in next 2 st, *(green)* (sc in next 3 st, dec, sc in next 2 st) repeat 3 times, sc in next 3 st, dec, *(petrol blue)* sc in next 5 st, dec [36]

Rnd 15 – 16: sc in next 8 st, *(green)* sc in next 23 st, *(petrol blue)* sc in next 5 st [36]

Rnd 17: sc in next 4 st, dec, sc in next 2 st, *(green)* (sc in next 2 st, dec, sc in next 2 st) repeat 4 times, *(petrol blue)* sc in next 2 st, dec [30]

Rnd 18: sc in next st, slst in next st [2] Leave the remaining stitches unworked.

Fasten off, leaving long tails for sewing. Stuff the body with fiberfill. Sew the body to the bottom of the head. Ensure that the green part of the body is at the front and the petrol blue part of the body is at the back. Sew the green part with the green yarn tail and the petrol blue part with the petrol blue yarn tail.

CREST *(in petrol blue yarn)*

Ch 3. Crochet in rows.

Row 1: start in second ch from hook, inc in next 2 st, ch 1, turn [4]

Row 2 – 3: sc in all 4 st, ch 1, turn [4]

Row 4: sc in next st, inc in next 2 st, sc in next st, ch 1, turn [6]

Row 5: sc in all 6 st, ch 1, turn [6]

Row 6: sc in next 2 st, inc in next 2 st, sc in next 2 st, ch 1, turn [8]

Row 7: sc in all 8 st, ch 1, turn [8]

Row 8: sc in next 3 st, inc in next 2 st, sc in next 3 st, ch 1, turn [10]

Row 9: sc in all 10 st, ch 1, turn [10]

Row 10: sc in next 4 st, inc in next 2 st, sc in next 4 st, ch 1, turn [12]

Row 11: sc in all 12 st, ch 1, turn [12]

Row 12: sc in next 5 st, inc in next 2 st, sc in next 5 st, ch 1, turn [14]

Row 13 – 16: sc in all 14 st, ch 1, turn [14]

Row 17: sc in next 4 st, hdc in next st, dc in next 4 st, hdc in next st, sc in next 4 st, ch 1, turn [14]

Row 18: sc in all 14 st, ch 1, turn [14]

Row 19: sc in next 4 st, hdc in next st, dc in next 4 st, hdc in next st, sc in next 4 st, ch 1, turn [14]

Row 20: sc in all 14 st, ch 1, turn [14]

Row 21: sc in next 2 st, hdc in next st, dc in next 8 st,

hdc in next st, sc in next 2 st, ch 1, turn [14]
Row 22: sc in all 14 st, ch 1, turn [14]
Row 23: sc in next 2 st, hdc in next st, dc in next 8 st, hdc in next st, sc in next 2 st, ch 1, turn [14]
Row 24: sc in all 14 st, ch 1, turn [14]
Row 25: sc in next 2 st, hdc in next st, dc in next 8 st, hdc in next st, sc in next 2 st, ch 1, turn [14]
Row 26: sc in all 14 st, ch 1, turn [14]
Row 27: inc in next st, sc in next 12 st, inc in next st, ch 1, turn [16]
Row 28: sc in all 16 st, ch 1, turn [16]
Row 29: inc in next st, sc in next 14 st, inc in next st, ch 1, turn [18]
Row 30: sc in all 18 st, ch 1, turn [18]
Row 31: inc in next st, sc in next 16 st, inc in next st, ch 1, turn [20]
Row 32: sc in all 20 st, ch 1, turn [20]
Row 33: sc in next 6 st, dec, sc in next 4 st, dec, sc in next 6 st, ch 1, turn [18]
Row 34: sc in all 18 st, ch 1, turn [18]
Row 35: sc in next 5 st, dec, sc in next 4 st, dec, sc in next 5 st, ch 1, turn [16]
Row 36: sc in next 4 st, dec, sc in next 4 st, dec, sc in next 4 st, ch 1, turn [14]
Row 37: sc in next 3 st, dec, sc in next 4 st, dec, sc in next 2 st, inc in next st [13]
Continue crocheting in the row-ends down the sides and around the entire head piece:
Down the first side: sc in next 3 st, dec, sc in next 2 st, dec, sc in next st, dec, (sc in next 2 st, dec) repeat 2 times, (sc in next 3 st, dec) repeat 2 times, sc in next

5 st [28] (picture 5)
In the beginning chains: inc in next 2 st [4]
Down the second side: sc in next 5 st, (dec, sc in next 3 st) repeat 2 times, (dec, sc in next 2 st) repeat 2 times, dec, sc in next st, dec, sc in next 2 st, dec, sc in next 4 st [29 – 61 stitches in total]
Slst in first st. Fasten off, leaving a long tail for sewing. Sew the bottom 12 stitches (the wide end) of the crest to the corresponding petrol blue stitches of round 17 of the body. Sew the tip of the crest to round 16 of the head, between the eyes. (picture 6)

BEAK (in black yarn)
Rnd 1: start 6 sc in a magic ring [6]
Rnd 2: sc in all 6 st [6]
Rnd 3: inc in next st, sc in next 5 st [7]
Rnd 4: inc in next 2 st, sc in next 5 st [9]
Rnd 5: sc in all 9 st [9]
Rnd 6: (sc in next st, inc in next st) repeat 2 times, sc in next 5 st [11]
Rnd 7 – 8: sc in all 11 st [11]
Rnd 9: sc in next 3 st, slst in next st [4] Leave the remaining stitches unworked.
Fasten off, leaving a long tail for sewing. Stuff the beak with fiberfill. Attach the beak to the head over the pointy end of the head piece, in between the eyes.

WING (make 2, in blue yarn)
Rnd 1: start 6 sc in a magic ring [6]
Rnd 2: inc in all 6 st [12]
Rnd 3: (sc in next 3 st, inc in next st) repeat 3 times [15]

Rnd 4: sc in all 15 st [15]
Rnd 5: (sc in next 3 st, dec) repeat 3 times [12]
Rnd 6: sc in all 12 st [12]
Rnd 7: (sc in next 2 st, dec) repeat 3 times [9]
Rnd 8: sc in all 9 st [9]
Rnd 9: (sc in next st, dec) repeat 3 times [6]
Fasten off, leaving a long tail for sewing. The wings don't need to be stuffed. Using your yarn needle, weave the yarn tail through the front loop of each remaining stitch and pull it tight to close. Sew round 2 of the wings to round 15 of the body.

FOOT (make 2, in gray yarn)
Start by making 2 toes for each foot.
Rnd 1: start 6 sc in magic ring [6]
Rnd 2 – 4: sc in all 6 st [6]
Fasten off and weave in the yarn end on the first toe. Don't fasten off on the second toe. In the next round, we'll join both toes together.
Rnd 5: sc in next 3 st on the second toe, continue on the first toe (picture 7), sc in next 6 st, continue on the second toe, sc in last 3 st [12] (picture 8)
Rnd 6: sc in next 2 st, dec, sc in next 4 st, dec, sc in next 2 st [10]
Rnd 7: sc in next st, sc3tog, sc in next 6 st [8]
Rnd 8: sc in all 8 st [8]
Stuff the foot lightly with fiberfill.
Rnd 9: (sc in next st, dec, sc in next st) repeat 2 times [6]
Fasten off, leaving a long tail for sewing. Using your yarn needle, weave the yarn tail through the front loop of each remaining stitch and pull it tight to close.

Sew both feet to the front of the body, about 3-4 stitches apart.

TAIL FEATHER (make 3, start in blue yarn)
Rnd 1: start 6 sc in a magic ring [6]
Rnd 2: (sc in next 2 st, inc in next st) repeat 2 times [8]
Rnd 3 – 8: sc in all 8 st [8]
Change to green yarn.
Rnd 9 – 10: sc in all 8 st [8]
Change to petrol blue yarn.
Rnd 11 – 14: sc in all 8 st [8]
Rnd 15: (sc in next 2 st, dec) repeat 2 times [6]
Fasten off, leaving a long tail for sewing. Trim 3 pipe cleaners (or sturdy wires) so that they are twice as long as the tail feathers. Fold them in half (picture 9) and insert one into each of the tail feathers. Flatten the tail feathers and sew the gaps closed with the leftover yarn tails. Attach 2 of the tail feathers to the back of the body, directly below the petrol blue patch. Then attach the third tail feather centered above the bottom 2 feathers (picture 10). With a strand of blue yarn, sew the tips of the tail feathers together. Weave in all yarn ends.

ANTI THE ANT-EATER

by Lemon Yarn Creations
(Andreia Ferreira)

SKILL LEVEL: ★ ★ ★

SIZE: 6" / 15 cm tall when made with the indicated yarn.

MATERIALS:

– Light worsted weight yarn in off-white, light brown and pink (leftover)
– B-1 / 2.5 mm crochet hook
– Safety eyes (10 mm)
– Yarn needle
– Stitch marker
– Fiberfill for stuffing

AMIGURUMI GALLERY

Scan or visit
www.amigurumi.com/3413
to share pictures and find inspiration.

BODY *(start in off-white yarn)*

Rnd 1: start 6 sc in a magic ring [6]

Rnd 2: inc in all 6 st [12]

Rnd 3: (sc in next st, inc in next st) repeat 6 times [18]

Rnd 4: (sc in next 2 st, inc in next st) repeat 6 times [24]

Rnd 5: (sc in next 3 st, inc in next st) repeat 6 times [30]

Rnd 6: (sc in next 4 st, inc in next st) repeat 6 times [36]

Rnd 7: (sc in next 5 st, inc in next st) repeat 6 times [42]

Rnd 8: (sc in next 6 st, inc in next st) repeat 6 times [48]

Rnd 9: (sc in next 7 st, inc in next st) repeat 6 times [54]

Rnd 10: (sc in next 8 st, inc in next st) repeat 6 times [60]

Rnd 11: (sc in next 9 st, inc in next st) repeat 6 times [66]

Rnd 12: (sc in next 10 st, inc in next st) repeat 6 times [72]

Rnd 13: (sc in next 11 st, inc in next st) repeat 6 times [78]

Rnd 14: (sc in next 12 st, inc in next st) repeat 6 times [84]

Rnd 15: skip 42 st, sc in next 42 st [42] (pictures 1-2)

You have now created a smaller round.

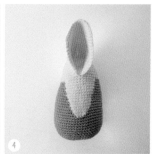

Work the next rounds with color changes. The color change is indicated in italics before each part.

Rnd 16: sc in next 6 st, *(light brown)* sc in next 12 st, *(off-white)* sc in next 6 st, *(light brown)* sc in next 12 st, *(off-white)* sc in next 6 st [42]

Rnd 17: sc in next 6 st, *(light brown)* inc in next st, sc in next 6 st, inc in next st, sc in next 4 st, *(off-white)* sc in next 2 st, inc in next st, sc in next 3 st, *(light brown)* sc in next 3 st, inc in next st, sc in next 6 st, inc in next st, sc in next st, *(off-white)* sc in next 5 st, inc in next st [48]

Rnd 18: sc in next 6 st, *(light brown)* sc in next 15 st, *(off-white)* sc in next 6 st, *(light brown)* sc in next 15 st, *(off-white)* sc in next 6 st [48]

Rnd 19: sc in next 6 st, *(light brown)* inc in next st, sc in next 8 st, inc in next st, sc in next 5 st, *(off-white)* sc in next 6 st, *(light brown)* inc in next st, sc in next 3 st, inc in next st, sc in next 7 st, inc in next st, sc in next 2 st, *(off-white)* sc in next 5 st, inc in next st [54]

Rnd 20: sc in next 6 st, *(light brown)* sc in next 18 st, *(off-white)* sc in next 5 st, *(light brown)* sc in next 19 st, *(off-white)* sc in next 6 st [54]

Rnd 21: sc in next 5 st, *(light brown)* dec, sc in next 16 st, inc in next st, *(off-white)* sc in next 4 st, *(light brown)* dec, sc in next 17 st, inc in next st, *(off-white)* sc in next 6 st [54]

Rnd 22: sc in next 5 st, *(light brown)* sc in next 20 st, *(off-white)* sc in next 3 st, *(light brown)* sc in next 21 st, *(off-white)* sc in next 5 st [54]

Rnd 23: sc in next 4 st, *(light brown)* dec, sc in next 18 st, inc in next st, *(off-white)* sc in next 2 st, *(light brown)* dec, sc in next 19 st, inc in next st, *(off-white)* sc in next 5 st [54]

Rnd 24: sc in next 4 st, *(light brown)* sc in next 46 st, *(off-white)* sc in next 4 st [54]

Rnd 25: sc in next st, inc in next st, sc in next 2 st, *(light brown)* inc in next st, sc in next 2 st, inc in next st, sc in next 38 st, inc in next st, sc in next 2 st, inc in next st, *(off-white)* sc in next 2 st, inc in next st, sc in next st [60]

Rnd 26: sc in next 5 st, *(light brown)* sc in next 51 st, *(off-white)* sc in next 4 st [60]

Rnd 27: sc in next 4 st, *(light brown)* sc in next 53 st, *(off-white)* sc in next 3 st [60]

Rnd 28: sc in next 3 st, *(light brown)* sc in next 55 st, *(off-white)* sc in next 2 st [60]

Rnd 29: sc in next 2 st, *(light brown)* sc in next 58 st [60]
Fasten off the off-white yarn and weave in the yarn end. Continue with light brown yarn (picture 3). Stuff the body with fiberfill and continue stuffing as you go.

Rnd 30 – 34: sc in all 60 st [60]

Rnd 35: (sc in next 8 st, dec) repeat 6 times [54]

Rnd 36: sc in all 54 st [54]

Rnd 37: (sc in next 7 st, dec) repeat 6 times [48]

Rnd 38: sc in all 48 st [48]

Rnd 39: (sc in next 6 st, dec) repeat 6 times [42]

Rnd 40: (sc in next 5 st, dec) repeat 6 times [36]

Rnd 41: (sc in next 4 st, dec) repeat 6 times [30]
Finish stuffing the body at this point to create a flat bottom.

Rnd 42: (sc in next 3 st, dec) repeat 6 times [24]

Rnd 43: (sc in next 2 st, dec) repeat 6 times [18]

Rnd 44: (sc in next st, dec) repeat 6 times [12]

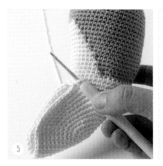

Rnd 45: dec 6 times [6]

Fasten off, leaving a yarn tail. Using your yarn needle, weave the yarn tail through the front loop of each remaining stitch and pull it tight to close. Weave in the yarn end (picture 4).

HEAD *(start in off-white yarn)*

Hold the body upside down, with the bottom away from you. Pull up a loop of off-white yarn in the first unworked stitch of round 14 (picture 5). Leave a long starting yarn tail, we'll use this to sew up the hole later on.

Rnd 15 – 17: sc in all 42 st [42]

Rnd 18: (sc in next 5 st, dec) repeat 6 times [36]

Rnd 19: sc in all 36 st [36]

Rnd 20: (sc in next 10 st, dec) repeat 3 times [33]

Rnd 21: sc in all 33 st [33]

Rnd 22: (sc in next 9 st, dec) repeat 3 times [30]

Rnd 23: sc in all 30 st [30]

Rnd 24: (sc in next 8 st, dec) repeat 3 times [27]

Rnd 25: sc in all 27 st [27]

Rnd 26: (sc in next 7 st, dec) repeat 3 times [24]

Rnd 27: sc in all 24 st [24]

Insert the safety eyes between rounds 20 and 21, with an interspace of 14 stitches. Make sure they are symmetrically placed (pictures 6).

Stuff the head with fiberfill. Make sure to stuff firmly where the head and body are joined and continue stuffing as you go.

Rnd 28: sc in next 8 st, (dec, sc in next 2 st) repeat 3 times, sc in next 4 st [21]

Rnd 29: sc in all 21 st [21]

Rnd 30: (sc in next 5 st, dec) repeat 3 times [18]

Rnd 31: sc in all 18 st [18]

Change to light brown yarn.

Rnd 32: (sc in next 4 st, dec) repeat 3 times [15]

Rnd 33: sc in all 15 st [15]

Rnd 34: (sc in next 3 st, dec) repeat 3 times [12]

Rnd 35: sc in all 12 st [12]

Rnd 36: (sc in next 2 st, dec) repeat 3 times [9]

Rnd 37: BLO sc in all 9 st [9]

Fasten off, leaving a yarn tail. Using your yarn needle,

weave the yarn tail through the front loop of each remaining stitch and pull it tight to close. Weave in the yarn end. Sew the hole between the head and the body closed with the starting yarn tail.

CHEEK *(make 2, in pink yarn)*
Rnd 1: start 6 sc in a magic ring [6]
Rnd 2: inc in all 6 st [12]
Slst in next st. Fasten off, leaving a long tail for sewing. Sew the cheeks below the eyes, between rounds 15 and 19.

TONGUE *(in pink yarn)*
Ch 10. Crochet in rows.
Row 1: start in third ch from hook, hdc in all 8 st [8]
Fasten off, leaving a long tail for sewing. Sew the tongue to round 37 of the head. Using your yarn needle, push round 37 of the head a bit inwards to make the mouth cavity for the tongue (pictures 7-8).

EAR *(make 2, in light brown yarn)*
Rnd 1: start 6 sc in a magic ring [6]
Rnd 2: (sc in next st, inc in next st) repeat 3 times [9]
Rnd 3 – 5: sc in all 9 st [9]
Rnd 6: (sc in next st, dec) repeat 3 times [6]
Fasten off, leaving a long tail for sewing. The ears don't need to be stuffed. Sew the ears between rounds 13 and 14, a bit above the eyes.

ARM *(make 2, in off-white yarn)*
Rnd 1: start 6 sc in a magic ring [6]

Rnd 2: (sc in next st, inc in next st) repeat 3 times [9]
Rnd 3 – 4: sc in all 9 st [9]
Rnd 5: (inc in next st, sc in next st) repeat 3 times, sc in next 3 st [12]
Rnd 6 – 7: sc in all 12 st [12]
Rnd 8: (inc in next st, sc in next 2 st) repeat 3 times, sc in next 3 st [15]
Rnd 9 – 18: sc in all 15 st [15]
Stuff the arms lightly with fiberfill. Flatten the opening of the arm and work the next round through both layers to close.
Rnd 19: sc in next 7 st [7] (picture 9)
Fasten off, leaving a long tail for sewing. Sew the arms to the body, between rounds 16 and 24, at 3 stitches from the color change of round 16. Secure the center of each arm to the body with a few stitches (picture 10).

LEG *(make 2, in off-white yarn)*
Ch 6. Stitches are worked around both sides of the foundation chain.
Rnd 1: start in second ch from hook, sc in next 4 st, 3 sc in next st. Continue on the other side of the foundation chain, sc in next 3 st, inc in next st [12]
Rnd 2: (sc in next st, inc in next st) repeat 6 times [18]
Rnd 3: (sc in next 2 st, inc in next st) repeat 6 times [24]
Rnd 4: sc in all 24 st [24]
Rnd 5: sc in next 8 st, dec 3 times, sc in next 10 st [21]
Rnd 6: sc in next 7 st, dec 3 times, sc in next 8 st [18]
Rnd 7 – 11: sc in all 18 st [18]
Stuff the leg firmly with fiberfill up to this point.
Rnd 12: sc in next 7 st, inc in next 3 st, sc in next 8 st [21]

Rnd 2: (sc in next st, inc in next st) repeat 3 times [9]
Rnd 3 – 4: sc in all 9 st [9]
Rnd 5: (sc in next 2 st, inc in next st) repeat 3 times [12]
Change to off-white yarn.
Rnd 6 – 7: sc in all 12 st [12]
Rnd 8: (sc in next 3 st, inc in next st) repeat 3 times [15]
Change to light brown yarn.
Rnd 9 – 10: sc in all 15 st [15]
Rnd 11: (sc in next 4 st, inc in next st) repeat 3 times [18]
Change to off-white yarn.
Rnd 12 – 13: sc in all 18 st [18]
Rnd 14: sc in next 6 st, (inc in next st, sc in next st) repeat 3 times, sc in next 6 st [21]
Rnd 15 – 16: sc in all 21 st [21]
Rnd 17: sc in next 6 st, (inc in next st, sc in next 2 st) repeat 3 times, sc in next 6 st [24]
Rnd 18 – 19: sc in all 24 st [24]
Rnd 20: sc in next 6 st, (inc in next st, sc in next 3 st) repeat 3 times, sc in next 6 st [27]
Rnd 21 – 22: sc in all 27 st [27]
Fasten off, leaving a long tail for sewing. Stuff the tail with fiberfill and sew it to the back of the body, between rounds 29 and 38 (picture 12).

Rnd 13: sc in next 7 st, (inc in next st, sc in next st) repeat 3 times, sc in next 8 st [24]
Rnd 14: sc in next 7 st, (inc in next st, sc in next 2 st) repeat 3 times, sc in next 8 st [27]
Rnd 15 – 19: sc in all 27 st [27]
Rnd 20: (sc in next 7 st, dec) repeat 3 times [24]
Rnd 21: (sc in next 6 st, dec) repeat 3 times [21]
Rnd 22: (sc in next 5 st, dec) repeat 3 times [18]
Rnd 23: (sc in next st, dec) repeat 6 times [12]
Rnd 24: dec 6 times [6]
Fasten off, leaving a long tail for sewing. Using your yarn needle, weave the yarn tail through the front loop of each remaining stitch and pull it tight to close. Flatten the unstuffed part of the leg and sew the legs to the sides of the body, between rounds 29 and 40, in a slight laid-back position. The feet should be slightly ahead of the hands (picture 11).

TAIL *(start in light brown yarn)*
Rnd 1: start 6 sc in a magic ring [6]

CEDRIC THE CRAB

by Elisa's Crochet
(Elisa Sartori)

SKILL LEVEL: ✳

SIZE: 6.5" / 17 cm tall when made with the indicated yarn.

MATERIALS

– Worsted weight yarn in red, coral, white (leftover) and black (leftover)
– Size D-3 / 3.25 mm crochet hook
– Black embroidery thread
– Yarn needle
– Stitch marker
– Fiberfill for stuffing

AMIGURUMI GALLERY

Scan or visit
www.amigurumi.com/3414
to share pictures and find inspiration.

EYE STALK (make 2, in red yarn)

Rnd 1: start 6 sc in a magic ring [6]

Rnd 2: inc in all 6 st [12]

Rnd 3: (sc in next st, inc in next st) repeat 6 times [18]

Rnd 4: (sc in next 2 st, inc in next st) repeat 6 times [24]

Rnd 5 – 9: sc in all 24 st [24]

Rnd 10: (sc in next 2 st, dec) repeat 6 times [18]

Rnd 11: dec 9 times [9]

Rnd 12: FLO sc in all 9 st [9]

Stuff the eye stalk with fiberfill and continue stuffing as you go.

Rnd 13 – 20: sc in all 9 st [9]

Fasten off and weave in the yarn ends on the first eye stalk. Make a second eye stalk, ch 6 on the second eye stalk and don't fasten off (picture 1). In the next round, we'll join the eye stalks to create the body.

BODY (start in red yarn)

Rnd 21: continue on the first eye stalk (picture 2), sc in next 9 st, hdc in next 6 ch (picture 3), continue on the second eye stalk, sc in next 9 st, hdc in the other side of next 6 ch [30] (picture 4)

Rnd 22: sc in next 3 st, inc in next 3 st, sc in next 12 st, inc in next 3 st, sc in next 9 st [36]

Rnd 23: sc in next 4 st, inc in next 3 st, sc in next 16 st, inc in next 3 st, sc in next 10 st [42]

Rnd 24: (sc in next st, inc in next st) repeat 21 times [63]

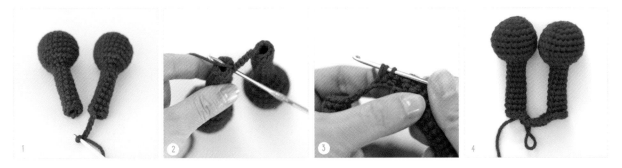

Rnd 25 – 27: sc in all 63 st [63]

Rnd 28: sc in next 10 st, inc in next 4 st, sc in next 13 st, inc in next st, sc in next 15 st, inc in next 4 st, sc in next 16 st [72]

Rnd 29: sc in all 72 st [72]

Rnd 30: sc in next 10 st, (inc in next st, sc in next st) repeat 3 times, inc in next st, sc in next 30 st, (inc in next st, sc in next st) repeat 3 times, inc in next st, sc in next 18 st [80]

Rnd 31 – 39: sc in all 80 st [80]

Rnd 40: FLO sc in all 80 st [80]

Fasten off the red yarn and weave in the yarn end. Pull up a loop of coral yarn in the back loop of the first stitch of round 39 (picture 5).

Rnd 41: BLO sc in all 80 st [80] (picture 6)

Rnd 42 – 43: sc in all 80 st [80]

Rnd 44: sc in next 10 st, (dec, sc in next st) repeat 3 times, dec, sc in next 30 st, (dec, sc in next st) repeat 3 times, dec, sc in next 18 st [72]

Rnd 45: sc in next 10 st, dec 4 times, sc in next 13 st, dec, sc in next 15 st, dec 4 times, sc in next 16 st [63]

Stuff the body with fiberfill and continue stuffing as you go.

Rnd 46: (sc in next st, dec) repeat 21 times [42]

Rnd 47: (sc in next 5 st, dec) repeat 6 times [36]

Rnd 48: (sc in next 4 st, dec) repeat 6 times [30]

Rnd 49: (sc in next 3 st, dec) repeat 6 times [24]

Rnd 50: (sc in next 2 st, dec) repeat 6 times [18]

Rnd 51: (sc in next st, dec) repeat 6 times [12]

Rnd 52: dec 6 times [6]

Fasten off and weave in the yarn end.

EYE *(make 2, in white yarn)*
Rnd 1: start 6 sc in a magic ring [6]
Rnd 2: inc in all 6 st [12]
Rnd 3: (sc in next st, inc in next st) repeat 6 times [18]
Fasten off, leaving a long tail for sewing. Using black embroidery thread, embroider an inversed U-shape on the eye, over rounds 2-3. Sew the eyes on the red eye stalks.
Use black embroidery thread to embroider the mouth toward the left side of the body, over rounds 31-36.

LARGE SHELL MARK *(in coral yarn)*
Rnd 1: start 6 sc in a magic ring [6]
Rnd 2: inc in all 6 st [12]
Fasten off, leaving a long tail for sewing. Sew the mark to the right side of the body, over rounds 24-29.

SMALL SHELL MARK *(in coral yarn)*
Rnd 1: start 6 sc in a magic ring [6]
Fasten off, leaving a long tail for sewing. Sew the mark to the right side of the body, over rounds 30-34.

LONG LEG *(make 2, in coral yarn)*
Rnd 1: start 8 sc in a magic ring [8]
Rnd 2: (sc in next 3 st, inc in next st) repeat 2 times [10]
Rnd 3 – 4: sc in all 10 st [10]
Rnd 5: (sc in next 3 st, dec) repeat 2 times [8]
Rnd 6: sc in all 8 st [8]
Rnd 7: (sc in next 2 st, dec) repeat 2 times [6]
Stuff the leg firmly with fiberfill and continue stuffing as you go.

Rnd 8 – 12: sc in all 6 st [6]
Fasten off, leaving a long tail for sewing.

MEDIUM LEG *(make 2, in coral yarn)*
Rnd 1: start 8 sc in a magic ring [8]
Rnd 2: (sc in next 3 st, inc in next st) repeat 2 times [10]
Rnd 3 – 4: sc in all 10 st [10]
Rnd 5: (sc in next 3 st, dec) repeat 2 times [8]
Rnd 6: sc in all 8 st [8]
Rnd 7: (sc in next 2 st, dec) repeat 2 times [6]
Stuff the leg firmly with fiberfill and continue stuffing as you go.
Rnd 8 – 11: sc in all 6 st [6]
Fasten off, leaving a long tail for sewing.

SHORT LEG *(make 2, in coral yarn)*
Rnd 1: start 8 sc in a magic ring [8]
Rnd 2: (sc in next 3 st, inc in next st) repeat 2 times [10]
Rnd 3 – 4: sc in all 10 st [10]
Rnd 5: (sc in next 3 st, dec) repeat 2 times [8]
Rnd 6: sc in all 8 st [8]
Rnd 7: (sc in next 2 st, dec) repeat 2 times [6]
Stuff the leg firmly with fiberfill and continue stuffing as you go.
Rnd 8 – 10: sc in all 6 st [6]
Fasten off, leaving a long tail for sewing. Secure the legs in place with pins, between rounds 41 and 44. Position the long leg at the back, the medium one in the center and the short one at the front (picture 7). Leave 1 stitch between each leg (picture 8). Sew them to the body.

PINCER *(make 2, in red yarn)*
Start by making a small and large finger for each pincer.

Small finger
Rnd 1: start 4 sc in a magic ring [4]
Rnd 2: (sc in next st, inc in next st) repeat 2 times [6]
Rnd 3: (sc in next 2 st, inc in next st) repeat 2 times [8]
Rnd 4: (sc in next 3 st, inc in next st) repeat 2 times [10]
Rnd 5: (sc in next 4 st, inc in next st) repeat 2 times [12]
Rnd 6: (sc in next 2 st, inc in next st) repeat 4 times [16]
Rnd 7: sc in all 16 st [16]
Stuff the finger with fiberfill. Fasten off and weave in the yarn end.

Large finger
Rnd 1: start 4 sc in a magic ring [4]
Rnd 2: (sc in next st, inc in next st) repeat 2 times [6]
Rnd 3: (sc in next 2 st, inc in next st) repeat 2 times [8]
Rnd 4: (sc in next st, inc in next st) repeat 4 times [12]
Rnd 5: (sc in next 2 st, inc in next st) repeat 4 times [16]
Rnd 6: (sc in next 7 st, inc in next st) repeat 2 times [18]
Rnd 7: (sc in next 8 st, inc in next st) repeat 2 times [20]
Rnd 8 – 9: sc in all 20 st [20]
Stuff the finger with fiberfill. Don't fasten off on the large finger. In the next round, we'll join both fingers together.
Rnd 10: sc in first st of the small finger to join (picture 9), sc in next 15 st, continue on the large finger, sc in next 20 st [36]
(pictures 10-11)
Rnd 11: (sc in next 4 st, dec) repeat 6 times [30]

Rnd 12: sc in all 30 st [30]
Rnd 13: (sc in next 3 st, dec) repeat 6 times [24]
Rnd 14: (sc in next 2 st, dec) repeat 6 times [18]
Rnd 15: (sc in next 7 st, dec) repeat 2 times [16]
Stuff the pincer with fiberfill and continue stuffing as you go.
Rnd 16: dec 8 times [8]
Rnd 17 – 27: sc in all 8 st [8]
Fasten off, leaving a long tail for sewing. Attach the pincers to the sides of the body with pins, between rounds 34 and 37 (picture 12). Make sure the small fingers are on the inside. Sew the pincers to the body.

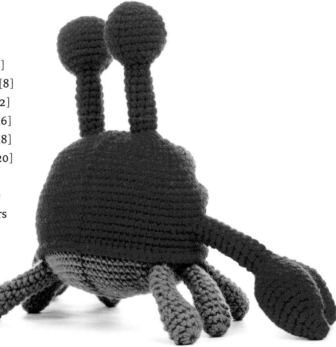

HENRY THE HIPPO

by Kamlin Patterns

SKILL LEVEL: ★ ★

SIZE: 12" / 30 cm tall when made with the indicated yarn.

MATERIALS:

– Worsted weight yarn in light gray, white, dark blue, light green, yellow and red (leftover)
– Size G-6 / 4 mm crochet hook
– Safety eyes (16 mm)
– Black embroidery thread
– 4 buttons for the legs and arms
– 2 beads for the swim ring
– A piece of white felt
– Yarn needle
– Pins
– Pipe cleaner
– Stitch marker
– Fiberfill for stuffing

 AMIGURUMI GALLERY
Scan or visit
www.amigurumi.com/302
to share pictures and find inspiration.

MUZZLE *(in light gray yarn)*

Rnd 1: start 6 sc in a magic ring [6]

Rnd 2: inc in all 6 st [12]

Rnd 3: (sc in next st, inc in next st) repeat 6 times [18]

Rnd 4: (sc in next 2 st, inc in next st) repeat 6 times [24]

Rnd 5: (sc in next 3 st, inc in next st) repeat 6 times [30]

Rnd 6: (sc in next 4 st, inc in next st) repeat 6 times [36]

Rnd 7: (sc in next 5 st, inc in next st) repeat 6 times [42]

Rnd 8: (sc in next 6 st, inc in next st) repeat 6 times [48]

Rnd 9: (sc in next 7 st, inc in next st) repeat 6 times [54]
Rnd 10: (sc in next 8 st, inc in next st) repeat 6 times [60]
Rnd 11: (sc in next 9 st, inc in next st) repeat 6 times [66]
Rnd 12: (sc in next 10 st, inc in next st) repeat 6 times [72]
Rnd 13 – 25: sc in all 72 st [72]
Rnd 26: (sc in next 10 st, dec) repeat 6 times [66]
Rnd 27: (sc in next 9 st, dec) repeat 6 times [60]
Rnd 28: (sc in next 8 st, dec) repeat 6 times [54]
Rnd 29: (sc in next 7 st, dec) repeat 6 times [48]
Fasten off, leaving a long tail for sewing. Stuff the muzzle with fiberfill.

HEAD *(in light gray yarn)*
Rnd 1: start 6 sc in a magic ring [6]
Rnd 2: inc in all 6 st [12]
Rnd 3: (sc in next st, inc in next st) repeat 6 times [18]
Rnd 4: (sc in next 2 st, inc in next st) repeat 6 times [24]
Rnd 5: (sc in next 3 st, inc in next st) repeat 6 times [30]
Rnd 6: (sc in next 4 st, inc in next st) repeat 6 times [36]
Rnd 7: (sc in next 5 st, inc in next st) repeat 6 times [42]
Rnd 8: (sc in next 6 st, inc in next st) repeat 6 times [48]
Rnd 9: (sc in next 7 st, inc in next st) repeat 6 times [54]
Rnd 10: (sc in next 8 st, inc in next st) repeat 6 times [60]
Rnd 11: (sc in next 9 st, inc in next st) repeat 6 times [66]
Rnd 12: (sc in next 10 st, inc in next st) repeat 6 times [72]
Rnd 13 – 24: sc in all 72 st [72]
Rnd 25: (sc in next 10 st, dec) repeat 6 times [66]
Rnd 26: (sc in next 9 st, dec) repeat 6 times [60]
Rnd 27: (sc in next 8 st, dec) repeat 6 times [54]
Rnd 28: (sc in next 7 st, dec) repeat 6 times [48]
Rnd 29: (sc in next 6 st, dec) repeat 6 times [42]
Rnd 30: (sc in next 5 st, dec) repeat 6 times [36]
Rnd 31: (sc in next 4 st, dec) repeat 6 times [30]
Rnd 32: (sc in next 3 st, dec) repeat 6 times [24]
Cut 2 round shapes from the white felt, slightly bigger than the safety eyes. Cut a slit in the center and insert the safety eyes. Attach the safety eyes with the felt pieces between round 8 and 9, with an interspace of about 7 stitches. Stuff the head with fiberfill and continue stuffing as you go.

Rnd 33: (sc in next 2 st, dec) repeat 6 times [18]
Rnd 34: (sc in next st, dec) repeat 6 times [12]
Rnd 35: dec 6 times [6]
Fasten off, leaving a yarn tail. Using your yarn needle, weave the yarn tail through the front loop of each remaining stitch and pull it tight to close. Pin and sew the muzzle to the head between rounds 11 and 30.

EAR *(make 2, in light gray yarn)*
Rnd 1: start 6 sc in a magic ring [6]
Rnd 2: inc in all 6 st [12]
Rnd 3: sc in all 12 st [12]
Fasten off, leaving a long tail for sewing. Sew the ears to the head, between rounds 7 and 10.

NOSTRIL *(make 2, in light gray yarn)*
Rnd 1: start 7 sc in a magic ring, ch 1, turn [7]
Continue crocheting in rows.
Row 2: sc in all 7 st, ch 1, turn [7]
Row 3: inc in next st, sc in next 5 st, inc in next st, ch 1, turn [9]
Row 4: sc in all 9 st [9]
Fasten off, leaving a long tail for sewing. Pull the starting round tightly closed. Sew the nostrils to the muzzle. Embroider the eyebrows and mouth using black embroidery thread.

BODY *(in light gray yarn)*
Rnd 1: start 6 sc in a magic ring [6]
Rnd 2: inc in all 6 st [12]
Rnd 3: (sc in next st, inc in next st) repeat 6 times [18]
Rnd 4: (sc in next 2 st, inc in next st) repeat 6 times [24]
Rnd 5: (sc in next 3 st, inc in next st) repeat 6 times [30]
Rnd 6: (sc in next 4 st, inc in next st) repeat 6 times [36]
Rnd 7: (sc in next 5 st, inc in next st) repeat 6 times [42]
Rnd 8: (sc in next 6 st, inc in next st) repeat 6 times [48]
Rnd 9: (sc in next 7 st, inc in next st) repeat 6 times [54]
Rnd 10: (sc in next 8 st, inc in next st) repeat 6 times [60]
Rnd 11: (sc in next 9 st, inc in next st) repeat 6 times [66]
Rnd 12: (sc in next 10 st, inc in next st) repeat 6 times [72]
Rnd 13: (sc in next 11 st, inc in next st) repeat 6 times [78]
Rnd 14: (sc in next 12 st, inc in next st) repeat 6 times [84]
Rnd 15: (sc in next 13 st, inc in next st) repeat 6 times [90]
Rnd 16 – 33: sc in all 90 st [90]
Rnd 34: (sc in next 13 st, dec) repeat 6 times [84]
Rnd 35: (sc in next 12 st, dec) repeat 6 times [78]
Rnd 36: (sc in next 11 st, dec) repeat 6 times [72]
Rnd 37: (sc in next 10 st, dec) repeat 6 times [66]
Rnd 38 – 42: sc in all 66 st [66]
Rnd 43: (sc in next 9 st, dec) repeat 6 times [60]
Rnd 44 – 46: sc in all 60 st [60]
Rnd 47: (sc in next 8 st, dec) repeat 6 times [54]
Rnd 48 – 49: sc in all 54 st [54]
Rnd 50: (sc in next 7 st, dec) repeat 6 times [48]

Rnd 51: sc in all 48 st [48]
Rnd 52: (sc in next 6 st, dec) repeat 6 times [42]
Rnd 53: sc in all 42 st [42]
Rnd 54: (sc in next 5 st, dec) repeat 6 times [36]
Rnd 55: (sc in next 4 st, dec) repeat 6 times [30]
Rnd 56: (sc in next 3 st, dec) repeat 6 times [24]
Stuff the body with fiberfill and continue stuffing as you go.
Rnd 57: (sc in next 2 st, dec) repeat 6 times [18]
Rnd 58: (sc in next st, dec) repeat 6 times [12]
Rnd 59: dec 6 times [6]
Fasten off, leaving a yarn tail. Using your yarn needle, weave the yarn tail through the front loop of each remaining stitch and pull it tight to close. Position the head and sew it to the body.

LEG *(make 2, in light gray yarn)*
Rnd 1: start 6 sc in a magic ring [6]
Rnd 2: inc in all 6 st [12]
Rnd 3: (sc in next st, inc in next st) repeat 6 times [18]
Rnd 4: (sc in next 2 st, inc in next st) repeat 6 times [24]
Rnd 5: (sc in next 3 st, inc in next st) repeat 6 times [30]
Rnd 6: (sc in next 4 st, inc in next st) repeat 6 times [36]
Rnd 7: BLO sc in all 36 st [36]
Rnd 8 – 12: sc in all 36 st [36]
Rnd 13: (sc in next 4 st, dec) repeat 6 times [30]
Rnd 14 – 18: sc in all 30 st [30]
Rnd 19: (sc in next 3 st, dec) repeat 6 times [24]
Rnd 20 – 30: sc in all 24 st [24]
Stuff the leg with fiberfill and continue stuffing as you go.
Rnd 31: (sc in next 2 st, dec) repeat 6 times [18]
Rnd 32: (sc in next st, dec) repeat 6 times [12]
Rnd 33: dec 6 times [6]
Fasten off, leaving a yarn tail. Using your yarn needle, weave the yarn tail through the front loop of each remaining stitch and pull it tight to close. Pin the legs to the body. If you would like to have movable legs, you can use strong embroidery thread and buttons. Sew the top center of each leg to the body at one point only. Go back and forth through the button, the leg and the body, pulling the thread tightly each time. Fasten off and weave in the yarn end.

ARM *(make 2, in light gray yarn)*
Rnd 1: start 6 sc in a magic ring [6]
Rnd 2: inc in all 6 st [12]
Rnd 3: (sc in next st, inc in next st) repeat 6 times [18]
Rnd 4: (sc in next 2 st, inc in next st) repeat 6 times [24]
Rnd 5: (sc in next 3 st, inc in next st) repeat 6 times [30]
Rnd 6: (sc in next 4 st, inc in next st) repeat 6 times [36]
Rnd 7: BLO sc in all 36 st [36]
Rnd 8 – 12: sc in all 36 st [36]
Rnd 13: (sc in next 4 st, dec) repeat 6 times [30]
Rnd 14 – 18: sc in all 30 st [30]

Rnd 19: (sc in next 3 st, dec) repeat 6 times [24]
Rnd 20 – 36: sc in all 24 st [24]
Stuff the arm with fiberfill and continue stuffing as you go.
Rnd 37: (sc in next 2 st, dec) repeat 6 times [18]
Rnd 38: (sc in next st, dec) repeat 6 times [12]
Rnd 39: dec 6 times [6]
Fasten off, leaving a yarn tail. Using your yarn needle, weave the yarn tail through the front loop of each remaining stitch and pull it tight to close. Pin the arms to the sides of the body and sew them on in the same way as the legs.

BATHING SUIT *(start in dark blue yarn)*
Start by making 2 trouser legs.

Trouser leg
Ch 42, join with a slst to form a ring. Make sure the ring isn't twisted. Work in a stripes pattern. The color change

is indicated in italics before each round.

Rnd 1 – 3: *(dark blue)* sc in all 42 st [42]

Rnd 4 – 6: *(white)* sc in all 42 st [42]

Rnd 7 – 9: *(dark blue)* sc in all 42 st [42]

Fasten off and weave in the yarn end on the first trouser leg. Don't fasten off on the second trouser leg. In the next round we'll join both trouser legs together.

Bathing suit body

Continue working in a stripe pattern.

Rnd 10: *(white)* sc in all 42 st on the second trouser leg, ch 6, sc in all 42 st on the first trouser leg, ch 6 and join to the second trouser leg with a slst [96]

Rnd 11 – 12: *(white)* sc in all 96 st [96]

Rnd 13 – 15: *(dark blue)* sc in all 96 st [96]

Rnd 16 – 18: *(white)* sc in all 96 st [96]

Rnd 19 – 21: *(dark blue)* sc in all 96 st [96]

Rnd 22 – 24: *(white)* sc in all 96 st [96]

Rnd 25 – 27: *(dark blue)* sc in all 96 st [96]

Rnd 28 – 30: *(white)* sc in all 96 st [96]

Rnd 31: *(dark blue)* sc in all 96 st [96]

Rnd 32: *(dark blue)* (sc in next 14 st, dec) repeat 6 times [90]

Rnd 33: *(dark blue)* sc in all 90 st [90]

Rnd 34 – 36: *(white)* sc in all 90 st [90]

Rnd 37 – 39: *(dark blue)* sc in all 90 st [90]

Rnd 40 – 42: *(white)* sc in all 90 st [90]

Fasten off and weave in the yarn end. Use a separate piece of white yarn to sew the hole between the trouser legs closed.

Shoulder straps

We'll now make the shoulder straps. Flatten the bathing suit. Count 6 stitches to the right and add a stitch marker in the next stitch. This is where the first shoulder strap will start. Pull up a loop of dark blue yarn in the marked stitch and ch 2. Crochet in rows. Continue working in a stripe pattern.

Row 1: *(dark blue)* sc in next 10 st, ch 1, turn [10]

Row 2: *(dark blue)* dec, sc in next 6 st, dec, ch 1, turn [8]

Row 3: *(dark blue)* dec, sc in next 4 st, dec, ch 1, turn [6]

Row 4 – 6: *(white)* sc in all 6 st, ch 1, turn [6]

Row 7 – 9: *(dark blue)* sc in all 6 st, ch 1, turn [6]

Row 10 – 12: *(white)* sc in all 6 st, ch 1, turn [6]

Row 13 – 15: *(dark blue)* sc in all 6 st, ch 1, turn [6]

Row 16 – 18: *(white)* sc in all 6 st, ch 1, turn [6]

Row 19 – 21: *(dark blue)* sc in all 6 st, ch 1, turn [6]

Row 22 – 24: *(white)* sc in all 6 st, ch 1, turn [6]

Row 25 – 27: *(dark blue)* sc in all 6 st, ch 1, turn [6]

Row 28 – 30: *(white)* sc in all 6 st, ch 1, turn [6]

Row 31 – 33: *(dark blue)* sc in all 6 st, ch 1, turn [6]

Row 34 – 36: *(white)* sc in all 6 st, ch 1, turn [6]

Row 37 – 39: *(dark blue)* sc in all 6 st, ch 1, turn [6]

Fasten off and weave in the yarn end. Start the next shoulder strap on the left side, with an interspace of 9 stitches to the first. Repeat the instructions for the first shoulder strap. Put the bathing suit on the hippo. Sew both shoulder straps to the back of the bathing suit, close to the center, with an interspace of 1 stitch.

SWIM RING *(in light green yarn)*

Ch 20, join with a slst to form a ring. Make sure the chain isn't twisted. Stuff the ring with fiberfill as you go.

Rnd 1 – 121: sc in all 20 st [20]

Fasten off, leaving a long tail for sewing. Sew the ends of the ring together.

Frog's head *(in light green yarn)*

Rnd 1: start 6 sc in a magic ring [6]

Rnd 2: inc in all 6 st [12]

Rnd 3: (sc in next st, inc in next st) repeat 6 times [18]

Rnd 4: (sc in next 2 st, inc in next st) repeat 6 times [24]

Rnd 5: (sc in next 3 st, inc in next st) repeat 6 times [30]

Rnd 6: (sc in next 4 st, inc in next st) repeat 6 times [36]

Rnd 7: (sc in next 5 st, inc in next st) repeat 6 times [42]

Rnd 8 – 12: sc in all 42 st [42]

Rnd 13: (sc in next 5 st, dec) repeat 6 times [36]

Rnd 14: (sc in next 4 st, dec) repeat 6 times [30]

Rnd 15: (sc in next 3 st, dec) repeat 6 times [24]

Stuff the head with fiberfill and continue stuffing as you go.

Rnd 16: (sc in next 2 st, dec) repeat 6 times [18]

Rnd 17: (sc in next st, dec) repeat 6 times [12]

Rnd 18: dec 6 times [6]

Fasten off, leaving a yarn tail. Using your yarn needle,

weave the yarn tail through the front loop of each remaining stitch and pull it tight to close.

Frog's eyelid *(make 2, in light green yarn)*

Rnd 1: start 6 sc in a magic ring [6]

Rnd 2: inc in all 6 st [12]

Rnd 3 – 5: sc in all 12 st [12]

Fasten off, leaving a long tail for sewing. Sew the eyelids on top of the frog's head. Sew a piece of white felt and a bead on each eyelid. Embroider the frog's mouth and nose using black embroidery thread. Sew the frog's head to the swim ring.

BOAT

Hull *(in yellow yarn)*

Ch 11. Stitches are worked around both sides of the foundation chain.

Rnd 1: start in second ch from hook, sc in next 9 st, inc in next st. Continue on the other side of the foundation chain, sc in next 9 st, inc in next st [22]

Rnd 2: sc in next 10 st, 3 sc in next st, sc in next 10 st, 3 sc in next st [26]

Rnd 3: inc in next st, sc in next 8 st, inc next 5 st, sc in next 8 st, inc in next 4 st [36]

Rnd 4: sc in all 36 st [36]

Rnd 5: BLO sc in all 36 st [36]

Rnd 6: sc in all 36 st [36]

Rnd 7: (sc in next 5 st, inc in next st) repeat 6 times [42]

Rnd 8: (sc in next 6 st, inc in next st) repeat 6 times [48]

Rnd 9 – 10: sc in all 48 st [48]

Fasten off and weave in the yarn end.

Deck *(in yellow yarn)*

Ch 11. Stitches are worked around both sides of the foundation chain.

Rnd 1: start in second ch from hook, sc in next 9 st, inc in next st. Continue on the other side of the foundation chain, sc in next 9 st, inc in next st [22]

Rnd 2: sc in next 10 st, 3 sc in next st, sc in next 10 st,

3 sc in next st [26]

Rnd 3: inc in next st, sc in next 8 st, inc next 5 st, sc in next 8 st, inc in next 4 st [36]

Rnd 4: (sc in next 5 st, inc in next st) repeat 6 times [42]

Rnd 5: (sc in next 6 st, inc in next st) repeat 6 times [48]

Fasten off, leaving a long tail for sewing. Sew the hull to the boat deck. Stuff the hull with fiberfill before closing the seam.

Sail *(make 2, in red yarn)*

Ch 3. Crochet in rows.

Row 1: start in third ch from hook, sc in this st, ch 1, turn [1]

Row 2: 3 sc in next st, ch 1, turn [3]

Row 3: sc in all 3 st, ch 1, turn [3]

Row 4: inc in next st, sc in next st, inc in next st, ch 1, turn [5]

Row 5: sc in all 5 st, ch 1, turn [5]

Row 6: inc in next st, sc in next 3 st, inc in next st, ch 1, turn [7]

Row 7: sc in all 7 st, ch 1, turn [7]

Row 8: inc in next st, sc in next 5 st, inc in next st, ch 1, turn [9]

Row 9: sc in all 9 st, ch 1, turn [9]

Row 10: inc in next st, sc in next 7 st, inc in next st, ch 1, turn [11]

Row 11: sc in all 11 st, ch 1, turn [11]

Row 12: inc in next st, sc in next 9 st, inc in next st, ch 1, turn [13]

Row 13: sc in all 13 st, ch 1, turn [13]

Fasten off and weave in the yarn end on the first sail. Don't fasten off on the second sail. Place both pieces with the wrong sides towards each other and crochet the next round through both layers to close.

Finishing Rnd: sc in next 13 row-ends, 4 sc in the top of the triangle to make a nice curve, sc in next 13 row-ends [30]

Fasten off, leaving a long tail for sewing.

Mast *(in white yarn)*

Rnd 1: start 6 sc in a magic ring [6]

Rnd 2 – 17: sc in all 6 st [6]

Fasten off, leaving a long tail for sewing. Fold a pipe cleaner and insert it in the mast. Sew the mast to the boat and sew the sail to the side of the mast. Finish by crocheting a long chain using white yarn and sewing it to the boat, so your hippo can pull his boat along.

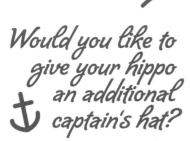

Would you like to give your hippo an additional captain's hat?

For the free pattern, check www.amigurumi.com/bonusfavorites

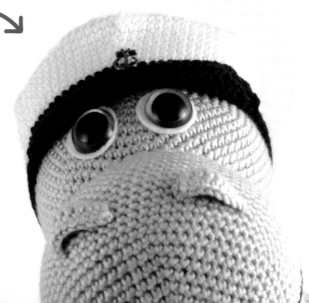

TOCO THE TOUCAN

by Airali Design (Ilaria Caliri)

SKILL LEVEL: ✷✷

SIZE: 5.5" / 14 cm tall when made with the indicated yarn.

MATERIALS:

– Light worsted weight yarn in black, white, red, pink, yellow, light blue
– Size C-2 / 3 mm crochet hook
– Safety eyes (15 mm)
– Yarn needle
– Pins
– Stitch markers
– Fiberfill for stuffing

AMIGURUMI GALLERY
Scan or visit
www.amigurumi.com/3002
to share pictures and find inspiration.

FACE PATCH *(in white yarn)*

Ch 16. Stitches are worked around both sides of the foundation chain.

Rnd 1: start in second ch from the hook, sc in next 14 st, 5 sc in next st. Continue on the other side of the foundation chain, sc in next 13 st, 4 sc in next st [36]

Rnd 2: (sc in next 15 st, inc in next 3 st) repeat 2 times [42]

Rnd 3: sc in next 15 st, (inc in next st, sc in next st) repeat 3 times, sc in next 15 st, (inc in next st, sc in next st) repeat 3 times [48]

Rnd 4: sc in next 15 st, (sc in next 2 st, inc in next st) repeat 3 times, sc in next 15 st, (sc in next 2 st, inc in next st) repeat 3 times [54]

Rnd 5: sc in next 15 st, (inc in next st, sc in next 3 st) repeat 3 times, sc in next 15 st, (inc in next st, sc in next 3 st) repeat 3 times [60]

Rnd 6: sc in next 15 st, (sc in next 4 st, inc in next st)

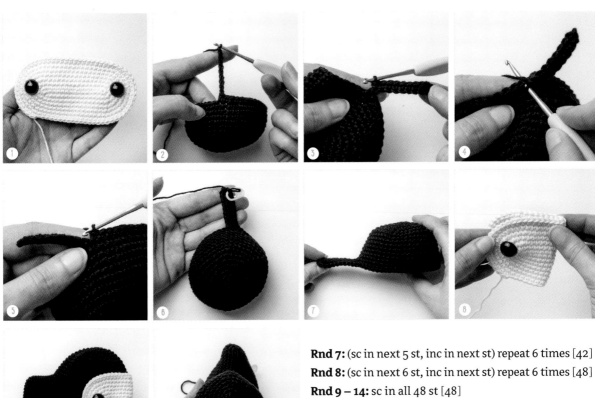

repeat 3 times, sc in next 15 st, (sc in next 4 st, inc in next st) repeat 3 times [66]

Rnd 7: sc in all 66 st [66]

Fasten off, leaving a long tail for sewing. Insert the safety eyes between rounds 3 and 4 (picture 1). Don't close the washers yet.

HEAD AND BODY *(in black yarn)*

Rnd 1: start 6 sc in a magic ring [6]

Rnd 2: inc in all 6 st [12]

Rnd 3: (sc in next st, inc in next st) repeat 6 times [18]

Rnd 4: (sc in next 2 st, inc in next st) repeat 6 times [24]

Rnd 5: (sc in next 3 st, inc in next st) repeat 6 times [30]

Rnd 6: (sc in next 4 st, inc in next st) repeat 6 times [36]

Rnd 7: (sc in next 5 st, inc in next st) repeat 6 times [42]

Rnd 8: (sc in next 6 st, inc in next st) repeat 6 times [48]

Rnd 9 – 14: sc in all 48 st [48]

Rnd 15: ch 10 (picture 2), start in second ch from hook, sc in next 9 ch (picture 3), continue along round 14 (picture 4), sc in all 48 st, continue on the other side of the chain, sc in next 9 st (picture 5) [66]

Mark the last stitch with a stitch marker (picture 6).

Rnd 16: 3 sc in next st, sc in next 64 st, 3 sc in next st [70] (picture 7)

Rnd 17: sc in next st, inc in next st, sc in next 66 st, inc in next st, sc in next st [72]

Rnd 18 – 32: sc in all 72 st [72]

Fold the face patch in half. Place it between rounds 11 and 26 of the head (pictures 8-10). Pass the safety eyes through the head and fix on the washers. Sew the face patch to the head using the white yarn tail.

Rnd 33: (sc in next 10 st, dec) repeat 6 times [66]

Rnd 34: (sc in next 9 st, dec) repeat 6 times [60]

Rnd 35: (sc in next 8 st, dec) repeat 6 times [54]

Rnd 36: (sc in next 7 st, dec) repeat 6 times [48]

Rnd 37: (sc in next 6 st, dec) repeat 6 times [42]

Rnd 38: (sc in next 5 st, dec) repeat 6 times [36]
Stuff the head and body with fiberfill and continue
stuffing as you go.
Rnd 39: (sc in next 4 st, dec) repeat 6 times [30]
Rnd 40: (sc in next 3 st, dec) repeat 6 times [24]
Rnd 41: (sc in next 2 st, dec) repeat 6 times [18]
Rnd 42: (sc in next st, dec) repeat 6 times [12]
Rnd 43: dec 6 times [6]
Fasten off and weave in the yarn ends.

BEAK *(start in red yarn)*
Rnd 1: start 6 sc in a magic ring [6]
Rnd 2: inc in all 6 st [12]
Rnd 3: (sc in next st, inc in next st) repeat
6 times [18]
Rnd 4: (sc in next 2 st, inc in next st) repeat 6 times [24]
Rnd 5: (sc in next 3 st, inc in next st) repeat 6 times [30]
Rnd 6: (dec, sc in next st) repeat 3 times, (inc in next st,
sc in next 6 st) repeat 3 times [30]
Rnd 7: dec 3 times, (inc in next st, sc in next 7 st)
repeat 3 times [30]
Rnd 8 – 9: sc in all 30 st [30]
Change to pink yarn.
Rnd 10 – 13: sc in all 30 st [30]
Change to yellow yarn.
Rnd 14 – 21: sc in all 30 st [30]
Fasten off, leaving a long tail for sewing. Stuff the beak
with fiberfill.

CHEEK *(make 2, in light blue yarn)*
Rnd 1: start 6 sc in a magic ring [6]
Rnd 2: inc in all 6 st [12]
Rnd 3: (sc in next st, inc in next st) repeat 6 times [18]
Slst in next st. Fasten off, leaving a long tail for sewing.

WING *(make 2, in black yarn)*
Rnd 1: start 6 sc in a magic ring [6]
Rnd 2: inc in all 6 st [12]
Rnd 3: (sc in next st, inc in next st) repeat 6 times [18]
Rnd 4 – 5: sc in all 18 st [18]

Rnd 6: (sc in next 7 st, dec) repeat 2 times [16]
Fasten off, leaving a long tail for sewing. The wings
don't need to be stuffed. Flatten the wings.

LONG TAIL FEATHER *(in black yarn)*
Rnd 1: start 6 sc in a magic ring [6]
Rnd 2: inc in all 6 st [12]
Rnd 3 – 5: sc in all 12 st [12]
Rnd 6: (sc in next 4 st, dec) repeat 2 times [10]
Rnd 7: (sc in next 3 st, dec) repeat 2 times [8]
Rnd 8: (sc in next 2 st, dec) repeat 2 times [6]
Fasten off, leaving a long tail for sewing. The long
tail feather doesn't need to be stuffed. Flatten the
feather.

SHORT TAIL FEATHER *(make 2, in black yarn)*
Rnd 1: start 5 sc in a magic ring [5]

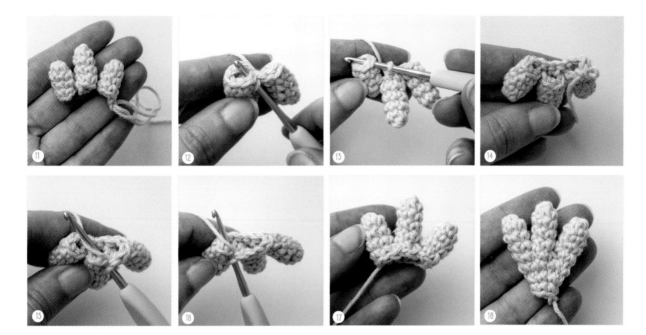

Rnd 2: inc in all 5 st [10]

Rnd 3 – 4: sc in all 10 st [10]

Rnd 5: (sc in next 3 st, dec) repeat 2 times [8]

Rnd 6: (sc in next 2 st, dec) repeat 2 times [6]

Fasten off, leaving a long tail for sewing. The short tail feather doesn't need to be stuffed. Flatten the feathers.

LEG *(make 2, in light blue yarn)*

Leave a long starting yarn tail.

Rnd 1: start 8 sc in a magic ring [8]

Rnd 2 – 8: sc in all 8 st [8]

Stuff the leg with fiberfill. Fasten off, leaving a long tail for sewing.

FOOT *(make 2, in light blue yarn)*

Start by making 3 toes for each foot.

Middle toe *(make 1 for each foot, 2 in total)*

Rnd 1: start 6 sc in a magic ring [6]

Rnd 2 – 5: sc in all 6 st [6]

Fasten off and weave in the yarn end.

Side toe *(make 2 for each foot, 4 in total)*

Rnd 1: start 6 sc in a magic ring [6]

Rnd 2 – 4: sc in all 6 st [6]

Fasten off and weave in the yarn end on the first side toe. Do not fasten off on the second side toe (picture 11). In the next round, we'll join the toes together.

Joining the toes

Rnd 5: sc in next 4 st on the second side toe, skip next st on this toe, (picture 12) sc in next 2 st on the middle toe, skip next st on this toe, sc in next 5 st on the first side toe (pictures 13-14), skip next st on this toe, skip 1 st on the middle toe, (picture 15) sc in next 2 st on the middle toe, skip next st on this toe, skip 1 st on the second side toe (picture 16), sc in next st on this toe [14] (picture 17)

There are little gaps between the toes. Since they are not stuffed and flat, they are invisible.

Rnd 6: (sc in next 5 st, dec) repeat 2 times [12]

Rnd 7: dec 6 times [6]

Rnd 8: sc in all 6 st [6] (picture 18)

The feet don't need to be stuffed. Fasten off, leaving a yarn tail. Using a yarn needle, weave the yarn tail

through the front loop of each remaining stitch and pull
it tight to close. Weave in the yarn end. Sew the feet to
the legs.

ASSEMBLY

– Sew the beak to the head, starting from the center
  top of the face patch.
– Sew the cheeks to the head, they're positioned over
  the face patch.
– Sew the wings to the sides of the body, between
  rounds 22 and 28, positioned at a slight angle.
– Sew the 3 feathers of the tail to the back of the
  body, with the long feather in the center (picture 19).

– Pin and sew the legs to the bottom of the body,
  across rounds 37 and 38, with an interspace of 5
  stitches (picture 20). Make sure the position of the
  feet allows the toucan to sit.

RAINDROP THE FOX

by Zipzipdreams (Anna Edina Tekten)

SKILL LEVEL: ✶ ✶

SIZE: 7.5" / 20 cm when made with the indicated yarn.

MATERIALS:

– Sport weight yarn in orange, black, white and pink (leftover)
– Size B-1 / 2.5 mm crochet hook
– Safety eyes (6 mm)
– Safety nose (12 mm)
– Black embroidery thread
– Yarn needle
– Stitch markers
– Fiberfill for stuffing

AMIGURUMI GALLERY

Scan or visit
www.amigurumi.com/2502
to share pictures and find inspiration.

HEAD *(in orange yarn)*

Rnd 1: start 6 sc in a magic ring [6]

Rnd 2: inc in all 6 st [12]

Rnd 3: (sc in next st, inc in next st) repeat 6 times [18]

Rnd 4: (sc in next 2 st, inc in next st) repeat 6 times [24]

Rnd 5: (sc in next 3 st, inc in next st) repeat 6 times [30]

Rnd 6: (sc in next 4 st, inc in next st) repeat 6 times [36]

Rnd 7: (sc in next 5 st, inc in next st) repeat 6 times [42]

Rnd 8: (sc in next 6 st, inc in next st) repeat 6 times [48]

Rnd 9: (sc in next 15 st, inc in next st) repeat 3 times [51]

Rnd 10: sc in all 51 st [51]

Rnd 11: (sc in next 16 st, inc in next st) repeat 3 times [54]

Rnd 12 – 15: sc in all 54 st [54]

Rnd 16: sc in next 12 st, inc in next 3 st, sc in next 24 st, inc in next 3 st, sc in next 12 st [60]

Rnd 17 – 21: sc in all 60 st [60]

Rnd 22: sc in next 13 st, dec 3 times, sc in next 24 st, dec 3 times, sc in next 11 st [54]

Rnd 23: sc in next 12 st, dec 3 times, sc in next 20 st, dec 3 times, sc in next 10 st [48]

Rnd 24: (sc in next 4 st, dec) repeat 8 times [40]

Rnd 25: (sc in next 3 st, dec) repeat 8 times [32]
Insert the safety eyes between rounds 16 and 17, with an interspace of 11 stitches. The eyes should be centered between both decrease sections of rounds 22-23 (picture 1).
Rnd 26: (sc in next 2 st, dec) repeat 8 times [24]
Rnd 27: (sc in next 2 st, dec) repeat 6 times [18]
Slst in next st. Fasten off, leaving a long tail for sewing. Stuff the head firmly with fiberfill.

MUZZLE *(in white yarn)*
Rnd 1: start 6 sc in a magic ring [6]
When you pull the yarn tail to tighten the magic ring, make sure you leave a hole large enough to fit the post of the safety nose in later.
Rnd 2: (sc in next st, inc in next 2 st) repeat 2 times [10]
Rnd 3: sc in next 2 st, inc in next 2 st, sc in next 3 st, inc in next 2 st, sc in next st [14]
Rnd 4: sc in next st, (sc in next st, inc in next st) repeat 2 times, sc in next 5 st, (inc in next st, sc in next st) repeat 2 times [18]
Rnd 5: inc in next 2 st, sc in next 2 st, inc in next st, hdc in next 9 st, inc in next st, sc in next 2 st, inc in next st [23]
Rnd 6: sc in next 4 st, inc in next 2 st, hdc in next 14 st, inc in next 2 st, sc in next st [27]
Rnd 7: slst in next 8 st, sc in next 2 st, hdc in next 10 st, sc in next 2 st, slst in next 5 st [27]
Slst in next st. Fasten off, leaving a long tail for sewing (picture 2). Insert the safety nose into the center of the magic ring and fix on the washer. Pull the yarn tail to tighten the ring around the post. Stuff the muzzle with fiberfill and sew it to the head, over rounds 17-22, between the eyes. Keep the slst at the upper corner of the muzzle. Add more stuffing just before closing the seam.

EAR *(make 2, start in black yarn)*
Rnd 1: start 6 sc in a magic ring [6]
Rnd 2: (sc in next st, inc in next st) repeat 3 times [9]

Rnd 3: (sc in next 2 st, inc in next st) repeat 3 times [12]
Change to orange yarn.
Rnd 4: (sc in next 2 st, inc in next st) repeat 4 times [16]
Rnd 5: sc in next st, (inc in next st, sc in next 3 st) repeat 3 times, inc in next st, sc in next 2 st [20]
Rnd 6: (sc in next 4 st, inc in next st) repeat 4 times [24]
Rnd 7: sc in next st, (inc in next st, sc in next 5 st) repeat 3 times, inc in next st, sc in next 4 st [28]
Rnd 8: (sc in next 6 st, inc in next st) repeat 4 times [32]
Rnd 9: sc in next 8 st, inc in next st, sc in next 15 st, inc in next st, sc in next 7 st [34]
Rnd 10 – 12: sc in all 34 st [34]
Rnd 13: (dec, sc in next 15 st) repeat 2 times [32]
Slst in next st. Fasten off, leaving a long tail for sewing. The ears don't need to be stuffed. Flatten the ears with the color change at the back. Fold a side of the ears and fix it with a couple of stitches (picture 3), then sew the ears to the head over rounds 4-11 (picture 4). Embroider eyebrows, eyelashes and a vertical line below the safety nose with black embroidery thread.

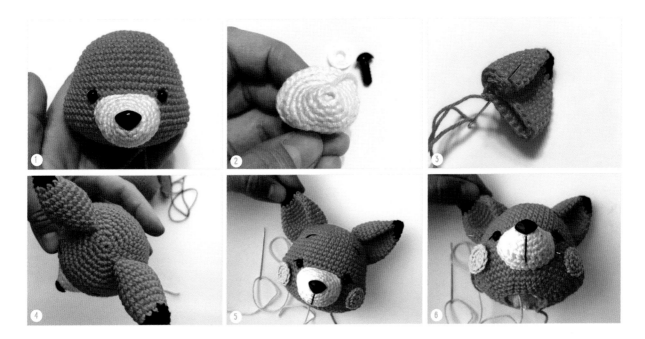

CHEEK *(make 2, in pink yarn)*

Work in joined rounds.

Rnd 1: start 6 sc in a magic ring, slst in first st, ch 1 [6]

Rnd 2: inc in all 6 st, slst in first st [12]

Fasten off, leaving a long tail for sewing. Sew the cheeks to the head over rounds 17-21, at 2 stitches from either side of the muzzle (pictures 5-6).

Rnd 17: sc in all 30 st [30]

Rnd 18: (sc in next 3 st, dec) repeat 6 times [24]

Rnd 19: sc in all 24 st [24]

Rnd 20: (sc in next 2 st, dec) repeat 6 times [18]

Rnd 21: sc in all 18 st [18]

Slst in next st. Fasten off, leaving a long tail for sewing. Stuff the body firmly with fiberfill. Sew the head to the

BODY *(in orange yarn)*

Rnd 1: start 6 sc in a magic ring [6]

Rnd 2: inc in all 6 st [12]

Rnd 3: (sc in next st, inc in next st) repeat 6 times [18]

Rnd 4: (sc in next 2 st, inc in next st) repeat 6 times [24]

Rnd 5: (sc in next 3 st, inc in next st) repeat 6 times [30]

Rnd 6: (sc in next 4 st, inc in next st) repeat 6 times [36]

Rnd 7: (sc in next 5 st, inc in next st) repeat 6 times [42]

Rnd 8 – 13: sc in all 42 st [42]

Rnd 14: sc in next 8 st, (dec, sc in next 3 st) repeat 5 times, dec, sc in next 7 st [36]

Rnd 15: sc in all 36 st [36]

Rnd 16: sc in next 8 st, (dec, sc in next 2 st) repeat 5 times, dec, sc in next 6 st [30]

body, making sure you keep the rounded belly at the front.

ARM *(make 2, start in black yarn)*
Rnd 1: start 6 sc in a magic ring [6]
Rnd 2: inc in all 6 st [12]
Rnd 3: (sc in next 5 st, inc in next st) repeat 2 times [14]
Rnd 4 – 5: sc in all 14 st [14]
Rnd 6: sc in next 5 st, dec, sc in next 7 st [13]
Rnd 7 – 8: sc in all 13 st [13]
Rnd 9: sc in next 6 st, dec, sc in next 5 st [12]
Stuff the arm with fiberfill and continue stuffing as you go.
Rnd 10 – 11: sc in all 12 st [12]
Rnd 12: sc in next st, *(change to orange yarn)*
sc in next 5 st, dec, sc in next 4 st [11]
Rnd 13 – 14: sc in all 11 st [11]
Rnd 15: sc in next 6 st, dec, sc in next 3 st [10]
Rnd 16 – 17: sc in all 10 st [10]
Rnd 18: sc in next 6 st, dec, sc in next 2 st [9]
Rnd 19 – 20: sc in all 9 st [9]
Rnd 21: (sc in next st, dec) repeat 3 times [6]
Slst in next st. Fasten off, leaving a long tail for sewing. Sew the arms to the sides of the body, over rounds 18-20. Embroider a cross-shaped belly button over rounds 8-9 using black embroidery thread.

LEG *(make 2, start in black yarn)*
Ch 5. Stitches are worked around both sides of the foundation chain.
Rnd 1: start in second ch from hook, inc in this st, sc in next 2 st, 3 sc in next st. Continue on the other side of the foundation chain, sc in next 3 st [10]
Rnd 2: inc in next 2 st, sc in next 2 st, inc in next 3 st, sc in next 2 st, inc in next st [16]
Rnd 3: (sc in next st, inc in next st) repeat 2 times, sc in next 2 st, (sc in next st, inc in next st) repeat 3 times, sc in next 3 st, inc in next st [22]
Rnd 4: (sc in next st, inc in next st) repeat 2 times, sc in next 6 st, (inc in next st, sc in next st) repeat 3 times, sc in next 5 st, inc in next st [28]
Rnd 5 – 6: sc in all 28 st [28]
Rnd 7: sc in next 12 st, (dec, sc in next st) repeat 4 times, sc in next 4 st [24]
Rnd 8: sc in next 10 st, dec 6 times, sc in next 2 st [18]
Rnd 9: sc in next 10 st, dec, sc in next st, dec, sc in next 3 st [16]
Stuff the leg firmly with fiberfill and continue stuffing as you go.
Rnd 10 – 14: sc in all 16 st [16]
Rnd 15: (sc in next 2 st, dec) repeat 4 times [12]
Rnd 16: sc in next 4 st [4] Leave the remaining stitches unworked.
Change to orange yarn.
Rnd 17 – 22: sc in next 12 st [12]
Rnd 23: (sc in next st, dec) repeat 4 times [8]
Slst in next st. Fasten off, leaving a long tail for sewing. Sew the legs to the sides of the body, over rounds 6-7.

TAIL *(start in white yarn)*

Rnd 1: start 6 sc in a magic ring [6]

Rnd 2: inc in next 3 st, sc in next 3 st [9]

Rnd 3: sc in all 9 st [9]

Rnd 4: sc in next 2 st, inc in next 3 st, sc in next 4 st [12]

Rnd 5: sc in all 12 st [12]

Rnd 6: sc in next 3 st, inc in next st, sc in next 2 st, *(change to orange yarn)* sc in next st, inc in next st, sc in next 3 st, inc in next st [15]

Rnd 7: (sc in next 2 st, inc in next st) repeat 5 times [20]

Rnd 8: sc in all 20 st [20]

Rnd 9: (sc in next 4 st, inc in next st) repeat 4 times [24]

Rnd 10 – 14: sc in all 24 st [24]

Rnd 15: (sc in next 6 st, dec) repeat 3 times [21]

Rnd 16: sc in next 2 st, (dec, sc in next 5 st) repeat 2 times, dec, sc in next 3 st [18]

Rnd 17: sc in all 18 st [18]

Rnd 18: (sc in next 4 st, dec) repeat 3 times [15]

Stuff this part of the tail firmly with fiberfill.

Rnd 19 – 20: sc in all 15 st [15]

Rnd 21: (sc in next 3 st, dec) repeat 3 times [12]

Rnd 22 – 23: sc in all 12 st [12]

Stuff this part of the tail only lightly with fiberfill. The end of the tail doesn't need to be stuffed.

Rnd 24: (sc in next 2 st, dec) repeat 3 times [9]

Rnd 25: sc in all 9 st [9]

Slst in next st. Fasten off, leaving a long tail for sewing. Flatten the end of the tail and sew it to the body, between the legs, over rounds 5-7.

GERTY THE GECKO

by Moji-Moji Design (Janine Holmes)

SKILL LEVEL: ✴ ✴

SIZE: 7" / 18 cm tall when made with the indicated yarn.

MATERIALS:

– Light worsted weight yarn in green, yellow and white (leftover)
– Size C-2 / 3 mm crochet hook
– Safety eyes (12 mm)
– Stitch marker
– Yarn needle
– Fiberfill for stuffing

AMIGURUMI GALLERY

Scan or visit
www.amigurumi.com/3001
to share pictures and find inspiration.

HEAD *(in green yarn)*

Rnd 1: start 6 sc in a magic ring [6]

Rnd 2: inc in all 6 st [12]

Rnd 3: (sc in next st, inc in next st) repeat 6 times [18]

Rnd 4: (sc in next 2 st, inc in next st) repeat 6 times [24]

Rnd 5: (sc in next 3 st, inc in next st) repeat 6 times [30]

Rnd 6 – 9: sc in all 30 st [30]

Rnd 10: inc in next 4 st, sc in next st (mark this stitch as a guide to place the eyes later) (picture 1), inc in next 4 st, sc in next 21 st [38]

Rnd 11: (sc in next st, inc in next st) repeat 4 times, sc in next st, (sc in next st, inc in next st) repeat 4 times, sc in next 21 st [46]

Rnd 12: (sc in next 22 st, inc in next st) repeat 2 times [48]

Rnd 13 – 16: sc in all 48 st [48]

Rnd 17: (sc in next 6 st, dec) repeat 6 times [42]

Rnd 18: sc in all 42 st [42]

Rnd 19: (sc in next 5 st, dec) repeat 6 times [36]
Rnd 20: sc in all 36 st [36]
Rnd 21: (sc in next 4 st, dec) repeat 6 times [30]
Rnd 22: sc in all 30 st [30]
Rnd 23: (sc in next 3 st, dec) repeat 6 times [24]
Rnd 24: sc in all 24 st [24]
Rnd 25: (sc in next 2 st, dec) repeat 6 times [18]
Stuff the head with fiberfill and continue stuffing as
you go.
Rnd 26: (sc in next st, dec) repeat 6 times [12]
Rnd 27: dec 6 times [6]
Fasten off, leaving a long tail for sewing. Using your
yarn needle, weave the yarn tail through the front
loop of each remaining stitch and pull it tight to close.
Weave in the yarn end.

EYE *(make 2, start in white yarn)*
Rnd 1: start 6 sc in a magic ring [6]
When you pull the yarn tail to tighten the magic ring,
make sure you leave a hole large enough to fit the post
of the safety eye in later.
Rnd 2: inc in all 6 st [12]

Change to yellow yarn.
Rnd 3: (sc in next st, inc in next st) repeat 6 times [18]
Change to green yarn.
Rnd 4 – 8: sc in all 18 st [18]
Insert the safety eye into the center of the magic ring
and close the washer. Pull the yarn tail to tighten
the ring around the post. Stuff the eye with fiberfill.
Flatten the eye and work the next round through both
layers to close.
Rnd 9: ch 1, sc in all 9 st [9] (picture 2)
Fasten off, leaving a long tail for sewing. Beginning at
the bottom center of the eye, work surface sc around
each of the yellow stitch posts (pictures 3-6). Fasten
off. Tie the yarn ends together and hide them inside
the eye. Pin the eyes to the top of the head with the
inside corners of the flat seams touching each other
at the marked stitch from round 10, and the outside
corners of the flat seams positioned between rounds
13 and 14, with an interspace of 18 stitches (picture 7).
Sew round 9 of the eye in place and, pinching the eye
and the head together, sew around all the edges where
the 2 pieces touch (picture 8).

BODY *(in yellow yarn)*

Rnd 1: start 6 sc in a magic ring [6]

Rnd 2: inc in all 6 st [12]

Rnd 3: (sc in next st, inc in next st) repeat 6 times [18]

Rnd 4: (sc in next 2 st, inc in next st) repeat 6 times [24]

Rnd 5: (sc in next 3 st, inc in next st) repeat 6 times [30]

Rnd 6: (sc in next 4 st, inc in next st) repeat 6 times [36]

Rnd 7: (sc in next 5 st, inc in next st) repeat 6 times [42]

Rnd 8: (sc in next 6 st, inc in next st) repeat 6 times [48]

Rnd 9 – 13: sc in all 48 st [48]

Rnd 14: (sc in next 6 st, dec) repeat 6 times [42]

Rnd 15 – 16: sc in all 42 st [42]

Rnd 17: (sc in next 5 st, dec) repeat 6 times [36]

Rnd 18 – 19: sc in all 36 st [36]

Rnd 20: (sc in next 4 st, dec) repeat 6 times [30]

Rnd 21 – 22: sc in all 30 st [30]

Rnd 23: (sc in next 3 st, dec) repeat 6 times [24]

Rnd 24 – 25: sc in all 24 st [24]

Rnd 26: (sc in next 4 st, dec) repeat 4 times [20]

Rnd 27 – 28: sc in all 20 st [20]

Rnd 29: (sc in next 8 st, dec) repeat 2 times [18]

Rnd 30 – 31: sc in all 18 st [18]

Fasten off, leaving a long tail for sewing. Stuff the body and sew it to the underside of the head, between rounds 15 and 22 (picture 9).

TAIL *(start in green yarn)*

Rnd 1: start 6 sc in a magic ring [6]

Rnd 2 – 3: sc in all 6 st [6]

Work in a stripes pattern, changing colors as indicated in italics for each round.

Rnd 4: *(yellow)* (sc in next st, inc in next st) repeat 3 times [9]

Rnd 5 – 6: *(yellow)* sc in all 9 st [9]

Rnd 7: *(green)* (sc in next 2 st, inc in next st) repeat 3 times [12]

Rnd 8 – 9: *(green)* sc in all 12 st [12]

Rnd 10: *(yellow)* (sc in next 3 st, inc in next st) repeat 3 times [15]

Rnd 11 – 12: *(yellow)* sc in all 15 st [15]

Rnd 13: *(green)* (sc in next 4 st, inc in next st) repeat 3 times [18]

Rnd 14 – 15: *(green)* sc in all 18 st [18]

Rnd 16 – 18: *(yellow)* sc in all 18 st [18]

Rnd 19 – 21: *(green)* sc in all 18 st [18]

Rnd 22 – 24: *(yellow)* sc in all 18 st [18]

Rnd 25: *(green)* (sc in next 5 st, inc in next st) repeat 3 times [21]

Rnd 26 – 27: *(green)* sc in all 21 st [21]

Rnd 28: *(yellow)* (sc in next 6 st, inc in next st) repeat 3 times [24]

Rnd 29 – 30: *(yellow)* sc in all 24 st [24]

Rnd 31: *(green)* (sc in next 3 st, inc in next st) repeat 6 times [30]

Rnd 32 – 33: *(green)* sc in all 30 st [30]

Rnd 34: *(yellow)* sc in all 30 st [30]

Fasten off, leaving a long tail for sewing. Stuff the tail and sew it between rounds 4 and 16 at the back of the body.

NOTE: At this point you can choose whether the head points straight forward or is twisted more to the side depending on where exactly you choose to place the tail.

CHIN PATCH *(in yellow yarn)*

Crochet in rows.

Row 1: start 3 sc in a magic ring, ch 1, turn [3]

Row 2: inc in all 3 st, ch 1, turn [6]

Row 3: (sc in next st, inc in next st) repeat 3 times, ch 1, turn [9]

Row 4: (sc in next 2 st, inc in next st) repeat 3 times, ch 1, turn [12]

Row 5: (sc in next 3 st, inc in next st) repeat 3 times, ch 1, turn [15]

Row 6: (sc in next 4 st, inc in next st) repeat 3 times, ch 1, turn [18]

Row 7: (sc in next 5 st, inc in next st) repeat 3 times, ch 1, turn [21]

Row 8: (sc in next 6 st, inc in next st) repeat 3 times, ch 1, turn [24]

Row 9: sc in all 24 st, ch 1, turn [24]

Work the next round all around the patch.

Rnd 10: (sc in next 2 st, dec) repeat 6 times, sc in next 18 row-ends down the flat side of the patch, slst in next st [36]

Fasten off, leaving a long tail for sewing. Sew the edge of the chin patch to the underside of the face with the center of the flat edge against the neck and the center of the curved edge between rounds 4 and 5 of the face (pictures 10-11).

ARM *(make 2, start in green yarn)*

Start by making 3 fingers for each hand.

Finger *(make 3 for each arm, in green yarn)*

Rnd 1: start 6 sc in a magic ring [6]

Rnd 2: (sc in next st, inc in next st) repeat 3 times [9]

Rnd 3: sc in all 9 st [9]

Rnd 4: (sc in next st, dec) repeat 3 times [6]

Fasten off and weave in the yarn ends on 2 fingers. Don't fasten off on the third finger. In the next round we'll join the fingers together.

Hand and arm

Rnd 5: sc in all 6 st on the third finger (picture 12), sc in next 3 st on the second finger (picture 13), sc in all 6 st on the first finger (picture 14), sc in next 3 st on the second finger (picture 15) [18]

Rnd 6: (sc in next st, dec) repeat 6 times [12]

Stuff the hand with fiberfill and continue stuffing the arm as you go.

Rnd 7: dec 6 times [6]

Work in a stripes pattern, changing colors as indicated in italics for each round.

Rnd 8 − 9: *(yellow)* sc in all 6 st [6]

Rnd 10 − 11: *(green)* sc in all 6 st [6]

Rnd 12 − 13: *(yellow)* sc in all 6 st [6]

Rnd 14: *(green)* (sc in next st, inc in next st) repeat 3 times [9]

Rnd 15: *(green)* sc in all 9 st [9]

Rnd 16 − 17: *(yellow)* sc in all 9 st [9]

Rnd 18: *(green)* sc in all 9 st [9]

Rnd 19: *(green)* (sc in next st, dec) repeat 3 times [6]

Fasten off, leaving a long tail for sewing. Flatten the top of the arm so that the seam runs from side to side in line with the 3 fingers and sew it closed. Sew the flat seam of the arms to the sides of the body, between rounds 29 and 30.

LEG *(make 2, start in green yarn)*

Start by making 3 toes for each foot.

Toe *(make 3 for each foot, in green yarn)*

Rnd 1: start 6 sc in a magic ring [6]

Rnd 2: (sc in next st, inc in next st) repeat 3 times [9]

Rnd 3 − 4: sc in all 9 st [9]

Rnd 5: (sc in next st, dec) repeat 3 times [6]

Fasten off and weave in the yarn ends on 2 toes. Don't fasten off on the third toe. In the next round, we'll join the toes together.

Foot and leg

Rnd 6: sc in all 6 st on the third toe (picture 12), sc in next 3 st on the second toe (picture 13), sc in all 6 st on the first toe (picture 14), sc in next 3 st on the second toe (picture 15) [18]

Rnd 7: (sc in next 4 st, dec) repeat 3 times [15]

Rnd 8: (sc in next 3 st, dec) repeat 3 times [12]

Work in a stripes pattern, changing colors as indicated in italics for each round.

Rnd 9: *(yellow)* sc in all 12 st [12]

Stuff the foot with fiberfill and continue stuffing the leg as you go.

Rnd 10: *(yellow)* (sc in next 2 st, dec) repeat 3 times [9]

Rnd 11 – 12: *(green)* sc in all 9 st [9]

Rnd 13 – 14: *(yellow)* sc in all 9 st [9]

Rnd 15 – 16: *(green)* sc in all 9 st [9]

Rnd 17: (sc in next st, dec) repeat 3 times [6]

Fasten off, leaving a long tail for sewing. Flatten the top of the leg so that the seam runs at a 90 degrees angle to the flat plane of the foot (picture 16) and sew it closed. Sew the flat seam vertically to the body between rounds 7 and 10, placing them 1 stitch in front of the tail. Sew the inside of the leg to the body where it touches.

JOHNNY THE MONKEY

by Pepika (Sanda Jelic Dobrosavljev)

HEAD *(in brown yarn)*

Starting at the front of the head.

Rnd 1: start 6 sc in a magic ring [6]

Rnd 2: inc in all 6 st [12]

Rnd 3: (sc in next st, inc in next st) repeat 6 times [18]

Rnd 4: (sc in next 2 st, inc in next st) repeat 6 times [24]

Rnd 5: (sc in next 3 st, inc in next st) repeat 6 times [30]

Rnd 6: (sc in next 4 st, inc in next st) repeat 6 times [36]

Rnd 7: (sc in next 5 st, inc in next st) repeat 6 times [42]

Rnd 8: (sc in next 6 st, inc in next st) repeat 6 times [48]

Rnd 9: (sc in next 7 st, inc in next st) repeat 6 times [54]

Rnd 10: (sc in next 8 st, inc in next st) repeat 6 times [60]

Rnd 11 – 16: sc in all 60 st [60]

Rnd 17: (sc in next 8 st, dec) repeat 6 times [54]

Rnd 18: (sc in next 7 st, dec) repeat 6 times [48]

Rnd 19: (sc in next 6 st, dec) repeat 6 times [42]

Rnd 20: (sc in next 5 st, dec) repeat 6 times [36]
Rnd 21: (sc in next 4 st, dec) repeat 6 times [30]
Rnd 22: (sc in next 3 st, dec) repeat 6 times [24]
Stuff the head with fiberfill and continue stuffing as you go.
Rnd 23: (sc in next 2 st, dec) repeat 6 times [18]
Rnd 24: (sc in next st, dec) repeat 6 times [12]
Rnd 25: dec 6 times [6]
Fasten off, leaving a yarn tail. Using your yarn needle, weave the yarn tail through the front loop of each remaining stitch and pull it tight to close. Weave in the yarn end.

FACE PATCH *(in yellow yarn)*
Rnd 1: start 6 sc in a magic ring [6]

Rnd 2: inc in all 6 st [12]
Rnd 3: (sc in next st, inc in next st) repeat 6 times [18]
Rnd 4: (sc in next 2 st, inc in next st) repeat 6 times [24]
Rnd 5: (sc in next 3 st, inc in next st) repeat 6 times [30]
Rnd 6 – 7: sc in all 30 st [30]
Rnd 8: (sc in next 4 st, inc in next st) repeat 3 times, sc in next 15 st [33]
Rnd 9: sc in next 5 st, sc + hdc + dc + hdc + sc in next st, slst in next 5 st, sc + hdc + dc + hdc + sc in next st, sc in next 21 st [41]
Rnd 10: sc in next 7 st, inc in next st, sc in next 2 st, dec, sc in next st, dec, sc in next 2 st, inc in next st, sc in next 23 st [41]
Fasten off, leaving a long tail for sewing. Insert the safety eyes in round 9 of the face patch, with an inter-

space of 5 stitches. Sew the face patch in the middle of the head, between rounds 7-8. Add stuffing before closing the seam.

EAR *(make 2, in yellow yarn)*
Rnd 1: start 5 sc in a magic ring [5]
Rnd 2: inc in all 5 st [10]
Rnd 3: (sc in next st, inc in next st) repeat 5 times [15]
Rnd 4: (sc in next 2 st, inc in next st) repeat 5 times [20]
Rnd 5: sc in all 20 st [20]
Rnd 6: (sc in next 2 st, dec) repeat 5 times [15]
Rnd 7: (sc in next st, dec) repeat 5 times [10]
Fasten off, leaving a long tail for sewing. Fold the ears, they don't need to be stuffed. Sew the ears between rounds 10 and 11, 2 rounds away from the face patch.

BODY *(in brown yarn)*
Rnd 1: start 5 sc in magic ring [5]
Rnd 2: inc in all 5 st [10]
Rnd 3: (sc in next st, inc in next st) repeat 5 times [15]
Rnd 4: (sc in next 2 st, inc in next st) repeat 5 times [20]
Rnd 5: (sc in next 3 st, inc in next st) repeat 5 times [25]
Rnd 6: (sc in next 4 st, inc in next st) repeat 5 times [30]
Rnd 7: (sc in next 5 st, inc in next st) repeat 5 times [35]
Rnd 8 – 13: sc in all 35 st [35]
Rnd 14: (sc in next 5 st, dec) repeat 5 times [30]
Rnd 15: (sc in next 4 st, dec) repeat 5 times [25]

Rnd 16: (sc in next 3 st, dec) repeat 5 times [20]
Rnd 17: sc in all 20 st [20]
Rnd 18: (sc in next 2 st, dec) repeat 5 times [15]
Rnd 19 – 20: sc in all 15 st [15]
Fasten off, leaving a long tail for sewing. Sew the head to the body.

ARM *(make 2, start in yellow yarn)*
Rnd 1: start 6 sc in a magic ring [6]
Rnd 2: inc in all 6 st [12]
Rnd 3: (sc in next 3 st, inc in next st) repeat 3 times [15]
Rnd 4 – 6: sc in all 15 st [15]
Rnd 7: dec 3 times, sc in next 9 st [12]
Change to brown yarn.
Rnd 8 – 19: sc in all 12 st [12]
Stuff the arm with fiberfill.
Rnd 20: dec 6 times [6]
Fasten off, leaving a long yarn tail. Using your yarn needle, weave the yarn tail through the front loop of each remaining stitch and pull it tight to close. Weave in the yarn end.
Take a piece of brown yarn on your yarn needle (leaving a long tail for securing). Insert the needle on the inside of the arm and bring it out on the outside. Insert the needle one stitch away from the place it came out, go back through the arm, through the body and through the second arm on the other side. Insert the needle back into the arm, one stitch from the place it came out, and go through the arm and the body again (picture 2). Take the yarn ends and make 2 tight knots. Weave in the yarn ends.

LEG *(make 2, start in yellow yarn)*
Ch 6. Stitches are worked around both sides of the foundation chain.
Rnd 1: start in second ch from hook, sc in next 4 st, 3 sc in next st. Continue on the other side of the foundation chain, sc in next 3 st, inc in next st [12]
Rnd 2: inc in next st, sc in next 3 st, inc in next 3 st, sc in next 3 st, inc in next 2 st [18]

Rnd 3: sc in next st, inc in next st, sc in next 4 st, inc in next st, sc in next 3 st, inc in next st, sc in next 5 st, inc in next st, sc in next st [22]

Rnd 4 – 5: sc in all 22 st [22]

Rnd 6: sc in next 6 st, dec 2 times, sc in next 2 st, dec 2 times, sc in next 6 st [18]

Rnd 7: sc in next 5 st, dec 4 times, sc in next 5 st [14]
Stuff the foot with fiberfill. Change to brown yarn.

Rnd 8 – 19: sc in all 14 st [14]

Rnd 20: dec 7 times [7]
Stuff the bottom part of the leg, but don't stuff the upper part of the leg. Fasten off, leaving a long yarn tail. Using your yarn needle, weave the yarn tail through the front loop of each remaining stitch and pull it tight to close. Leave a yarn tail for sewing. Sew the legs to rounds 1-7 of the body, making sure that the monkey sits balanced.

TAIL *(in brown yarn)*

Rnd 1: start 6 sc in a magic ring [6]

Rnd 2: inc in all 6 st [12]
Stuff the tail with fiberfill as you go.

Rnd 3 – 39: sc in all 12 st [12]
Fasten off, leaving a long tail for sewing. Sew the tail to the center of the back, over rounds 3-7. Shape the tail so that the end is curved.

MEYER
THE MALLARD DUCK & HIS BABIES
by Little Muggles (Amy Lin)

SKILL LEVEL: ★ ★ ★

SIZE: the mallard duck is 7.5" / 19 cm tall and the baby duck is 3.5" / 9 cm tall when made with the indicated yarn.

MATERIALS MEYER THE MALLARD DUCK:
- Worsted weight yarn in green, yellow, beige, warm brown, dark brown, blue (leftover) and white (leftover)
- Size E-4 / 3.5 mm crochet hook
- Safety eyes (12 mm)

MATERIALS BABY DUCK:
- Light worsted weight yarn in yellow
- Worsted weight yarn in orange
- Size C-2 / 3 mm crochet hook
- Safety eyes (7 mm)

MATERIALS BOTH:
- Yarn needle
- Stitch marker
- Fiberfill for stuffing

AMIGURUMI GALLERY
Scan or visit
www.amigurumi.com/2212
to share pictures and find inspiration.

MEYER THE MALLARD DUCK

HEAD AND BODY (*start in green yarn*)

Rnd 1: start 6 sc in a magic ring [6]

Rnd 2: inc in all 6 st [12]

Rnd 3: (sc in next st, inc in next st) repeat 6 times [18]

Rnd 4: sc in all 18 st [18]

Rnd 5: (sc in next 2 st, inc in next st) repeat 6 times [24]

Rnd 6: (sc in next 3 st, inc in next st) repeat 6 times [30]

Rnd 7: sc in next 2 st, inc in next st, (sc in next 4 st, inc in next st) repeat 5 times, sc in next 2 st [36]

Rnd 8: (sc in next 5 st, inc in next st) repeat 6 times [42]

Rnd 9: sc in all 42 st [42]

Rnd 10: sc in next 3 st, inc in next st, (sc in next 6 st, inc in next st) repeat 5 times, sc in next 3 st [48]

Rnd 11: (sc in next 7 st, inc in next st) repeat 6 times [54]

Rnd 12 – 17: sc in all 54 st [54]

Rnd 18: (sc in next 7 st, dec) repeat 6 times [48]

Rnd 19: sc in next 3 st, dec, (sc in next 6 st, dec) repeat 5 times, sc in next 3 st [42]

Rnd 20: sc in all 42 st [42]

Rnd 21: (sc in next 5 st, dec) repeat 6 times [36]

Rnd 22: sc in next 2 st, dec, (sc in next 4 st, dec) repeat 5 times, sc in next 2 st [30]

Rnd 23: (sc in next 3 st, dec) repeat 6 times [24]

Rnd 24: (sc in next 2 st, dec) repeat 6 times [18]

Stuff the head firmly with fiberfill. Change to white yarn.

Rnd 25 – 27: sc in all 18 st [18]

Rnd 28: sc in next 6 st, *(change to beige yarn)* ch 15, start in second ch from hook, sc in next 14 ch. This will bring you back to the point where you branched off with the chain. Continue into the round, make a sc into the same stitch from which you branched off, *(change to warm brown yarn)* sc in next 12 st [47]

Insert the safety eyes. To position them so they are looking forward, you need to approximate the posi-

tion of where the body will be. Take the chain (which is basically the backbone of the body) and pull it straight towards the top of the head (picture 1). To extend the chain, you can use an extra bit of yarn – pull it all the way around to the other side and this will give you the midline of the face (picture 2). Place the eyes symmetrically to either side of this yarn midline. The eyes are placed between rounds 14 and 15, with an interspace of 11 stitches (picture 3).

Work the next rounds with color changes. The color change is indicated in italics before each part.

Rnd 29: *(warm brown)* sc in next 6 st, *(beige)* sc in next 13 st, inc in next 2 st, sc in next 15 st, *(warm brown)* sc in next 11 st [49]

Rnd 30: (inc in next st, sc in next 2 st) repeat 2 times, *(beige)* sc in next 14 st, inc in next 2 st, sc in next 15 st, inc in next st, *(warm brown)* sc in next 2 st, (inc in next st, sc in next 2 st) repeat 3 times [57]

Rnd 31: (inc in next st, sc in next 3 st) repeat 2 times *(beige)* sc in next 14 st, inc in next st, sc in next 2 st, inc in next st, sc in next 15 st, inc in next st, sc in next st, *(warm brown)* sc in next 2 st, (inc in next st, sc in next 3 st) repeat 3 times [65]

Rnd 32: sc in next 10 st, *(beige)* sc in next 15 st, inc in next st, sc in next 3 st, inc in next st, sc in next 18 st, *(warm brown)* sc in next 17 st [67]

Rnd 33 – 34: sc in next 10 st, *(beige)* sc in next 40 st, *(warm brown)* sc in next 17 st [67]

Rnd 35: sc in next 10 st, *(beige)* inc in next st, (sc in next 10 st, inc in next st) repeat 3 times, sc in next 6 st, *(warm brown)* sc in next 4 st, inc in next st, sc in next 11 st, inc in next st [73]

Rnd 36 – 38: sc in next 10 st, *(beige)* sc in next 44 st, *(warm brown)* sc in next 19 st [73]

Rnd 39: dec, sc in next 8 st, *(beige)* (dec, sc in next 9 st) repeat 4 times, *(warm brown)* dec, sc in next 8 st, dec, sc in next 7 st [66]

Rnd 40: sc in next 9 st, *(beige)* sc in next 40 st, *(warm brown)* sc in next 17 st [66]

Rnd 41: dec, sc in next 7 st, *(beige)* (dec, sc in next 8 st) repeat 4 times, *(warm brown)* dec, sc in next 7 st, dec, sc in next 6 st [59]

Rnd 42: dec, sc in next 6 st, *(beige)* (dec, sc in next 7 st) repeat 4 times, *(warm brown)* dec, sc in next 6 st, dec, sc in next 5 st [52]

Rnd 43: sc in next 7 st, *(beige)* sc in next 32 st, *(warm brown)* sc in next 13 st [52]

Rnd 44: dec, sc in next 5 st, *(beige)* (dec, sc in next 6 st) repeat 4 times, *(warm brown)* dec, sc in next 5 st, dec, sc in next 4 st [45]

Rnd 45 – 46: sc in next 6 st, *(beige)* sc in next 28 st, *(warm brown)* sc in next 11 st [45]

Rnd 47: dec, sc in next 4 st, *(beige)* sc in next 9 st, dec, sc in next 12 st, dec, sc in next 3 st, *(warm brown)* sc in next 11 st [42]

Rnd 48: BPsc in next 5 st, *(beige)* BPsc in next 26 st, *(warm brown)* BPsc in next 11 st [42]
Change to beige yarn.

Rnd 49: (sc in next 5 st, dec) repeat 6 times [36]

Rnd 50: (sc in next 4 st, dec) repeat 6 times [30]
Stuff the body firmly with fiberfill.

Rnd 51: (sc in next 3 st, dec) repeat 6 times [24]

Rnd 52: (sc in next 2 st, dec) repeat 6 times [18]

Rnd 53: (sc in next st, dec) repeat 6 times [12]

Rnd 54: dec 6 times [6]
Fasten off and weave in the yarn end.

BILL *(in yellow yarn)*
Ch 8. Stitches are worked around both sides of the foundation chain.

Rnd 1: start in second ch from hook, sc in next 6 st, inc in next st. Continue on the other side of the foundation chain, sc in next 6 st, inc in next st [16]

Rnd 2: inc in next st, sc in next 5 st, inc in next st, sc in next st, inc in next st, sc in next 6 st, inc in next st [20]

Rnd 3 – 5: sc in all 20 st [20]
Fasten off, leaving a long tail for sewing. Stuff the bill with fiberfill. Center it between the eyes and sew it to the head over rounds 15-18 (picture 4).

RIGHT WING *(start in beige yarn)*

Rnd 1: start 6 sc in a magic ring [6]

Rnd 2: inc in all 6 st [12]

Rnd 3: (sc in next st, inc in next st) repeat 6 times [18]

Rnd 4 – 8: sc in all 18 st [18]
Change to dark brown yarn.

Rnd 9: sc in next 8 st, *(change to blue yarn)*, sc in next 10 st [18]
Change to dark brown yarn.

Rnd 10: sc in all 18 st [18]

Rnd 11: (sc in next st, dec) repeat 6 times [12]
Rnd 12 – 13: sc in all 12 st [12]
Rnd 14: (sc in next st, dec) repeat 4 times [8]
Rnd 15: (sc in next st, dec) repeat 2 times, sc in next 2 st [6]
Rnd 16: dec 2 times [4] Leave the remaining stitches unworked.
Fasten off and weave in the yarn end. The wing doesn't need to be stuffed.

LEFT WING *(start in beige yarn)*
Rnd 1: start 6 sc in a magic ring [6]
Rnd 2: inc in all 6 st [12]
Rnd 3: (sc in next st, inc in next st) repeat 6 times [18]
Rnd 4 – 8: sc in all 18 st [18]
Change to blue yarn.
Rnd 9: sc in next 10 st, *(change to dark brown yarn)*, sc in next 8 st [18]
Rnd 10: sc in all 18 st [18]
Rnd 11: (sc in next st, dec) repeat 6 times [12]
Rnd 12 – 13: sc in all 12 st [12]
Rnd 14: (sc in next st, dec) repeat 4 times [8]

Rnd 15: (sc in next st, dec) repeat 2 times, sc in next 2 st [6]
Rnd 16: dec 2 times [4] Leave the remaining stitches unworked.
Fasten off and weave in the yarn end. The wing doesn't need to be stuffed. Sew the wings to the sides of the duck's body. The blue stripe should be towards the bottom of each wing when sewing it on.

BABY DUCK

HEAD AND BODY *(in yellow yarn)*
Rnd 1: start 6 sc in a magic ring [6]
Rnd 2: inc in all 6 st [12]
Rnd 3: (sc in next st, inc in next st) repeat 6 times [18]
Rnd 4: sc in all 18 st [18]
Rnd 5: (sc in next 2 st, inc in next st) repeat 6 times [24]
Rnd 6: sc in all 24 st [24]
Rnd 7: (sc in next 3 st, inc in next st) repeat 6 times [30]
Rnd 8: (sc in next 4 st, inc in next st) repeat 6 times [36]
Rnd 9: sc in all 36 st [36]
Rnd 10: (sc in next 4 st, dec) repeat 6 times [30]
Rnd 11: (sc in next 3 st, dec) repeat 6 times [24]
Rnd 12: (sc in next 2 st, dec) repeat 6 times [18]
Rnd 13: (sc in next st, dec) repeat 6 times [12]
Stuff the head with fiberfill. Insert the safety eyes. To position them so they are looking forward, you need to approximate the position of where the body will be. Pull the yarn so that there is a big long loop (picture 5).

Pull the loop of yarn straight down towards the top of the head and then over to the other side. This gives you the approximate midline of the face (picture 6). Place the eyes symmetrically to either side of this yarn midline. The eyes are placed between rounds 8 and 9, with an interspace of 6 stitches (pictures 7-8).

Rnd 14: (sc in next 3 st, dec) repeat 2 times, sc in next 2 st [10]

Rnd 15 – 16: sc in all 10 st [10]

Rnd 17: sc in all 10 st, ch 12, start in second ch from hook, sc in next 11 ch [21]

Rnd 18: (sc in next 2 st, inc in next st) repeat 3 times, sc in next st, continue on the chain, sc in next 10 st, inc in next 2 st, sc in next 10 st [37]

Rnd 19: (sc in next 3 st, inc in next st) repeat 3 times, sc in next 12 st, inc in next st, sc in next st, inc in next st, sc in next 10 st [42]

Rnd 20: (sc in next 4 st, inc in next st) repeat 3 times, sc in next 12 st, inc in next st, sc in next 2 st, inc in next st, sc in next 11 st [47]

Rnd 21 – 22: sc in all 47 st [47]

Rnd 23: sc in next 31 st, dec, sc in next 2 st, dec, sc in next 10 st [45]

Rnd 24 – 25: sc in all 45 st [45]

Rnd 26: (sc in next 4 st, dec) repeat 3 times, sc in next 14 st, dec, sc in next st, dec, sc in in next 8 st [40]

Rnd 27: (sc in next 3 st, dec) repeat 3 times, sc in next 13 st, dec, sc in next st, dec, sc in next 7 st [35]

Rnd 28: (sc in next 2 st, dec) repeat 4 times, sc in next 8 st, dec, sc in next 2 st, dec, sc in next 5 st [29]

Rnd 29: (sc in next 2 st, dec) repeat 3 times, sc in next 7 st, dec, sc in next 2 st, dec, sc in next 4 st [24]

Stuff the body with fiberfill.

Rnd 30: BPsc in all 24 st [24]

Rnd 31: (sc in next 2 st, dec) repeat 6 times [18]

Rnd 32: (sc in next st, dec) repeat 6 times [12]

Rnd 33: dec 6 times [6]

Fasten off and weave in the yarn end.

BABY DUCK BILL *(in orange yarn)*

Ch 5. Stitches are worked around both sides of the foundation chain.

Rnd 1: start in second ch from hook, sc in next 3 st, inc in next st. Continue on the other side of the foundation chain, sc in next 3 st, inc in next st [10]

Rnd 2 – 3: sc in all 10 st [10]

Fasten off, leaving a tail for sewing. Sew the bill to the head over rounds 9-10.

BABY DUCK WING *(make 2, in yellow yarn)*

Rnd 1: start 6 sc in a magic ring [6]

Rnd 2: inc in all 6 st [12]

Rnd 3 – 4: sc in all 12 st [12]

Rnd 5: (sc in next 2 st, dec) repeat 3 times [9]

Rnd 6: sc in all 9 st [9]

Rnd 7: (sc in next 2 st, dec) repeat 2 times, sc in next st [7]

Rnd 8: sc in next 2 st, dec, sc in next 3 st [6]

Rnd 9: sc in next 2 st, dec, sc in next 2 st [5]

Rnd 10: dec 2 times [2] Leave the remaining stitches unworked.

Fasten off and weave in the yarn end. The wings don't need to be stuffed. Sew the wings to the sides of the body.

SAMMY
THE
SEAHORSE

by A Morning Cup of Jo Creations
(Josephine Wu)

SKILL LEVEL: ★ ★

SIZE: 8" / 20 cm tall when made with the
indicated yarn.

MATERIALS:

– Worsted weight yarn in light blue, blue and
  orange (leftover)
– Size F-5 /3.75 mm crochet hook
– Safety eyes (12 mm)
– White felt
– Orange and blue embroidery thread
– Small orange beads
– Yarn needle
– Pins
– Fabric glue
– Stitch marker
– Fiberfill for stuffing

AMIGURUMI GALLERY
Scan or visit
www.amigurumi.com/413
to share pictures and find inspiration.

HEAD *(in light blue yarn)*

Rnd 1: start 6 sc in a magic ring [6]

Rnd 2: inc in all 6 st [12]

Rnd 3: (inc in next st, sc in next st) repeat 6 times [18]

Rnd 4: BLO sc in all 18 st [18]

Rnd 5: sc in all 18 st [18]

Rnd 6: (dec, sc in next st) repeat 6 times [12]

Rnd 7: sc in all 12 st [12]

Rnd 8: inc in next 6 st, FLO sc in next 6 st [18]

Rnd 9: (inc in next st, sc in next st) repeat 6 times, sc in next 6 st [24]

Rnd 10: (inc in next st, sc in next 2 st) repeat 6 times,

sc in next 6 st [30]

Rnd 11: (inc in next st, sc in next 3 st) repeat 6 times, sc in next 6 st [36]

Rnd 12: (inc in next st, sc in next 4 st) repeat 6 times, sc in next 6 st [42]

Rnd 13: sc in all 42 st [42]

Rnd 14: (inc in next st, sc in next 6 st) repeat 6 times [48]

Rnd 15: (inc in next st, sc in next 7 st) repeat 6 times [54]

Rnd 16: (inc in next st, sc in next 8 st) repeat 6 times [60]

Cut 2 ovals from the white felt, slightly bigger than the safety eyes. Cut a hole in the center and insert the safety eyes. Hold the head with the seahorse's snout towards you. The section that contains the increases in rounds 8 to 12 is held upward. Attach the safety eyes with the felt pieces between rounds 12 and 13 of the head.

Rnd 17 – 19: sc in all 60 st [60]

Rnd 20: (dec, sc in next 8 st) repeat 6 times [54]

Rnd 21: (dec, sc in next 7 st) repeat 6 times [48]

Rnd 22: (dec, sc in next 6 st) repeat 6 times [42]

Stuff the head with fiberfill and continue stuffing as you go.

Rnd 23: (dec, sc in next 5 st) repeat 6 times [36]

Rnd 24: (dec, sc in next 4 st) repeat 6 times [30]

Rnd 25: (dec, sc in next 3 st) repeat 6 times [24]

Rnd 26: (dec, sc in next 2 st) repeat 6 times [18]

Rnd 27: (dec, sc in next st) repeat 6 times [12]

Rnd 28: dec 6 times [6]

Fasten off, leaving a yarn tail. Using your yarn needle, weave the yarn tail through the front loop of each remaining stitch and pull it tight to close. Weave in the yarn end.

BODY *(in light blue yarn)*

NOTE: The body is crocheted using joined rounds, as they help the curve of the belly and tail line up properly.

Work in joined rounds. Make the first stitch of the next round in the same stitch where you made the last slst. We start at the tip of the tail.

Rnd 1: start 4 sc in a magic ring [4]

Rnd 2 – 3: ch 1, sc in all 4 st, slst in first st, ch 1 [4]

Rnd 4: inc in next st, sc in next 3 st, slst in first st, ch 1 [5]

Rnd 5: inc in next st, sc in next 4 st, slst in first st, ch 1 [6]

Rnd 6: sc in all 6 st, slst in first st, ch 1 [6]

Rnd 7: inc in next st, sc in next 5 st, slst in first st, ch 1 [7]

Rnd 8: sc in all 7 st, slst in first st, ch 1 [7]

Rnd 9: inc in next st, sc in next 6 st, slst in first st, ch 1 [8]

Rnd 10: sc in all 8 st, slst in first st, ch 1 [8]
Rnd 11: inc in next st, sc in next 7 st, slst in first st, ch 1 [9]
Rnd 12: sc in all 9 st, slst in first st, ch 1 [9]
Rnd 13: inc in next st, sc in next 8 st, slst in first st, ch 1 [10]
Rnd 14: sc in all 10 st, slst in first st, ch 1 [10]
Rnd 15: inc in next st, sc in next 9 st, slst in first st, ch 1 [11]
Rnd 16: sc in all 11 st, slst in first st, ch 1 [11]
Rnd 17: inc in next st, sc in next 10 st, slst in first st, ch 1 [12]
Rnd 18: sc in next 6 st, inc in next 6 st, slst in first st, ch 1 [18]
Rnd 19: sc in next 6 st, (inc in next st, sc in next st) repeat 6 times, slst in first st, ch 1 [24]
Rnd 20: sc in next 6 st, (inc in next st, sc in next 2 st) repeat 6 times, slst in first st, ch 1 [30]
Rnd 21: sc in next 6 st, (inc in next st, sc in next 3 st) repeat 6 times, slst in first st, ch 1 [36]
Rnd 22: sc in all 36 st, slst in first st, ch 1 [36]
Rnd 23: sc in next 6 st, (dec, sc in next 3 st) repeat 6 times, slst in first st, ch 1 [30]
Rnd 24: sc in all 30 st, slst in first st, ch 1 [30]
Rnd 25: sc in next 6 st, (dec, sc in next 2 st) repeat 6 times, slst in first st, ch 1 [24]
Rnd 26: sc in all 24 st, slst in first st, ch 1 [24]
Stuff with fiberfill and continue stuffing as you go. The tip of the tail doesn't need to be stuffed.
Rnd 27: (dec, sc in next 2 st) repeat 6 times, slst in first st, ch 1 [18]
Rnd 28: sc in all 18 st, slst in first st, ch 1 [18]
Rnd 29: (dec, sc in next st) repeat 6 times, slst in first st, ch 1 [12]
Rnd 30: hdc in next 3 st, slst in next 9 st, slst in first st, ch 1 [12]
Rnd 31: sc in all 12 st, slst in first st [12]
Fasten off, leaving a long tail for sewing. Sew the body to rounds 17 to 19 of the head. Curl the tail and fix it with a few stitches to keep it in place.

MANE *(in blue yarn)*

Ch 42. Crochet in rows.

Row 1: start in second chain from hook, sc in next st, dc in next 2 st, sc in next st, slst in next st, (sc in next st, dc in next st, tr in next 2 st, dc in next st, sc in next st, slst in next st) repeat 2 times, sc in next st, dc in next 2 st, sc in next st, slst in next st, sc in next st, dc in next st, sc in next st, slst in next 3 st *(mark the first of these 3 slst)*, (sc in next st, dc in next st, sc in next st, slst in next st) repeat 2 times, sc in next st, slst in next 2 st [41]

Fasten off, leaving a long tail for sewing. Pin the stitch you marked to the base of the seahorse's head where it meets the neck. Pin the rest of the mane so the first stitch of row 1 reaches the seahorse's forehead, and the last stitch is stretched down the seahorse's back. Make sure the mane is in line with the seahorse's snout and eyes (evenly dividing the body in half). Sew the mane in place.

LOWER FIN *(make 2, in orange yarn)*

Rnd 1: start a magic ring with ch 2, dc, ch 2, slst, ch 3, tr, ch 1, dc, ch 1, dc.

Tighten the ring. Fasten off, leaving a tail for sewing. One half of the fin is larger than the other. The larger side is the top of the fin. Sew the fins to the sides of the body, between rounds 22 and 25.

UPPER FIN *(make 2, in orange yarn)*

Rnd 1: start a magic ring with ch 3, 2 tr, ch 1, 2 dc, ch 2, slst.

Tighten the ring. Fasten off, leaving a tail for sewing. Sew the fins to the sides of the head, diagonally between rounds 24 and 27.

ASSEMBLY

– Sew orange beads to the mane using blue embroidery thread.

– Cut 1 oval piece of felt for the seahorse's belly. Glue the belly to the seahorse's body. Use orange embroidery thread to sew stripes across the belly.

STANLEY THE GIRAFFE

by Little Muggles (Amy Lin)

SKILL LEVEL: ✶

SIZE: 10" / 25 cm tall when made with the indicated yarn.

MATERIALS:

– Worsted weight yarn in yellow, beige and dark brown
– Size G-6 / 4 mm crochet hook
– Safety eyes (12 mm)
– 2 small buttons or black embroidery thread for the nostrils
– Yarn needle
– Red ribbon
– Stitch marker
– Fiberfill for stuffing

AMIGURUMI GALLERY

Scan or visit
www.amigurumi.com/405
to share pictures and find inspiration.

HEAD *(in yellow yarn)*

Rnd 1: start 6 sc in a magic ring [6]

Rnd 2: inc in all 6 st [12]

Rnd 3: (sc in next st, inc in next st) repeat 6 times [18]

Rnd 4: (sc in next 2 st, inc in next st) repeat 6 times [24]

Rnd 5: sc in all 24 st [24]

Rnd 6: (sc in next 3 st, inc in next st) repeat 6 times [30]

Rnd 7: (sc in next 4 st, inc in next st) repeat 6 times [36]

Rnd 8: (sc in next 5 st, inc in next st) repeat 6 times [42]

Rnd 9: sc in all 42 st [42]

Rnd 10: (sc in next 6 st, inc in next st) repeat 6 times [48]

Rnd 11: sc in all 48 st [48]

Rnd 12: (sc in next 7 st, inc in next st) repeat 6 times [54]

Rnd 13 – 17: sc in all 54 st [54]

Rnd 18: (sc in next 7 st, dec) repeat 6 times [48]

Rnd 19: sc in all 48 st [48]

Rnd 20: (sc in next 6 st, dec) repeat 6 times [42]
Rnd 21: (sc in next 5 st, dec) repeat 6 times [36]
Rnd 22: (sc in next 4 st, dec) repeat 6 times [30]
Rnd 23: sc in all 30 st [30]
Rnd 24: (sc in next 3 st, dec) repeat 6 times [24]
Rnd 25 – 29: sc in all 24 st [24]
Fasten off and weave in the yarn end. Insert the safety
eyes between rounds 13 and 14, with an interspace of
11 stitches. Stuff the head with fiberfill.

HORN *(make 2, start in brown yarn)*
Rnd 1: start 6 sc in a magic ring [6]
Rnd 2: inc in all 6 st [12]
Rnd 3: sc in all 12 st [12]
Rnd 4: (sc in next st, dec) repeat 4 times [8]
Change to yellow yarn.
Rnd 5 – 9: sc in all 8 st [8]
Fasten off, leaving a long tail for sewing. The horns
don't need to be stuffed. Sew the horns to the head
between rounds 4 and 5.

EAR *(make 2, in yellow yarn)*
Rnd 1: start 4 sc in a magic ring [4]
Rnd 2: sc in all 4 st [4]
Rnd 3: inc in all 4 st [8]
Rnd 4: sc in all 8 st [8]
Rnd 5: (sc in next st, inc in next st) repeat 4 times [12]
Rnd 6: (sc in next 2 st, inc in next st) repeat 4 times [16]
Rnd 7: (sc in next 3 st, inc in next st) repeat 4 times [20]
Rnd 8: sc in all 20 st [20]
Rnd 9: (sc in next 3 st, dec) repeat 4 times [16]
Rnd 10: (sc in next 2 st, dec) repeat 4 times [12]
Rnd 11: (sc in next st, dec) repeat 4 times [8]
Fasten off, leaving a long tail for sewing. Flatten the
ears, they don't need to be stuffed. Sew the ears to the
head between rounds 9 and 11.

SNOUT *(in beige yarn)*
Ch 9. Stitches are worked around both sides of the
foundation chain.

Rnd 1: start in second ch from hook, sc in next 7 st,
inc in next st. Continue on the other side of the foundation chain, sc in next 7 st, inc in next st [18]
Rnd 2: (sc in next st, inc in next st, sc in next 6 st,
inc in next st) repeat 2 times [22]
Rnd 3: (sc in next 2 st, inc in next st, sc in next 7 st,
inc in next st) repeat 2 times [26]
Rnd 4: sc in all 26 st [26]
Rnd 5: (sc in next 3 st, inc in next st, sc in next 8 st,
inc in next st) repeat 2 times [30]
Rnd 6: sc in all 30 st [30]
Rnd 7: (sc in next 4 st, inc in next st, sc in next 9 st,
inc in next st) repeat 2 times [34]

Rnd 8: sc in all 34 st [34]

Rnd 9: sc in next 4 st, dec, sc in next 8 st, dec, sc in next 5 st, dec, sc in next 9 st, dec [30]

Fasten off, leaving a long tail for sewing. Stuff the snout with fiberfill. Sew the snout to the head between rounds 14 and 23. Sew on the buttons for the nostrils or embroider them with black embroidery thread.

BODY *(in yellow yarn)*

Rnd 1: start 6 sc in a magic ring [6]

Rnd 2: inc in all 6 st [12]

Rnd 3: (sc in next st, inc in next st) repeat 6 times [18]

Rnd 4: (sc in next 2 st, inc in next st) repeat 6 times [24]

Rnd 5: (sc in next 3 st, inc in next st) repeat 6 times [30]

Rnd 6: (sc in next 4 st, inc in next st) repeat 6 times [36]

Rnd 7: (sc in next 5 st, inc in next st) repeat 6 times [42]

Rnd 8: sc in all 42 st [42]

Rnd 9: (sc in next 6 st, inc in next st) repeat 6 times [48]

Rnd 10: (sc in next 7 st, inc in next st) repeat 6 times [54]

Rnd 11: (sc in next 8 st, inc in next st) repeat 6 times [60]

Rnd 12: (sc in next 9 st, inc in next st) repeat 6 times [66]

Rnd 13 – 14: sc in all 66 st [66]

Rnd 15: (sc in next 9 st, dec) repeat 6 times [60]

Rnd 16 – 17: sc in all 60 st [60]

Rnd 18: (sc in next 8 st, dec) repeat 6 times [54]

Rnd 19: sc in all 54 st [54]

Rnd 20: (sc in next 7 st, dec) repeat 6 times [48]

Rnd 21: sc in all 48 st [48]

Rnd 22: (sc in next 6 st, dec) repeat 6 times [42]

Rnd 23: sc in all 42 st [42]

Stuff the body with fiberfill and continue stuffing as you go.

Rnd 24: (sc in next 5 st, dec) repeat 6 times [36]

Rnd 25: (sc in next 4 st, dec) repeat 6 times [30]

Rnd 26 – 28: sc in all 30 st [30]

Rnd 29: (sc in next 3 st, dec) repeat 6 times [24]

Rnd 30 – 34: sc in all 24 st [24]

Fasten off, leaving a long tail for sewing. Sew the head to the body. Add extra stuffing before closing the seam.

ARM *(make 2, start in brown yarn)*

Rnd 1: start 6 sc in a magic ring [6]

Rnd 2: inc in all 6 st [12]

Rnd 3: (sc in next st, inc in next st) repeat 6 times [18]

Rnd 4: (sc in next 2 st, inc in next st) repeat 6 times [24]

Rnd 5: BLO sc in all 24 st [24]

Rnd 6 – 7: sc in all 24 st [24]

Rnd 8: (sc in next 2 st, dec) repeat 6 times [18]

Change to yellow yarn.

Rnd 9: BLO sc in all 18 st [18]

Rnd 10: sc in all 18 st [18]

Rnd 11: (sc in next 3 st, dec, sc in next 2 st, dec) repeat 2 times [14]

Rnd 12 – 14: sc in all 14 st [14]

Stuff the arm with fiberfill and continue stuffing as

you go.

Rnd 15: (sc in next 2 st, dec) repeat 3 times, sc in next 2 st [11]

Rnd 16 – 17: sc in all 11 st [11]

Rnd 18: (sc in next 2 st, dec) repeat 2 times, sc in next 3 st [9]

Rnd 19 – 20: sc in all 9 st [9]

Fasten off, leaving a long tail for sewing. Sew the arms to the body, about 9 rounds down from where you attached the head.

LEG *(make 2, start in brown yarn)*

Rnd 1: start 6 sc in a magic ring [6]

Rnd 2: inc in all 6 st [12]

Rnd 3: (sc in next st, inc in next st) repeat 6 times [18]

Rnd 4: (sc in next 2 st, inc in next st) repeat 6 times [24]

Rnd 5: (sc in next 3 st, inc in next st) repeat 6 times [30]

Rnd 6: (sc in next 4 st, inc in next st) repeat 6 times [36]

Rnd 7: BLO sc in all 36 st [36]

Rnd 8 – 9: sc in all 36 st [36]

Rnd 10: (sc in next 4 st, dec) repeat 6 times [30]

Change to yellow yarn.

Rnd 11: BLO sc in all 30 st [30]

Rnd 12: sc in all 30 st [30]

Rnd 13: (sc in next 3 st, dec) repeat 6 times [24]

Rnd 14 – 15: sc in all 24 st [24]

Rnd 16: (sc in next 2 st, dec) repeat 6 times [18]

Rnd 17 – 20: sc in all 18 st [18]

Stuff the leg with fiberfill up to this point.

Rnd 21: (sc in next st, dec) repeat 6 times [12]

Rnd 22: sc in all 12 st [12]

Fasten off, leaving a long tail for sewing. Flatten the legs and sew them to round 8 of the body.

TAIL *(start in brown yarn)*

Rnd 1: start 4 sc in a magic ring [4]

Rnd 2: sc in all 4 st [4]

Rnd 3: inc in all 4 st [8]

Rnd 4: sc in all 8 st [8]

Rnd 5: (sc in next st, inc in next st) repeat 4 times [12]

Rnd 6: (sc in next 2 st, inc in next st) repeat 4 times [16]

Rnd 7: (sc in next 2 st, dec) repeat 4 times [12]

Stuff the tail lightly with fiberfill. Change to yellow yarn.

Rnd 8 – 15: sc in all 12 st [12]

Fasten off, leaving a long tail for sewing. Sew the tail to the back of the body, on round 8.

SPOT *(make 3, in brown yarn)*

Rnd 1: start 6 sc in magic ring [6]

Rnd 2: (sc in next st, inc in next st) repeat 3 times [9]

Rnd 3: (sc in next st, inc in next 2 st) repeat 3 times [15]

Fasten off, leaving a long tail for sewing. Sew the 3 spots on the back of the giraffe. Tie the red ribbon around the neck using a classic tie knot.

SCRAPS
THE
SEAGULL

by Crochetbykim
(Kim Bengtsson Friis)

SKILL LEVEL: ★

SIZE: 8" / 20 cm tall when made with the indicated yarn.

MATERIALS:
– Worsted weight yarn in white, gray, black and
  yellow
– Size G-6 / 4 mm crochet hook
– Safety eyes (8 mm)
– Black embroidery thread
– Yarn needle
– Stitch marker
– Fiberfill for stuffing

AMIGURUMI GALLERY
Scan or visit
www.amigurumi.com/2203
to share pictures and find inspiration.

HEAD AND BODY *(in white yarn)*

Rnd 1: start 6 sc in a magic ring [6]

Rnd 2: inc in all 6 st [12]

Rnd 3: (sc in next st, inc in next st) repeat 6 times [18]

Rnd 4: (sc in next 2 st, inc in next st) repeat 6 times [24]

Rnd 5: (sc in next 3 st, inc in next st) repeat 6 times [30]

Rnd 6: (sc in next 4 st, inc in next st) repeat 6 times [36]

Rnd 7: (sc in next 5 st, inc in next st) repeat 6 times [42]

Rnd 8 – 23: sc in all 42 st [42]

Rnd 24: ch 10, start in second ch from hook, inc in next st, sc in next 8 st, continue on the body, sc in next 41 st, continue on the other side of the chain, sc in next 8 st, inc in next st [61]

Insert the safety eyes between rounds 12 and 13, with an interspace of 2 stitches.

Rnd 25: sc in next st, inc in next st, sc in next 57 st, inc in next st, sc in next st [63]

Rnd 26 – 30: sc in all 63 st [63]

Rnd 31: sc in next 3 st, dec 2 times, sc in next 23 st, dec, sc in next 27 st, dec 2 times [58]

Rnd 32: sc in next 27 st, dec 2 times, sc in next 27 st [56]

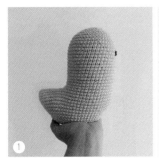   

Rnd 33: sc in all 56 st [56]

Rnd 34: (dec 2 times, sc in next 22 st) repeat 2 times, dec 2 times [50]

Rnd 35: sc in all 50 st [50]

Stuff with fiberfill and continue stuffing as you go.

Rnd 36: dec, sc in next 46 st, dec [48]

Rnd 37: (sc in next 6 st, dec) repeat 6 times [42]

Rnd 38: (sc in next 5 st, dec) repeat 6 times [36]

Rnd 39: (sc in next 4 st, dec) repeat 6 times [30]

Rnd 40: (sc in next 3 st, dec) repeat 6 times [24]

Rnd 41: (sc in next 2 st, dec) repeat 6 times [18]

Rnd 42: (sc in next st, dec) repeat 6 times [12]

Rnd 43: dec 6 times [6]

Fasten off, leaving a yarn tail. Using your yarn needle, weave the yarn tail through the front loop of each remaining stitch and pull it tight to close. Weave in the yarn end (picture 1).

BEAK *(in yellow yarn)*

Rnd 1: start 6 sc in a magic ring [6]

Rnd 2: inc in all 6 st [12]

Rnd 3 – 8: sc in all 12 st [12]

Fasten off, leaving a long tail for sewing. Stuff the beak with fiberfill. Sew the beak to the head, 1 round below the eyes (picture 2). Embroider eyebrows over rounds 10 and 11 using black embroidery thread (picture 3).

WING *(make 2, start in black yarn)*

Rnd 1: start 6 sc in a magic ring [6]

Rnd 2: sc in all 6 st [6]

Rnd 3: inc in all 6 st [12]

Rnd 4: sc in all 12 st [12]

Rnd 5: (sc in next st, inc in next st) repeat 6 times [18]

Rnd 6: sc in all 18 st [18]

Change to gray yarn.

Rnd 7: (sc in next 2 st, inc in next st) repeat 6 times [24]

Rnd 8: sc in all 24 st [24]

Rnd 9: (sc in next 3 st, inc in next st) repeat 6 times [30]

Rnd 10 – 14: sc in all 30 st [30]

Rnd 15: (sc in next 3 st, dec) repeat 6 times [24]

Rnd 16: sc in all 24 st [24]

Rnd 17: (sc in next 2 st, dec) repeat 6 times [18]

Rnd 18 – 19: sc in all 18 st [18]

Rnd 20: (sc in next st, dec) repeat 6 times [12]

Rnd 21 – 22: sc in all 12 st [12]

Fasten off, leaving a long tail for sewing. The wings don't need to be stuffed.

LEG *(make 2, in yellow yarn)*
Rnd 1: start 6 sc in a magic ring [6]
Rnd 2: inc in all 6 st [12]
Rnd 3: (sc in next st, inc in next st) repeat 6 times [18]
Rnd 4: (sc in next 2 st, inc in next st) repeat 6 times [24]
Rnd 5 – 8: sc in all 24 st [24]
Rnd 9: sc in next 6 st, dec 6 times, sc in next 6 st [18]
Rnd 10: sc in next 3 st, dec 6 times, sc in next 3 st [12]
Rnd 11 – 20: sc in all 12 st [12]
Fasten off, leaving a long tail for sewing. Stuff the feet

with fiberfill. The legs don't need to be stuffed.

TAIL FEATHER *(make 2, in black yarn)*
Rnd 1: start 6 sc in a magic ring [6]
Rnd 2: inc in all 6 st [12]
Rnd 3: (sc in next st, inc in next st) repeat 6 times [18]
Rnd 4: (sc in next 2 st, inc in next st) repeat 6 times [24]
Rnd 5: (sc in next 3 st, inc in next st) repeat 6 times [30]
Rnd 6: (sc in next 4 st, inc in next st) repeat 6 times [36]
Fold the circle to a semicircle. Work the next round through both layers to close.
Rnd 7: sc in next 18 st around the semicircle [18]
Fasten off, leaving a long tail for sewing.

ASSEMBLY
– Sew the legs to the body with an interspace of 2 stitches (picture 4).
– Sew the tail feathers to the body (picture 5).
– Position the wings on row 24, and tilt them backwards. Pin the wings in place (picture 6) and sew them to the body.
– Add a few tufts of gray hair on top of the head.

MONTY THE MOOSE

by LittleAquaGirl
(Erinna Lee)

SKILL LEVEL: ✦ ✦

SIZE: 6" /15 cm tall when made with the indicated yarn.

MATERIALS:

– Fingering weight yarn in beige, medium blue, light blue, soft brown
– Size B-1 / 2.5 mm crochet hook
– Safety eyes (7.5 mm)
– Black embroidery thread
– Yarn needle
– Stitch markers
– Fiberfill for stuffing

AMIGURUMI GALLERY

Scan or visit
www.amigurumi.com/2204
to share pictures and find inspiration.

HEAD *(start in beige yarn)*

Rnd 1: start 8 sc in a magic ring [8]

Rnd 2: inc in all 8 st [16]

Rnd 3: (sc in next st, inc in next st) repeat 8 times [24]

Rnd 4: (sc in next 2 st, inc in next st) repeat 8 times [32]

Rnd 5: (sc in next 3 st, inc in next st) repeat 8 times [40]

Rnd 6: (sc in next 4 st, inc in next st) repeat 8 times [48]

Rnd 7: (sc in next 5 st, inc in next st) repeat 8 times [56]

Rnd 8 – 13: sc in all 56 st [56]

Rnd 14: sc in next 13 st, dec *(mark this dec with a stitch marker)*, sc in next 26 st, dec *(mark this dec with a stitch marker)*, sc in next 13 st [54]

The 2 decreases marked in round 14 indicate the sides of the head.

Rnd 15: sc in all 54 st [54]

Rnd 16: sc in next 13 st, dec, sc in next 25 st, dec, sc in next 12 st [52]

Rnd 17: sc in next 12 st, dec, sc in next 24 st, dec, sc in

next 12 st [50]

Rnd 18: sc in next 12 st, dec, sc in next 23 st, dec, sc in next 11 st [48]

Change to light blue yarn.

Rnd 19: (sc in next 11 st, inc in next st) repeat 4 times [52]

Rnd 20: (sc in next 12 st, inc in next st) repeat 4 times [56]

Rnd 21: sc in next 14 st, (sc in next 6 st, inc in next st) repeat 4 times, sc in next 14 st [60]

Rnd 22: sc in next 6 st, inc in next st, sc in next 7 st, (sc in next 7 st, inc in next st) repeat 5 times, sc in next 6 st [66]

Rnd 23: (sc in next 10 st, inc in next st) repeat 6 times [72]

Rnd 24 – 30: sc in all 72 st [72]

Use the marked stitches of round 14 as a guide and insert the safety eyes between rounds 19 and 20, with an interspace of 5 stitches. Using black embroidery thread, embroider the eyebrows diagonally over round 21, with each eyebrow being about 3 stitches long.

Rnd 31: (sc in next 10 st, dec) repeat 6 times [66]

Rnd 32: (sc in next 9 st, dec) repeat 6 times [60]

Rnd 33: (sc in next 8 st, dec) repeat 6 times [54]

Rnd 34: (sc in next 7 st, dec) repeat 6 times [48]

Rnd 35: sc in all 48 st [48]

Rnd 36: (sc in next 6 st, dec) repeat 6 times [42]

Rnd 37: (sc in next 5 st, dec) repeat 6 times [36]

Rnd 38: (sc in next 4 st, dec) repeat 6 times [30]

Rnd 39: (sc in next 3 st, dec) repeat 6 times [24]

Stuff the head with fiberfill and continue stuffing as you go.

Rnd 40: (sc in next 2 st, dec) repeat 6 times [18]

Rnd 41: (sc in next st, dec) repeat 6 times [12]

Rnd 42: dec 6 times [6]

Slst in next st. Fasten off, leaving a yarn tail. Using your yarn needle, weave the yarn tail through the front loop of each remaining stitch and pull it tight to close. Weave in the yarn end.

MAIN ANTLER *(make 2, in beige yarn)*
Rnd 1: start 6 sc in a magic ring [6]
Rnd 2: inc in all 6 st [12]
Rnd 3: (sc in next st, inc in next st) repeat 6 times [18]
Rnd 4: (sc in next 2 st, inc in next st) repeat 6 times [24]
Rnd 5: (sc in next 3 st, inc in next st) repeat 6 times [30]
Rnd 6 – 10: sc in all 30 st [30]
Rnd 11: sc in next 10 st, dec, sc in next 2 st, dec *(mark this dec with a stitch marker, it indicates the top side of the antler)*, sc in next 2 st, dec, sc in next 10 st [27]
Rnd 12: sc in next 11 st, dec, sc in next st, dec, sc in next 11 st [25]
Rnd 13: sc in next 7 st, (dec, sc in next st) repeat 4 times, sc in next 6 st [21]
Stuff the main antler with fiberfill and continue stuffing as you go.
Rnd 14: sc in next 7 st, (dec, sc in next st) repeat 3 times, sc in next 5 st [18]
Rnd 15: sc in all 18 st [18]
Rnd 16: sc in next 7 st, (dec, sc in next st) repeat 2 times, sc in next 5 st [16]
Rnd 17 – 31: sc in all 16 st [16]
Slst in next st. Fasten off, leaving a long tail for sewing.

MEDIUM ANTLER BRANCH *(make 2, in beige yarn)*
Rnd 1: start 6 sc in a magic ring [6]
Rnd 2: inc in all 6 st [12]
Rnd 3: sc in all 12 st [12]
Rnd 4: (sc in next 5 st, inc in next st) repeat 2 times [14]
Rnd 5 – 8: sc in all 14 st [14]
Slst in next st. Fasten off, leaving a long tail for sewing. Stuff the medium antler branch with fiberfill.

SMALL ANTLER BRANCH *(make 2, in beige yarn)*
Rnd 1: start 6 sc in a magic ring [6]

Rnd 2: inc in all 6 st [12]
Rnd 3 – 7: sc in all 12 st [12]
Slst in next st. Fasten off, leaving a long tail for sewing. Stuff the small antler branch with fiberfill.

ASSEMBLY ANTLERS
– Sew the medium antler branch over rounds 17-22 of the main antler. Note that the marked stitch at round 11 of the main antler is the top side of the antler (picture 1).
– Sew the small antler branch over rounds 25-29 of the main antler (picture 1).
– Sew the main antlers to the sides of the head, over rounds 29-33. The insides of the main antlers should be 20 stitches apart if you count the stitches between rounds 30 and 31 of the head.

INNER EAR *(make 2, in soft brown yarn)*
Rnd 1: start 6 sc in a magic ring [6]
Rnd 2: inc in all 6 st [12]
Rnd 3: (sc in next st, inc in next st) repeat 6 times [18]
Rnd 4: (sc in next 2 st, inc in next st) repeat 6 times [24]
Rnd 5: (sc in next 3 st, inc in next st) repeat 6 times [30]
Rnd 6: (sc in next 4 st, inc in next st) repeat 6 times [36]
Rnd 7: (sc in next 5 st, inc in next st) repeat 6 times [42]
Slst in next st. Fasten off and weave in the yarn end.

OUTER EAR *(make 2, in light blue yarn)*
Rnd 1: start 6 sc in a magic ring [6]
Rnd 2: inc in all 6 st [12]
Rnd 3: (sc in next st, inc in next st) repeat 6 times [18]
Rnd 4: (sc in next 2 st, inc in next st) repeat 6 times [24]
Rnd 5: (sc in next 3 st, inc in next st) repeat 6 times [30]
Rnd 6: (sc in next 4 st, inc in next st) repeat 6 times [36]
Rnd 7: (sc in next 5 st, inc in next st) repeat 6 times [42]
Don't fasten off. In the next round, we'll join the outer and inner ears. Place together the outer and inner ears, with the wrong sides towards each other (picture 2).
Continue from the outer ear.
Rnd 8: ch 1, sc in all 42 st [42]
Fold the ear in half and work the next round through both layers to close.
Rnd 9: sc in next 2 st, slst in next st [3] (picture 3)
Fasten off, leaving a long tail for sewing.

BODY *(in light blue yarn)*
Rnd 1: start 6 sc in a magic ring [6]
Rnd 2: inc in all 6 st [12]
Rnd 3: (sc in next st, inc in next st) repeat 6 times [18]
Rnd 4: (sc in next 2 st, inc in next st) repeat 6 times [24]
Rnd 5: (sc in next 3 st, inc in next st) repeat 6 times [30]
Rnd 6: (sc in next 4 st, inc in next st) repeat 6 times [36]
Rnd 7: (sc in next 5 st, inc in next st) repeat 6 times [42]
Rnd 8: (sc in next 6 st, inc in next st) repeat 6 times [48]
Rnd 9: (sc in next 7 st, inc in next st) repeat 6 times [54]

Rnd 10: (sc in next 8 st, inc in next st) repeat 6 times [60]
Rnd 11: (sc in next 9 st, inc in next st) repeat 6 times [66]
Rnd 12: (sc in next 10 st, inc in next st) repeat 6 times [72]
Rnd 13 – 18: sc in all 72 st [72]
Rnd 19: (sc in next 16 st, dec) repeat 4 times [68]
Rnd 20: sc in all 68 st [68]
Rnd 21: (sc in next 15 st, dec) repeat 4 times [64]
Rnd 22: sc in all 64 st [64]
Rnd 23: (sc in next 14 st, dec) repeat 4 times [60]
Rnd 24: sc in all 60 st [60]
Rnd 25: (sc in next 13 st, dec) repeat 4 times [56]
Rnd 26: (sc in next 12 st, dec) repeat 4 times [52]
Rnd 27: (sc in next 11 st, dec) repeat 4 times [48]
Rnd 28: (sc in next 10 st, dec) repeat 4 times [44]
Rnd 29: (sc in next 9 st, dec) repeat 4 times [40]
Rnd 30: sc in all 40 st [40]
Rnd 31: (sc in next 8 st, dec) repeat 4 times [36]

Rnd 32: sc in all 36 st [36]
Rnd 33: (sc in next 7 st, dec) repeat 4 times [32]
Rnd 34: sc in all 32 st [32]
Rnd 35: (sc in next 6 st, dec) repeat 4 times [28]
Rnd 36: sc in all 28 st [28]
Slst in next st. Fasten off, leaving a long tail for sewing.
Stuff the body with fiberfill.

ARM *(make 2, start in beige yarn)*
Rnd 1: start 6 sc in a magic ring [6]
Rnd 2: inc in all 6 st [12]
Rnd 3: (sc in next st, inc in next st) repeat 6 times [18]
Rnd 4: (sc in next 2 st, inc in next st) repeat 6 times [24]
Rnd 5 – 8: sc in all 24 st [24]
Rnd 9: dec 2 times, sc in next 16 st, dec 2 times [20]
Rnd 10: dec, sc in next 16 st, dec [18]
Rnd 11: sc in next st, dec, sc in next 13 st, dec [16]
Rnd 12: sc in next st, dec, sc in next 11 st, dec [14]
Change to light blue yarn.
Rnd 13 – 30: sc in all 14 st [14]
Stuff the hands firmly with fiberfill. Stuff the rest of
the arm only lightly.
Rnd 31: sc in next 9 st [9] Leave the remaining stitches
unworked.
Flatten the opening of the arm and work the next
round through both layers to close.
Rnd 32: sc in next 7 st [7]
Fasten off, leaving a long tail for sewing.

LEG *(make 2, start in beige yarn)*
Rnd 1: start 6 sc in a magic ring [6]
Rnd 2: inc in all 6 st [12]
Rnd 3: (sc in next st, inc in next st) repeat 6 times [18]
Rnd 4: (sc in next 2 st, inc in next st) repeat 6 times [24]
Rnd 5: (sc in next 3 st, inc in next st) repeat 6 times [30]
Rnd 6 – 10: sc in all 30 st [30]
Rnd 11: sc in next 9 st, (dec, sc in next st) repeat
4 times, sc in next 9 st [26]
Rnd 12: sc in next 7 st, (dec, sc in next st) repeat
4 times, sc in next 7 st [22]
Rnd 13: sc in next 8 st, (dec, sc in next st) repeat
2 times, sc in next 8 st [20]
Rnd 14: sc in all 20 st [20]
Change to light blue yarn.
Rnd 15 – 22: sc in all 20 st [20]
Rnd 23: sc in next 11 st, inc in next 2 st, sc in next
7 st [22]
Rnd 24: sc in next 11 st, inc in next st, sc in next 2 st,
inc in next st, sc in next 7 st [24]
Rnd 25 – 26: sc in all 24 st [24]
Stuff the leg with fiberfill and continue stuffing as
you go.
Rnd 27: (sc in next 2 st, dec) repeat 6 times [18]
Rnd 28: (sc in next st, dec) repeat 6 times [12]
Rnd 29: dec 6 times [6]
Slst in next st. Fasten off, leaving a long tail. Using
your yarn needle, weave the yarn tail through the front
loop of each remaining stitch and pull it tight to close.
Bring the yarn tail out between rounds 21 and 22, on
the inside of the leg (picture 4).

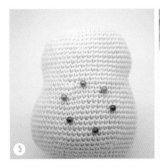
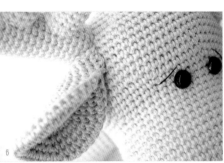

TAIL *(in light blue yarn)*
Rnd 1: start 4 sc in a magic ring [4]
Rnd 2: (sc in next st, inc in next st) repeat 2 times [6]
Rnd 3: (sc in next st, inc in next st) repeat 3 times [9]
Rnd 4: (sc in next 2 st, inc in next st) repeat 3 times [12]
Rnd 5: sc in all 12 st [12]
Rnd 6: (sc in next st, inc in next st) repeat 6 times [18]
Rnd 7 – 8: sc in all 18 st [18]
Rnd 9: (sc in next 4 st, dec) repeat 3 times [15]
Rnd 10: sc in all 15 st [15]
Rnd 11: (sc in next 3 st, dec) repeat 3 times [12]
Rnd 12: sc in all 12 st [12]
Rnd 13: (sc in next 2 st, dec) repeat 3 times [9]
Flatten the opening of the tail and work the next round through both layers to close. The tail doesn't need to be stuffed.
Rnd 14: sc in next 4 st [4]
Fasten off, leaving a long tail for sewing.

BOW *(in medium blue yarn)*
Leave a long starting yarn tail. Ch 55. Crochet in rows.
Row 1: start in second ch from hook, sc in all 54 st, ch 1, turn [54]
Row 2 – 9: sc in all 54 st, ch 1, turn [54]
Row 10: sc in all 54 st [54]
Fasten off, leaving a long tail for sewing.

CENTER OF BOW *(in medium blue yarn)*
Leave a long starting yarn tail. Ch 11. Crochet in rows.
Row 1: start in second ch from hook, sc in all 10 st, ch 1, turn [10]

Row 2: sc in all 10 st, ch 1, turn [10]
Row 3: sc in all 10 st [10]
Fasten off, leaving a long tail for sewing.

ASSEMBLY
– Pin and sew the head to the body. You can tilt it slightly to give Monty a cuter look. The opening of the body should fall over rounds 20-28 of the head (picture 5).
– Sew the arms between rounds 35 and 36 of the body. The arms should be 8 stitches apart in the front with the hand curving inwards towards the body.
– Sew the ears with the flat seam over rounds 26-29 of the head (picture 6). The front corners of the ears should be 23 stitches apart.
– Sew the legs to the sides of the body. Sew around the top of the curve of the leg (picture 7). To secure the legs against the body, sew the inner side of each leg to the body with a few stitches. The top side of the thigh should fall between rounds 16 and 17 of the body. The back side of the leg should fall behind the midline of the body (picture 7).
– Sew the flat seam of the tail between rounds 13 and 14 of the back, between the legs (picture 7).
– Sew the short edges of the bow together. The side where you joined the edges will be the side facing the body.
– Wrap the center of the bow around the bow so that it covers the seam. Sew the ends together on the back side of the bow. Pass a few stitches through the bow itself to prevent the center from sliding around. Sew the bow to the body, below his head.

HAMISH THE HAMSTER
by Moji-Moji Design (Janine Holmes)

SKILL LEVEL: ★ ★ ★

SIZE: 5" / 13 cm tall when made with the indicated yarn.

MATERIALS:
– Light worsted weight yarn in light brown, white, light pink, red (leftover), green (leftover) and black (leftover)
– Size C-2 / 3 mm crochet hook
– Safety eyes (12 mm)
– Safety nose (15 mm)
– Yarn needle
– Stitch marker
– Fiberfill for stuffing

FACE PATCH *(in white yarn)*
Start by making 2 separate cheeks.

Cheek *(make 2, in white yarn)*
Rnd 1: start 6 sc in a magic ring [6]
Rnd 2: inc in all 6 st [12]
Rnd 3: (sc in next st, inc in next st) repeat 6 times [18]
Fasten off and weave in the yarn end on the first cheek. Don't fasten off on the second cheek. In the next round, we'll join both cheeks together.

Joining the cheeks
Rnd 4: ch 5, sc in next 18 st on the first cheek, BLO sc in next 5 ch, sc in next 18 st on the second cheek, sc in

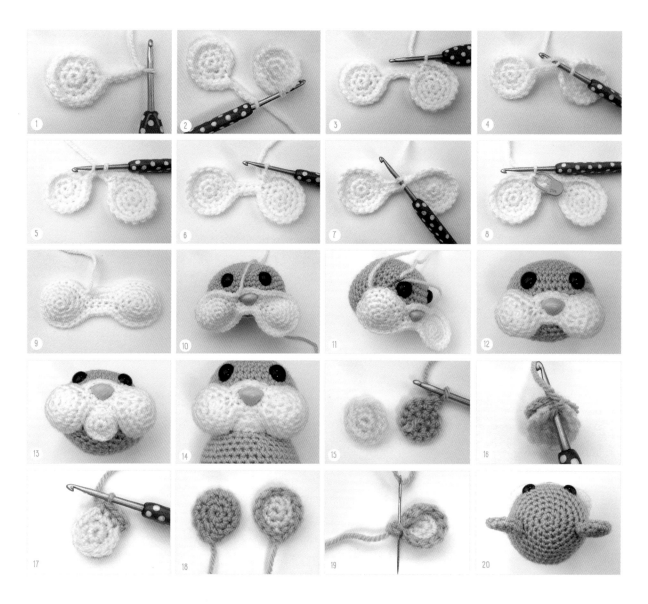

other side of next 5 ch [46] (pictures 1-7)

Rnd 5: sc in all 46 st [46] (pictures 8-9)

Fasten off, leaving a long tail for sewing.

HEAD *(in light brown yarn)*

Rnd 1: start 6 sc in a magic ring [6]

Rnd 2: inc in all 6 st [12]

Rnd 3: (sc in next st, inc in next st) repeat 6 times [18]

Rnd 4: (sc in next 2 st, inc in next st) repeat 6 times [24]

Rnd 5: (sc in next 3 st, inc in next st) repeat 6 times [30]

Rnd 6: (sc in next 4 st, inc in next st) repeat 6 times [36]

Rnd 7: (sc in next 5 st, inc in next st) repeat 6 times [42]

Rnd 8 – 14: sc in all 42 st [42]

Insert the safety eyes between rounds 8 and 9, with an interspace of 7 stitches.

Rnd 15: (sc in next 5 st, dec) repeat 6 times [36]

Rnd 16: (sc in next 4 st, dec) repeat 6 times [30]

Insert the safety nose into the center of the face patch,

then insert the stem of the nose between rounds 11 and 12 of the head, making sure it's placed in the center below the eyes. Close the washers, but don't sew the edges of the face patch down yet (picture 10).

Rnd 17: (sc in next 3 st, dec) repeat 6 times [24]
Rnd 18: (sc in next 2 st, dec) repeat 6 times [18]
Stuff the head with fiberfill.
Rnd 19: (sc in next st, dec) repeat 6 times [12]
Rnd 20: dec 6 times [6]
Fasten off, leaving a yarn tail. Using your yarn needle, weave the yarn tail through the front loop of each remaining stitch and pull it tight to close. Weave in the yarn end. Put a small amount of stuffing into each cheek. Sew the edges of the face patch down, adding more stuffing to each cheek just before closing the seam (pictures 11-12).

CHIN PATCH *(in white yarn)*
Rnd 1: start 6 sc in a magic ring [6]
Rnd 2: inc in all 6 st [12]
Fasten off, leaving a long tail for sewing. Sew the chin patch to the lower space between the cheeks (picture 13).

BODY *(in light brown yarn)*
Rnd 1: start 6 sc in a magic ring [6]
Rnd 2: inc in all 6 st [12]
Rnd 3: (sc in next st, inc in next st) repeat 6 times [18]
Rnd 4: (sc in next 2 st, inc in next st) repeat 6 times [24]
Rnd 5: (sc in next 3 st, inc in next st) repeat 6 times [30]
Rnd 6: (sc in next 4 st, inc in next st) repeat 6 times [36]
Rnd 7: (sc in next 5 st, inc in next st) repeat 6 times [42]
Rnd 8: (sc in next 6 st, inc in next st) repeat 6 times [48]
Rnd 9 – 11: sc in all 48 st [48]
Rnd 12: (sc in next 6 st, dec) repeat 6 times [42]
Rnd 13 – 15: sc in all 42 st [42]
Rnd 16: (sc in next 5 st, dec) repeat 6 times [36]
Rnd 17 – 18: sc in all 36 st [36]

Fasten off, leaving a long tail for sewing. Stuff the body and sew it between rounds 15 and 16 of the head (picture 14).

EAR *(make 4, 2 in light pink and 2 in light brown yarn)*
Rnd 1: start 6 sc in a magic ring [6]
Rnd 2: inc in all 6 st [12]
Fasten off and weave in the yarn end on the light pink piece. Don't fasten off on the light brown piece (picture 15). Place the light pink piece on top of the light brown piece, with the wrong sides towards each other. Work the next round through both layers to close.
Rnd 3: ch 1, sc in all 12 st [12] (pictures 16-18)
Slst in first st. Fasten off, leaving a long tail for sewing. Pinch the base of the ear and use the yarn tail to sew the lower edge together (picture 19). Sew the tips of the lower edges to the top of the head over rounds 5-6 (picture 20).

ARM (make 2, start in light pink yarn)

Rnd 1: start 6 sc in a magic ring [6]

Change to light brown yarn.

Rnd 2: sc in all 6 st [6]

Rnd 3: (sc in next st, inc in next st) repeat 3 times [9]

Rnd 4: (sc in next 2 st, inc in next st) repeat 3 times [12]

Rnd 5 – 7: sc in all 12 st [12]

Rnd 8: (sc in next 3 st, inc in next st) repeat 3 times [15]

Rnd 9 – 11: sc in all 15 st [15]

Rnd 12: (sc in next 3 st, dec) repeat 3 times [12]

Stuff the arm with fiberfill.

Rnd 13: dec 6 times [6]

Fasten off, leaving a long yarn tail. Using your yarn needle, weave the yarn tail through the front loop of each remaining stitch and pull it tight to close. Leave a long tail for sewing. Sew round 13 of the arms to the sides of the body, at the neck crease (picture 21).

HAND (make 2, in light pink yarn)

Ch 3. Crochet in rows.

Row 1: start in second ch from hook, slst in this st, slst in next st, (ch 3, slst in second ch from hook, slst in next st) repeat 5 times [6 fingers]

Fasten off, leaving a long tail for sewing. Fold the hand in half, lining up the two sets of 3 fingers, and sew around all the edges of the fingers (picture 22). Sew the base of the hands to round 1 of the arms (picture 23).

TUMMY PATCH *(in white yarn)*

Ch 11. Crochet in rows.

Row 1: start in second ch from hook, sc in all 10 st, ch 1, turn [10]

Row 2: sc in all 10 st, ch 1, turn [10]

Row 3: inc in next st, sc in next 8 st, inc in next st, ch 1, turn [12]

Row 4 – 5: sc in all 12 st, ch 1, turn [12]

Row 6: inc in next st, sc in next 10 st, inc in next st, ch 1, turn [14]

Row 7 – 9: sc in all 14 st, ch 1, turn [14]

Row 10: skip 1 st, sc in next 11 st, skip 1 st, sc in next st, ch 1, turn [12]

Row 11: skip 1 st, sc in next 9 st, skip 1 st, sc in next st, ch 1, turn [10]

Row 12: skip 1 st, sc in next 7 st, skip 1 st, sc in next st, ch 1, turn [8]

Row 13: skip 1 st, sc in next 5 st, skip 1 st, sc in next st [6]

Fasten off, leaving a long tail for sewing. Sew row 1 of the tummy patch to the body just underneath the chin, then sew the rest of the edges in place (pictures 24-26).

HAUNCHES *(make 2, in light brown yarn)*

Rnd 1: start 6 sc in a magic ring [6]

Rnd 2: inc in all 6 st [12]

Rnd 3: (sc in next st, inc in next st) repeat 6 times [18]

Rnd 4: (sc in next 2 st, inc in next st) repeat 6 times [24]

Rnd 5 – 6: sc in all 24 st [24]

Fasten off, leaving a long tail for sewing. Stuff lightly and position the haunches to the sides of the body between rounds 6 and 14, so that each haunch slightly overlaps the tummy patch. Make alternate stitches into the

haunch and then into the body (pictures 27-29), adding more stuffing just before closing the seam.

FOOT *(make 4, in light pink yarn, 2 pieces for each foot)*

Rnd 1: start 6 sc in a magic ring [6]

Rnd 2: (sc in next st, ch 3, start in second ch from hook, slst in next 2 st) repeat 3 times, slst in next st [3 toes]

Leave the remaining stitches unworked.

Fasten off and weave in the yarn ends on 2 of the pieces. Leave a long tail for sewing on the other 2 pieces. Stack 2 of the pieces, one on top of the other, with the wrong sides towards each other. Sew the edges of the foot together, all the way around (picture 30). Make small stitches around the toes to help define the shape. Sew the top of each foot to the underside of each haunch, towards the front of the body (picture 31).

TAIL *(start in light pink yarn)*
Rnd 1: start 3 sc in a magic ring [3]
Rnd 2: inc in all 3 st [6]
Change to light brown yarn.
Rnd 3: sc in all 6 st [6]
Rnd 4: (sc in next st, inc in next st) repeat 3 times [9]
Rnd 5: sc in all 9 st [9]
Fasten off, leaving a long tail for sewing. Stuff the tail with fiberfill and sew it to rounds 6-8 on the lower back (picture 32).

FINISHING
Embroider a single vertical running stitch from the base of the chin to the lower tip of the nose using black yarn. At this point you can either sew the arms to the body in your desired position or you can make a juicy strawberry for your hamster's lunch and sew the palm of each hand to either side of it.

STRAWBERRY *(in red yarn)*
Rnd 1: start 3 sc in a magic ring [3]
Rnd 2: inc in all 3 st [6]
Rnd 3: (sc in next st, inc in next st) repeat 3 times [9]
Rnd 4: (sc in next 2 st, inc in next st) repeat 3 times [12]
Rnd 5: (sc in next 3 st, inc in next st) repeat 3 times [15]
Rnd 6: (sc in next 4 st, inc in next st) repeat 3 times [18]
Rnd 7: sc in all 18 st [18]
Rnd 8: (sc in next st, dec) repeat 6 times [12]
Stuff the strawberry with fiberfill.

Rnd 9: dec 6 times [6]
Fasten off, leaving a yarn tail. Using your yarn needle, weave the yarn tail through the front loop of each remaining stitch and pull it tight to close. Weave in the yarn end.

LEAVES *(in green yarn)*
Ch 4. Crochet in rows.
Row 1: start in second ch from hook, slst in this st, slst in next 2 st *(mark the last slst)*, (3 ch, start in second ch from hook, slst in next 2 st, slst in marked st) repeat 4 times [5 leaves]
Fasten off, leaving a long tail for sewing. Sew the leaves to the top of the strawberry. Embroider small stitches using white yarn to make the seeds.

ANNA THE SWAN AND HER BABY PETER

by Pica Pau (Yan Schenkel)

SKILL LEVEL: ✦ ✦ ✦

SIZE: Anna: 9.5" / 24 cm tall, **Peter:** 6.5" / 16 cm tall when made with the indicated yarn.

MATERIALS ANNA:

– Light worsted weight yarn in off-white, black (leftover) and yellow (leftover)

– Safety eyes (8 mm)

MATERIALS PETER:

– Light worsted weight yarn in light gray, dark gray (leftover) and pink (leftover)

– Safety eyes (10 mm)

MATERIALS BOTH:

– Size D-3 / 3 mm crochet hook

– Yarn needle

– Stitch marker

– Fiberfill for stuffing

AMIGURUMI GALLERY

Scan or visit
www.amigurumi.com/1415
to share pictures and find inspiration.

ANNA THE MOTHER SWAN

BEAK *(in yellow yarn)*

Rnd 1: start 5 sc in a magic ring [5]

Rnd 2: sc in all 5 st [5]

Rnd 3: inc in all 5 st [10]

Rnd 4: sc in all 10 st [10]

Rnd 5: sc in next 9 st, inc in next st [11]

Rnd 6: sc in next 10 st, inc in next st [12]

Rnd 7: sc in next 11 st, inc in next st [13]

Rnd 8: sc in next 12 st, inc in next st [14]

Rnd 9: sc in next 13 st, inc in next st [15]

Rnd 10: sc in all 15 st [15]

Fasten off, leaving a long tail for sewing. Stuff the beak with fiberfill.

BLACK CIRCLE *(in black yarn)*
Rnd 1: start 6 sc in a magic ring [6]
Rnd 2: inc in all 6 st [12]
Rnd 3: (sc in next st, inc in next st) repeat 6 times [18]
Rnd 4: (sc in next 2 st, inc in next st) repeat 6 times [24]
Rnd 5: sc in all 24 st [24]
Fasten off, leaving a long tail for sewing.

HEAD AND BODY *(in off-white yarn)*
Rnd 1: start 6 sc in a magic ring [6]
Rnd 2: inc in all 6 st [12]
Rnd 3: (sc in next st, inc in next st) repeat 6 times [18]
Rnd 4: (sc in next 2 st, inc in next st) repeat 6 times [24]
Rnd 5: (sc in next 3 st, inc in next st) repeat 6 times [30]
Rnd 6: (sc in next 4 st, inc in next st) repeat 6 times [36]
Rnd 7: (sc in next 5 st, inc in next st) repeat 6 times [42]
Rnd 8: (sc in next 6 st, inc in next st) repeat 6 times [48]
Rnd 9: (sc in next 7 st, inc in next st) repeat 6 times [54]
Rnd 10 – 16: sc in all 54 st [54]
Rnd 17: (sc in next 7 st, dec) repeat 6 times [48]
Rnd 18: (sc in next 6 st, dec) repeat 6 times [42]
Rnd 19: (sc in next 5 st, dec) repeat 6 times [36]
Rnd 20: (sc in next 4 st, dec) repeat 6 times [30]
Rnd 21: (sc in next 3 st, dec) repeat 6 times [24]
Rnd 22: (sc in next 2 st, dec) repeat 6 times [18]
Rnd 23 – 32: sc in all 18 st [18]
Rnd 33: sc in next 8 st, inc in next 2 st, sc in next 8 st [20]
Rnd 34 – 35: sc in all 20 st [20]
Rnd 36: sc in next 9 st, inc in next st, sc in next st, inc in next st, sc in next 8 st [22]
Rnd 37 – 38: sc in all 22 st [22]
Rnd 39: dec, sc in next 8 st, inc in next 4 st, sc in next 6 st, dec [24]
Rnd 40 – 41: sc in all 24 st [24]
Rnd 42: ch 19 to start the body of the swan. Place the stitch marker in the next stitch, this will be the new beginning of the round (picture 1). Crochet back on the

chain, start in second ch from the hook, inc in this st, sc in next 17 st, continue on the neck, sc in next 24 st, continue on the other side of the chain, sc in next 17 st, inc in next st [62]
Rnd 43: inc in next 2 st, sc in next 27 st, inc in next st, sc in next 3 st, inc in next st, sc in next 26 st, inc in next 2 st [68]
Sew the black circle of the beak to the head between rounds 12 and 21. Keep the position of the body of the swan in mind. Sew the yellow beak to the black circle. Add more stuffing before closing the seam. Insert the safety eyes between rounds 14 and 15, at 5 stitches from the beak. Stuff the head and neck firmly with fiberfill and continue stuffing as you go.
Rnd 44: inc in next 3 st, sc in next 62 st, inc in next 3 st [74]
Rnd 45: sc in all 74 st [74]
Rnd 46: sc in next 35 st, inc in next st, sc in next 4 st, inc in next st, sc in next 33 st [76]
Rnd 47 – 48: sc in all 76 st [76]
Rnd 49: sc in next 4 st, dec, sc in next 30 st, inc in next st, sc in next 5 st, inc in next st, sc in next 28 st, dec, sc in next 3 st [76]
Rnd 50: sc in all 76 st [76]
Rnd 51: sc in next 4 st, dec, sc in next 30 st, inc in next st, sc in next 6 st, inc in next st, sc in next 27 st, dec, sc in next 3 st [76]
Rnd 52: sc in all 76 st [76]
Rnd 53: sc in next 4 st, dec, sc in next 30 st, inc in next st, sc in next 7 st, inc in next st, sc in next 26 st, dec, sc in next 3 st [76]

Rnd 54: sc in next 34 st, dec, sc in next 9 st, dec, sc in next 29 st [74]

Rnd 55: sc in next 4 st, dec, sc in next 27 st, dec, sc in next 9 st, dec, sc in next 23 st, dec, sc in next 3 st [70]

Rnd 56: sc in next 31 st, dec, sc in next 9 st, dec, sc in next 26 st [68]

Rnd 57: sc in next 4 st, dec, sc in next 24 st, dec, sc in next 9 st, dec, sc in next 20 st, dec, sc in next 3 st [64]

Rnd 58: sc in next 4 st, dec, sc in next 22 st, dec, sc in next 9 st, dec, sc in next 18 st, dec, sc in next 3 st [60]

Rnd 59: BLO (sc in next 8 st, dec) repeat 6 times [54]

Rnd 60: (sc in next 7 st, dec) repeat 6 times [48]

Rnd 61: (sc in next 6 st, dec) repeat 6 times [42]

Rnd 62: (sc in next 5 st, dec) repeat 6 times [36]

Rnd 63: (sc in next 4 st, dec) repeat 6 times [30]

Rnd 64: (sc in next 3 st, dec) repeat 6 times [24]

Stuff the body with fiberfill up to this point.

Rnd 65: (sc in next 2 st, dec) repeat 6 times [18]

Rnd 66: (sc in next st, dec) repeat 6 times [12]

Rnd 67: dec 6 times [6]

Fasten off. Using your yarn needle, weave the yarn tail through the front loop of each remaining stitch and pull it tight to close.

Sew a stitch from the bottom of the body to the back, so that the body doesn't inflate like a ball. This way, the swan will sit better.

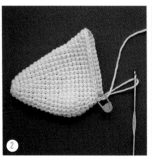
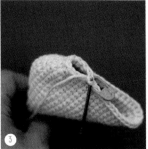

WING *(make 2, in off-white yarn)*

Rnd 1: start 6 sc in a magic ring [6]

Rnd 2: inc in all 6 st [12]

Rnd 3: sc in all 12 st [12]

Rnd 4: (sc in next st, inc in next st) repeat 6 times [18]

Rnd 5 – 6: sc in all 18 st [18]

Rnd 7: (sc in next 2 st, inc in next st) repeat 6 times [24]

Rnd 8 – 9: sc in all 24 st [24]

Rnd 10: (sc in next 3 st, inc in next st) repeat 6 times [30]

Rnd 11 – 12: sc in all 30 st [30]

Rnd 13: (sc in next 4 st, inc in next st) repeat 6 times [36]

Rnd 14 – 16: sc in all 36 st [36]

Rnd 17: dec 2 times, sc in next 12 st, inc in next 4 st, sc in next 12 st, dec 2 times [36]

Rnd 18 – 19: sc in all 36 st [36]

Rnd 20: dec 2 times, sc in next 12 st, inc in next 4 st, sc in next 12 st, dec 2 times [36]

Rnd 21: sc in all 36 st [36] (picture 2) Mark the 32nd stitch of round 21 with a stitch marker.

Next, we will divide the wing to make 3 feathers: use 10 stitches for the small feather, 12 stitches for the medium feather and 14 stitches for the large feather.

Small feather

Sc in next 5 st. Skip 26 st and work the first stitch of the next round in the 32nd marked stitch of the previous round to create a smaller round (picture 3).

Rnd 1: inc in next st, sc in next 3 st, dec, sc in next 4 st [10]

Rnd 2: inc in next st, sc in next 4 st, dec, sc in next 3 st [10]

Rnd 3: sc in next st, inc in next st, sc in next 3 st, dec, sc in next 3 st [10]

Rnd 4: sc in next 2 st, inc in next st, sc in next 3 st, dec, sc in next 2 st [10] (picture 4)

Rnd 5: (dec, sc in next st) repeat 3 times, sc in next st [7]

Rnd 6: (dec, sc in next st) repeat 2 times, sc in next st [5]

Fasten off. Using your yarn needle, weave the yarn tail through the front loop of each remaining stitch and pull it tight to close. Weave in the yarn end.

Medium feather

Pull up a loop of off-white yarn in the next stitch to the left on the main wing shape (picture 5).

Sc in next 6 st (picture 6). Skip 14 st and work the first stitch of the next round in the 6th stitch to the right side of the small feather to create a smaller round.

Rnd 1: sc in all 12 st [12]

Rnd 2: inc in next st, sc in next 4 st, dec, sc in next 5 st [12] (picture 7)

Rnd 3: inc in next st, sc in next 5 st, dec, sc in next 4 st [12]

Rnd 4: sc in next st, inc in next st, sc in next 4 st, dec, sc in next 4 st [12]

Rnd 5: sc in next st, inc in next st, sc in next 5 st, dec, sc in next 3 st [12]

Rnd 6: (dec, sc in next st) repeat 4 times [8]

Rnd 7: sc in next st, inc in next st, sc in next 3 st, dec, sc in next st [8]

Rnd 8: dec 4 times [4]

Fasten off. Using your yarn needle, weave the yarn tail through the front loop of each remaining stitch and

pull it tight to close. Weave in the yarn end.

Large feather

Pull up a loop of off-white yarn in the next stitch to the left on the main wing shape.

Rnd 1: sc in next 14 st, sc in the first stitch of the large feather (picture 8).

Rnd 2: sc in next 6 st, inc in next st, sc in next 5 st, dec [14]

Rnd 3: sc in next 6 st, inc in next st, sc in next 7 st [15]

Rnd 4: dec, sc in next 5 st, inc in next st, sc in next 5 st, dec [14]

Rnd 5: sc in next 7 st, inc in next st, sc in next 6 st [15]

Rnd 6: dec, sc in next 5 st, inc in next st, sc in next 5 st, dec [14]

Rnd 7: (dec, sc in next st) repeat 4 times, sc in next 2 st [10]

Rnd 8: dec, sc in next 3 st, inc in next st, sc in next 4 st [10]

Rnd 9: dec 5 times [5]

Fasten off. Using your yarn needle, weave the yarn tail through the front loop of each remaining stitch and pull it tight to close (picture 9). Weave in the yarn end. Sew the wings to the sides of the body.

PETER THE BABY SWAN

BEAK *(in dark gray yarn)*

Ch 4. Stitches are worked around both sides of the foundation chain.

Rnd 1: start in second ch from hook, inc in this st,

sc in next st, 4 sc in next st. Continue on the other side of the foundation chain, sc in next st, inc in next st [10]

Rnd 2 – 3: sc in all 10 st [10]

Rnd 4: (sc in next st, inc in next st) repeat 5 times [15]

Rnd 5: sc in all 15 st [15]

Fasten off, leaving a long tail for sewing. The beak doesn't need to be stuffed.

HEAD AND BODY *(in light gray yarn)*

Rnd 1: start 6 sc in a magic ring [6]

Rnd 2: inc in all 6 st [12]

Rnd 3: (sc in next st, inc in next st) repeat 6 times [18]

Rnd 4: (sc in next 2 st, inc in next st) repeat 6 times [24]

Rnd 5: (sc in next 3 st, inc in next st) repeat 6 times [30]

Rnd 6: (sc in next 4 st, inc in next st) repeat 6 times [36]

Rnd 7: (sc in next 5 st, inc in next st) repeat 6 times [42]

Rnd 8 – 13: sc in all 42 st [42]

Rnd 14: (sc in next 5 st, dec) repeat 6 times [36]

Rnd 15: (sc in next 4 st, dec) repeat 6 times [30]

Rnd 16: (sc in next 3 st, dec) repeat 6 times [24]

Sew the beak to the head between rounds 11 and 13. Insert the safety eyes between rounds 11 and 12, at 4 stitches from the beak. Embroider the little cheeks under the eyes using pink yarn.

Rnd 17: (sc in next 2 st, dec) repeat 6 times [18]

Rnd 18: (sc in next st, dec) repeat 6 times [12]

Stuff the head firmly with fiberfill and continue stuffing as you go.

Rnd 19 – 20: sc in all 12 st [12]

Rnd 21: dec, sc in next 4 st, inc in next st, sc in next

5 st [12]

Rnd 22: sc in all 12 st [12]

Rnd 23: sc in next 5 st, inc in next st, sc in next 4 st, dec [12]

Rnd 24: sc in all 12 st [12]

Rnd 25: dec, sc in next 4 st, inc in next st, sc in next 5 st [12]

Rnd 26 – 27: sc in all 12 st [12]

Note: Your hook should be positioned at the back of the head, on the opposite side of the beak. If this is not the case, add a few more sc or undo a few. This way the body of the swan will be positioned as seen in the example images, with the beak facing forward.

Rnd 28: ch 12 to start the body of the swan. Place the stitch marker in the next st (this will be the new beginning of the round). Crochet back on the chain, start in second ch from hook, inc in this st, sc in next 10 st, continue on the neck, sc in next 12 st, continue on the other side of the chain, sc in next 10 st, inc in next st [36]

Rnd 29: inc in next 2 st, sc in next 15 st, inc in next 3 st, sc in next 15 st, inc in next st [42]

Rnd 30: inc in next 3 st, sc in next 38 st, inc in next st [46]

Rnd 31: (sc in next st, inc in next st) repeat 2 times, sc in next 42 st [48]

Rnd 32: sc in all 48 st [48]

Rnd 33: (sc in next 7 st, inc in next st) repeat 6 times [54]

Rnd 34 – 35: sc in all 54 st [54]

Rnd 36: sc in next 6 st, dec, sc in next 19 st, inc in next st, sc in next 4 st, inc in next st, sc in next 18 st, dec, sc in next st [54]

Rnd 37: sc in next 6 st, dec, sc in next 18 st, dec, sc in next 5 st, dec, sc in next 16 st, dec, sc in next st [50]

Rnd 38: sc in next 6 st, dec, sc in next 39 st, dec, sc in next st [48]

Rnd 39: sc in next 6 st, dec, sc in next 15 st, dec, sc in next 5 st, dec, sc in next 13 st, dec, sc in next st [44]

Rnd 40: sc in next 6 st, dec, sc in next 33 st, dec, sc in next st [42]

Rnd 41: sc in all 42 st [42]

Rnd 42: (sc in next 5 st, dec) repeat 6 times [36]

Rnd 43: (sc in next 4 st, dec) repeat 6 times [30]

Rnd 44: (sc in next 3 st, dec) repeat 6 times [24]

Stuff the body with fiberfill up to this point.

Rnd 45: (sc in next 2 st, dec) repeat 6 times [18]

Rnd 46: (sc in next st, dec) repeat 6 times [12]

Rnd 47: dec 6 times [6]

Fasten off. Using your yarn needle, weave the yarn tail through the front loop of each remaining stitch and pull it tight to close. Weave in the yarn end.

Sew a stitch from the bottom of the body to the back, so that the body doesn't inflate like a ball. This way, the baby swan will sit better.

WING *(make 2, in light gray yarn)*

Rnd 1: start 5 sc in a magic ring [5]

Rnd 2: sc in all 5 st [5]

Rnd 3: inc in all 5 st [10]

Rnd 4: sc in all 10 st [10]

Rnd 5: (sc in next st, inc in next st) repeat 5 times [15]

Rnd 6 – 7: sc in all 15 st [15]

Rnd 8: (sc in next 2 st, inc in next st) repeat 5 times [20]

Rnd 9 – 10: sc in all 20 st [20]

Rnd 11: (sc in next 3 st, inc in next st) repeat 5 times [25]

Rnd 12 – 14: sc in all 25 st [25]

Rnd 15: (sc in next 3 st, dec) repeat 5 times [20]

Rnd 16: (sc in next 2 st, dec) repeat 5 times [15]

Rnd 17: (sc in next st, dec) repeat 5 times [10]

Rnd 18: dec 5 times [5]

Fasten off, leaving a long tail for sewing. The wings don't need to be stuffed. Sew the wings to the sides of the body.

SAMMY THE SEAL

by DIY Fluffies
(Mariska Vos-Bolman)

SKILL LEVEL: ✶ ✶

SIZE: 8.5"/ 21 cm when made with the indicated yarn.

MATERIALS:

– Sport weight yarn in gray, pink and black (leftover)
– Size B-1 / 2.5 mm crochet hook
– Safety eyes (13 mm)
– Yarn needle
– Pins
– Stitch markers
– Fiberfill for stuffing

AMIGURUMI GALLERY

Scan or visit
www.amigurumi.com/2507
to share pictures and find inspiration.

BODY *(in gray yarn)*

Rnd 1: start 6 sc in a magic ring [6]

Rnd 2: inc in all 6 st [12]

Rnd 3: (sc in next st, inc in next st) repeat 6 times [18]

Rnd 4: (sc in next 2 st, inc in next st) repeat 6 times [24]

Rnd 5: (sc in next 3 st, inc in next st) repeat 6 times [30]

Rnd 6: (sc in next 4 st, inc in next st) repeat 6 times [36]

Rnd 7: (sc in next 5 st, inc in next st) repeat 6 times [42]

Rnd 8: (sc in next 6 st, inc in next st) repeat 6 times [48]

Rnd 9: (sc in next 7 st, inc in next st) repeat 6 times [54]

Rnd 10: (sc in next 8 st, inc in next st) repeat 6 times [60]

Rnd 11 – 14: sc in all 60 st [60]

Rnd 15: sc in next 28 st, dec, sc in next 8 st, dec, sc in next 20 st [58]

Rnd 16: sc in next 9 st, inc in next st, sc in next 47 st, inc in next st [60]

Rnd 17: sc in next 31 st, inc in next 6 st, sc in next 23 st [66]

Rnd 18: sc in next 34 st, inc in next st, sc in next 5 st, inc in next st, sc in next 25 st [68]

Mark stitches 28 and 46 of round 18 as a guide to place the safety eyes later.

Rnd 19: sc in next 10 st, inc in next st, sc in next 16 st, inc in next st, sc in next st, inc in next st, sc in next 19 st, inc in next st, sc in next st, inc in next st, sc in next 15 st, inc in next st [74]

Rnd 20 – 21: sc in all 74 st [74]

Rnd 22: sc in next 11 st, inc in next st, sc in next 61 st, inc in next st [76]

Insert the safety eyes between rounds 17 and 18, one between stitches 28-29 and one between stitches 46-47.

Rnd 23: sc in next 34 st, (dec, sc in next 3 st) repeat 3 times, dec, sc in next 25 st [72]

Rnd 24: sc in next 35 st, (dec, sc in next st) repeat 3 times, dec, sc in next 26 st [68]

Rnd 25: sc in next 12 st, inc in next st, sc in next 13 st, (sc in next st, dec) repeat 8 times, sc in next 17 st, inc in next st [62]

Rnd 26: sc in next 21 st, dec, sc in next st, (sc in next st, dec) repeat 4 times, (dec, sc in next st) repeat 4 times, sc in next st, dec, sc in next 11 st [52]

Rnd 27: sc in all 52 st [52]

Rnd 28: sc in next 13 st, inc in next st, sc in next 37 st, inc in next st [54]

Rnd 29: sc in all 54 st [54]

Rnd 30: (sc in next 8 st, inc in next st) repeat 6 times [60]

Rnd 31 – 32: sc in all 60 st [60]

Rnd 33: (sc in next 9 st, inc in next st) repeat 6 times [66]

Rnd 34 – 43: sc in all 66 st [66]

Rnd 44: (sc in next 9 st, dec) repeat 6 times [60]

Rnd 45: (sc in next 8 st, dec) repeat 6 times [54]

Rnd 46: (sc in next 7 st, dec) repeat 6 times [48]

Rnd 47: (sc in next 6 st, dec) repeat 6 times [42]

Rnd 48: (sc in next 5 st, dec) repeat 6 times [36]

Rnd 49: (sc in next 4 st, dec) repeat 6 times [30]

Stuff the body with fiberfill and continue stuffing as you go.

Rnd 50: (sc in next 3 st, dec) repeat 6 times [24]

Rnd 51: (sc in next 2 st, dec) repeat 6 times [18]
Rnd 52: (sc in next st, dec) repeat 6 times [12]
Rnd 53: dec 6 times [6]
Fasten off, leaving a yarn tail. Using your yarn needle, weave the yarn tail through the front loop of each remaining stitch and pull it tight to close. Weave in the yarn end.

TAIL *(in gray yarn)*
Start by making 2 separate back flippers.

Back flipper *(make 2, in gray yarn)*
Rnd 1: start 4 sc in a magic ring [4]
Rnd 2: inc in all 4 st [8]
Rnd 3: (sc in next st, inc in next st) repeat 4 times [12]
Rnd 4: sc in all 12 st [12]
Rnd 5: (sc in next 2 st, inc in next st) repeat 4 times [16]
Rnd 6: sc in all 16 st [16]
Rnd 7: (sc in next 7 st, inc in next st) repeat 2 times [18]

Rnd 8: sc in all 18 st [18]
Rnd 9: (sc in next 7 st, dec) repeat 2 times [16]
Rnd 10: (sc in next 2 st, dec) repeat 4 times [12]
Rnd 11: sc in all 12 st [12]
Rnd 12: (sc in next st, dec) repeat 4 times [8]
Rnd 13: sc in all 8 st [8]
Fasten off and weave in the yarn tail on the first flipper. Don't fasten off on the second flipper. The back flippers don't need to be stuffed. In the next round, we'll join both flippers together.

Tail part
Rnd 14: sc in next 4 st on the second flipper, continue on the first flipper, sc in next 8 st, continue on the second flipper, sc in next 4 st [16]
Rnd 15 – 16: sc in all 16 st [16]
Rnd 17: (sc in next 3 st, inc in next st) repeat 4 times [20]
Rnd 18: sc in all 20 st [20]
Rnd 19: (sc in next 4 st, inc in next st) repeat 4 times [24]

Rnd 20: sc in all 24 st [24]
Rnd 21: (sc in next 3 st, inc in next st) repeat 6 times [30]
Rnd 22: sc in all 30 st [30]
Rnd 23: (sc in next 4 st, inc in next st) repeat 6 times [36]
Rnd 24: sc in all 36 st [36]
Rnd 25: (sc in next 5 st, inc in next st) repeat 6 times [42]
Rnd 26: sc in all 42 st [42]
Rnd 27: (sc in next 6 st, inc in next st) repeat 6 times [48]
Rnd 28: sc in all 48 st [48]
Rnd 29: (sc in next 7 st, inc in next st) repeat 6 times [54]
Rnd 30: sc in all 54 st [54]
Fasten off, leaving a long tail for sewing. Stuff the tail part with fiberfill. Sew it to the back of the body, between rounds 33-52.

FRONT FLIPPER *(make 2, in gray yarn)*
Rnd 1: start 6 sc in a magic ring [6]
Rnd 2: inc in all 6 st [12]
Rnd 3: (sc in next 3 st, inc in next st) repeat 3 times [15]
Rnd 4 – 8: sc in all 15 st [15]
Rnd 9: (sc in next 3 st, dec) repeat 3 times [12]
Rnd 10 – 11: sc in all 12 st [12]
Rnd 12: (sc in next 2 st, dec) repeat 3 times [9]
Rnd 13: sc in all 9 st [9]
Fasten off, leaving a long tail for sewing. The front flippers don't need to be stuffed. Sew the flippers to the body, on round 39, with an interspace of 21 stitches at the front.

NOSE *(in black yarn)*
Rnd 1: start 4 sc in a magic ring [4]

Rnd 2: (sc in next st, inc in next st) repeat 2 times [6]
Fasten off, leaving a long tail for sewing. Sew the nose on rounds 18-19, between the eyes.

STRAP *(in pink yarn)*
Ch 61 (try on the strap around Sammy's neck and adjust the number of chains if necessary). Crochet in rows.
Row 1: start in second ch from hook, sc in next 60 st, ch 1, turn [60]
Row 2: sc in next 60 st, ch 1, turn [60]
Row 3: sc in next 60 st [60]
Fasten off, leaving a long tail for sewing. Wrap the strap around the seal's neck and sew the ends together.

BOW *(in pink yarn)*
Ch 30. Join with a slst to form a ring (pictures 1-2). Make sure the ring isn't twisted. Work in joined rounds.
Rnd 1 – 3: ch 3, dc in all 30 st, slst in first dc [30] (pictures 3-4)
Fasten off and weave in the yarn end.

CENTER OF BOW *(in pink yarn)*
Ch 11. Crochet in rows.
Row 1: start in second ch from hook, sc in next 10 st, ch 1, turn [10]
Row 2: sc in next 10 st, ch 1, turn [10]
Row 3: sc in next 10 st [10]
Fasten off, leaving a long tail for sewing. Fold the center of the bow around the bow and strap, and sew the ends together.

KIRK
THE
FROG

by Lisa Jestes Designs
(Lisa Jestes)

AMIGURUMI GALLERY
Scan or visit
www.amigurumi.com/406
to share pictures and find inspiration.

SKILL LEVEL: ✶ ✶

SIZE: 9" / 23 cm tall when made with the indicated yarn.

MATERIALS:

– Worsted weight yarn in green, white (leftover) and black (leftover)
– Size F-5 / 3.75 mm crochet hook
– Yarn needle
– Fabric glue
– Leftover piece of black and white felt
– Stitch marker
– Fiberfill for stuffing

HEAD *(in green yarn)*

Rnd 1: start 6 sc in a magic ring [6]

Rnd 2: inc in all 6 st [12]

Rnd 3: (sc in next st, inc in next st) repeat 6 times [18]

Rnd 4: (sc in next 2 st, inc in next st) repeat 6 times [24]

Rnd 5: (sc in next 3 st, inc in next st) repeat 6 times [30]

Rnd 6: (sc in next 4 st, inc in next st) repeat 6 times [36]

Rnd 7: (sc in next 5 st, inc in next st) repeat 6 times [42]

Rnd 8: sc in all 42 st [42]

Rnd 9: (sc in next 6 st, inc in next st) repeat 6 times [48]

Rnd 10: sc in all 48 st [48]

Rnd 11: sc in next 7 st, inc in next st, (sc in next st, inc in next st) repeat 4 times, sc in next 16 st, inc in next st, (sc in next st, inc in next st) repeat 4 times, sc in next 7 st [58]

Rnd 12: sc in all 58 st [58]

Rnd 13: sc in next 7 st, inc in next st, (sc in next 2 st, inc in next st) repeat 4 times, sc in next 18 st, inc in next st, (sc in next 2 st, inc in next st) repeat 4 times, sc in next 7 st [68]

Rnd 14 – 19: sc in all 68 st [68]

Rnd 20: sc in next 7 st, dec, (sc in next 2 st, dec) repeat 4 times, sc in next 18 st, dec, (sc in next 2 st, dec) repeat 4 times, sc in next 7 st [58]

Rnd 21: sc in all 58 st [58]

Rnd 22: sc in next 7 st, dec, (sc in next st, dec) repeat 4 times, sc in next 16 st, dec, (sc in next st, dec) repeat 4 times, sc in next 7 st [48]

Rnd 23: sc in all 48 st [48]

Rnd 24: (sc in next 6 st, dec) repeat 6 times [42]

Rnd 25: sc in all 42 st [42]

Rnd 26: (sc in next 5 st, dec) repeat 6 times [36]
Stuff the head with fiberfill and continue stuffing as you go.

Rnd 27: (sc in next 4 st, dec) repeat 6 times [30]

Rnd 28: (sc in next 3 st, dec) repeat 6 times [24]

Rnd 29: (sc in next 2 st, dec) repeat 6 times [18]

Rnd 30: (sc in next st, dec) repeat 6 times [12]

Rnd 31: dec 6 times [6]
Fasten off and weave in the yarn ends.

BODY *(in green yarn)*

Rnd 1: start 6 sc in a magic ring [6]

Rnd 2: inc in all 6 st [12]

Rnd 3: (sc in next st, inc in next st) repeat 6 times [18]

Rnd 4: (sc in next 2 st, inc in next st) repeat 6 times [24]

Rnd 5: (sc in next 3 st, inc in next st) repeat 6 times [30]

Rnd 6: (sc in next 4 st, inc in next st) repeat 6 times [36]

Rnd 7: (sc in next 5 st, inc in next st) repeat 6 times [42]

Rnd 8 – 11: sc in all 42 st [42]

Rnd 12: (sc in next 5 st, dec) repeat 6 times [36]

Rnd 13 – 16: sc in all 36 st [36]

Rnd 17: (sc in next 4 st, dec) repeat 6 times [30]

Rnd 18 – 20: sc in all 30 st [30]

Rnd 21: (sc in next 3 st, dec) repeat 6 times [24]

Rnd 22 – 24: sc in all 24 st [24]
Fasten off, leaving a long tail for sewing. Stuff the body with fiberfill.

EYE *(make 2, in white yarn)*

Rnd 1: start 6 sc in a magic ring [6]

Rnd 2: inc in all 6 st [12]

Rnd 3: (sc in next st, inc in next st) repeat 6 times [18]

Rnd 4 – 5: sc in all 18 st [18]

Rnd 6: (sc in next st, dec) repeat 6 times [12]
Stuff the eye with fiberfill.

Rnd 7: dec 6 times [6]
Fasten off and weave in the yarn ends.

EYELID *(make 2, in green yarn)*

Crochet in rows.

Row 1: start 5 sc in a magic ring, ch 1, turn [5]

Row 2: (sc in next st, inc in next st) repeat 2 times, sc in next st, ch 1, turn [7]

Row 3: (sc in next st, inc in next st) repeat 3 times, sc in next st, ch 1, turn [10]

Row 4: (sc in next 4 st, inc in next st) repeat 2 times, ch 1, turn [12]

Row 5: (sc in next 3 st, inc in next st) repeat 3 times, ch 1, turn [15]

Row 6: (sc in next 4 st, inc in next st) repeat 3 times, ch 1, turn [18]

Row 7: (sc in next 5 st, inc in next st) repeat 3 times, ch 1, turn [21]

Row 8: sc in all 21 st, ch 1, turn [21]

Row 9: (sc in next 5 st, dec) repeat 3 times, ch 1, turn [18]

Row 10: (sc in next 4 st, dec) repeat 3 times [15]

Fasten off, leaving a long tail for sewing.

ARM *(make 2, in green yarn)*

Rnd 1: start 5 sc in a magic ring [5]

Rnd 2: inc in all 5 st [10]

Rnd 3 – 13: sc in all 10 st [10]

Rnd 14: (sc in next 3 st, dec) repeat 2 times [8]

Rnd 15 – 18: sc in all 8 st [8]

Rnd 19: (inc in next 2 st, sc in next 2 st) repeat 2 times [12]

Rnd 20: (sc in next st, inc in next st) repeat 6 times [18]

Rnd 21 – 22: sc in all 18 st [18]

Stuff the arm with fiberfill.

Rnd 23: (sc in next 2 st, inc in next st) repeat 6 times [24]

Continue working the first finger.

First finger

Rnd 1: sc in next 8 st, sc in the last stitch of round 23 [9]

You have now created a smaller round.

(picture 1) Continue working in these 9 stitches only.

Rnd 2: sc in all 9 st [9]

Rnd 3: (sc in next st, dec) repeat 3 times [6]

Stuff the first finger with fiberfill and continue stuffing as you go.

Rnd 4: sc in all 6 st [6]

Rnd 5: (sc in next st, inc in next st) repeat 3 times [9]

Rnd 6: (sc in next 2 st, inc in next st) repeat 3 times [12]

Rnd 7: sc in all 12 st [12]

Rnd 8: (sc in next 2 st, dec) repeat 3 times [9]

Rnd 9: (sc in next st, dec) repeat 3 times [6]

Rnd 10: dec 3 times [3]

Fasten off, leaving a yarn tail. Using your yarn needle, weave the yarn tail through the front loop of each remaining stitch and pull it tight to close. Weave in the yarn end (picture 2).

Second finger

Pull up a loop of green yarn in the first stitch to the left of the first finger (picture 3).

Rnd 1: ch 1, sc in same st where you joined your yarn,

sc in next 3 st, skip next 7 st (picture 4), sc in next 4 st, inc in the bottom of the first finger (picture 5) [10]
You have now created a smaller round.
Rnd 2: sc in all 10 st [10]
Stuff the second finger with fiberfill and continue stuffing as you go.
Rnd 3: (sc in next 3 st, dec) repeat 2 times [8]
Rnd 4 – 5: sc in all 8 st [8]
Rnd 6: (sc in next st, inc in next st) repeat 4 times [12]
Rnd 7: (sc in next 2 st, inc in next st) repeat 4 times [16]
Rnd 8: sc in all 16 st [16]
Rnd 9: (sc in next 2 st, dec) repeat 4 times [12]
Rnd 10: (sc in next st, dec) repeat 4 times [8]
Rnd 11: dec 4 times [4]
Fasten off, leaving a yarn tail. Using your yarn needle, weave the yarn tail through the front loop of each remaining stitch and pull it tight to close. Weave in the yarn end (picture 6).

Third finger
Pull up a loop of green yarn in the first stitch to the left of the second finger (picture 7).

Rnd 1: ch 1, sc in same st as where you joined your yarn, sc in next 6 st, 2 sc in the bottom of the second finger (picture 8) [9]
Rnd 2: (sc in next st, dec) repeat 3 times [6]
Stuff the third finger with fiberfill and continue stuffing as you go.
Rnd 3: sc in all 6 st [6]
Rnd 4: (sc in next st, inc in next st) repeat 3 times [9]
Rnd 5: (sc in next 2 st, inc in next st) repeat 3 times [12]
Rnd 6: sc in all 12 st [12]
Rnd 7: (sc in next 2 st, dec) repeat 3 times [9]
Rnd 8: (sc in next st, dec) repeat 3 times [6]
Rnd 9: dec 3 times [3]
Fasten off, leaving a yarn tail. Using your yarn needle, weave the yarn tail through the front loop of each remaining stitch and pull it tight to close. Weave in the yarn end. Sew up any holes between the fingers.

LEG (make 2, in green yarn)
Rnd 1: start 5 sc in a magic ring [5]
Rnd 2: inc in all 5 st [10]
Rnd 3: (sc in next st, inc in next st) repeat 5 times [15]

Rnd 4: (sc in next 2 st, inc in next st) repeat 5 times [20]

Rnd 5 – 14: sc in all 20 st [20]

Rnd 15: (sc in next 2 st, dec) repeat 5 times [15]

Rnd 16 – 20: sc in all 15 st [15]

Stuff the leg with fiberfill and continue stuffing as you go.

Rnd 21: (sc in next st, dec) repeat 5 times [10]

Rnd 22: sc in all 10 st [10]

Rnd 23: (sc in next 3 st, dec) repeat 2 times [8]

Don't overstuff the middle section of the leg. You should be able to bend it later.

Rnd 24: sc in all 8 st [8]

Rnd 25: (sc in next 3 st, inc in next st) repeat 2 times [10]

Rnd 26 – 27: sc in all 10 st [10]

Rnd 28: (sc in next 4 st, inc in next st) repeat 2 times [12]

Rnd 29 – 32: sc in all 12 st [12]

Rnd 33: (sc in next 3 st, inc in next st) repeat 3 times [15]

Rnd 34 – 39: sc in all 15 st [15]

Rnd 40: (sc in next 3 st, dec) repeat 3 times [12]

Rnd 41 – 45: sc in all 12 st [12]

Fasten off, leaving a long tail for sewing.

FOOT (make 2, in green yarn)

Leave a long starting yarn tail.

Rnd 1: start 6 sc in a magic ring [6]

Rnd 2: inc in all 6 st [12]

Rnd 3: (sc in next st, inc in next st) repeat 6 times [18]

Rnd 4 – 5: sc in all 18 st [18]

Rnd 6: (sc in next 2 st, inc in next st) repeat 6 times [24]

Rnd 7 – 9: sc in all 24 st [24]

Repeat the instructions to make the first, second and third finger to complete the toes. Stuff the toes and feet with fiberfill as you go.

ASSEMBLY

– Position the head on the body and sew them together.

– Sew the eyelids to the white eyeball with the edge touching round 4. Add some fiberfill under the eyelids, behind the eyes.

– Pin the eyes to the head between round 4 and 11 and sew them on. Add a few stitches under the white parts of the eye, because the stuffing behind the eyelids might come out if you don't.

– Pin the arms to the body and sew them in place.

– Sew the top back part of the feet to the legs, so that the feet are at a right angle.

– If you want to bend the legs, you can sew them together with one stitch under the knee so that they'll stay put.

– Sew round 3-11 of the legs to the body. If you want to bend the legs, like in the pictured example, you can sew them to the body pointing upwards. If you want the legs to be straight, you can sew them to the body pointing downwards.

– Cut 2 small circles from black felt for the frog's pupils and 2 smaller circles from white felt to add some 'shine' to his eyes. Use fabric glue to attach these.

– For the frog's mouth, take a long strand of green yarn and insert your needle into the back of the frog's head. Bring the needle out on the front side between rounds 17 and 18, where you want the mouth to start. Run the strand across the face and insert the needle on the other side of the face. Run the needle back through the head, to where you started on the back of the frog's head. Pull both ends tight to make the indentation of the mouth. Tie a couple of knots to secure, cut the ends and stuff the knots back into the head to hide them.

LEO
THE
LION

by Amalou Designs
(Marielle Maag)

NOTE: Use a size B-1 / 2.5 mm crochet hook unless the pattern states differently.

BODY *(start in yellow yarn)*

Leg *(make 2, in yellow yarn)*

Start by making 2 separate legs.

Rnd 1: start 6 sc in a magic ring [6]

Rnd 2: inc in all 6 st [12]

Rnd 3: (sc in next st, inc in next st) repeat 6 times [18]

Rnd 4: (sc in next 2 st, inc in next st) repeat 6 times [24]

Rnd 5: sc in all 24 st [24]

Rnd 6: dec 2 times, sc in next 9 st, inc in next 2 st, sc in next 9 st [24]

Rnd 7: sc in all 24 st [24]

Rnd 8: dec 2 times, sc in next 9 st, inc in next 2 st, sc in next 9 st [24]

Rnd 9 – 10: sc in all 24 st [24]

Rnd 11: dec 2 times, sc in next 9 st, inc in next 2 st, sc in next 9 st [24]

Rnd 12: sc in all 24 st [24]

Mark the last stitch with a stitch marker. Fasten off

SKILL LEVEL: ✶ ✶

SIZE: 7.5" / 19 cm tall when made with the indicated yarn.

MATERIALS:

– Sport weight yarn in yellow, brown, orange and white (leftover)

– Size B-1 / 2.5 mm crochet hook

– Size C-2 / 3 mm crochet hook

– Safety eyes (8 mm)

– Yarn needle

– Stitch marker

– Fiberfill for stuffing

AMIGURUMI GALLERY

Scan or visit
www.amigurumi.com/2215
to share pictures and find inspiration.

and weave in the yarn end on the first leg. Don't fasten off on the second leg, sc in next 2 st, ch 6. In the next round we'll join both legs together.

Joining the legs

Rnd 13: sc in the stitch next to the marked last st of round 12 of the first leg (make sure that the feet face each other, (picture 1)) sc in next 23 st on the first leg, sc in next 6 ch (picture 2), sc in next 24 st on the second leg, sc in the other side of next 6 ch [60]

Rnd 14 – 18: sc in all 60 st [60]

Rnd 19: sc in next 12 st, dec, sc in next 28 st, dec, sc in next 16 st [58]

Rnd 20: sc in all 58 st [58]

Rnd 21: sc in next 12 st, dec, sc in next 27 st, dec, sc in next 15 st [56]

Rnd 22: sc in all 56 st [56]

Rnd 23: sc in next 12 st, dec, sc in next 26 st, dec, sc in next 14 st [54]

Rnd 24: sc in all 54 st [54]

Change to brown yarn.

Rnd 25: sc in next 12 st, dec, sc in next 25 st, dec, sc in next 13 st [52]

Rnd 26: sc in all 52 st [52]

Rnd 27: sc in next 12 st, dec, sc in next 24 st, dec, sc in next 12 st [50] (picture 3)

Rnd 28: sc in all 50 st [50]

Rnd 29: sc in next 12 st, dec, sc in next 23 st, dec, sc in next 11 st [48]

Rnd 30: sc in all 48 st [48]

Rnd 31: sc in next 12 st, dec, sc in next 22 st, dec, sc in next 10 st [46]

Rnd 32: sc in all 46 st [46]

Rnd 33: sc in next 12 st, dec, sc in next 21 st, dec, sc in next 9 st [44]

Rnd 34: sc in all 44 st [44]

Rnd 35: sc in next 12 st, dec, sc in next 20 st, dec, sc in next 8 st [42]

Rnd 36: sc in next 12 st, dec, sc in next 19 st, dec, sc in

next 7 st [40]

Rnd 37: sc in next 12 st, dec, sc in next 18 st, dec, sc in next 6 st [38]

Rnd 38: sc in next 12 st, dec, sc in next 17 st, dec, sc in next 5 st [36]

Rnd 39: sc in next 12 st, dec, sc in next 16 st, dec, sc in next 4 st [34]

Rnd 40: sc in next 12 st, dec, sc in next 15 st, dec, sc in next 3 st [32]

Rnd 41: sc in next 12 st, dec, sc in next 14 st, dec, sc in next 2 st [30]

Fasten off, leaving a long tail for sewing. Stuff the body with fiberfill.

HEAD *(in yellow yarn)*
Rnd 1: start 6 sc in a magic ring [6]
Rnd 2: inc in all 6 st [12]
Rnd 3: (sc in next st, inc in next st) repeat 6 times [18]
Rnd 4: (sc in next 2 st, inc in next st) repeat 6 times [24]
Rnd 5: (sc in next 3 st, inc in next st) repeat 6 times [30]
Rnd 6: (sc in next 4 st, inc in next st) repeat 6 times [36]
Rnd 7: (sc in next 5 st, inc in next st) repeat 6 times [42]

Rnd 8: (sc in next 6 st, inc in next st) repeat 6 times [48]
Rnd 9: sc in all 48 st [48]
Rnd 10: (sc in next 7 st, inc in next st) repeat 6 times [54]
Rnd 11: sc in all 54 st [54]
Rnd 12: (sc in next 8 st, inc in next st) repeat 6 times [60]
Rnd 13: (sc in next 9 st, inc in next st) repeat 6 times [66]
Rnd 14: (sc in next 10 st, inc in next st) repeat 6 times [72]
Rnd 15: sc in all 72 st [72]
Rnd 16: (sc in next 11 st, inc in next st) repeat 6 times [78]
Rnd 17: sc in all 78 st [78]
Rnd 18: (sc in next 12 st, inc in next st) repeat 6 times [84]
Rnd 19 – 20: sc in all 84 st [84]
Rnd 21: (sc in next 12 st, dec) repeat 6 times [78]
Rnd 22: (sc in next 11 st, dec) repeat 6 times [72]
Rnd 23: (sc in next 10 st, dec) repeat 6 times [66]
Rnd 24: (sc in next 9 st, dec) repeat 6 times [60]
Rnd 25: (sc in next 8 st, dec) repeat 6 times [54]
Rnd 26: (sc in next 7 st, dec) repeat 6 times [48]
Rnd 27: (sc in next 6 st, dec) repeat 6 times [42]
Rnd 28: (sc in next 5 st, dec) repeat 6 times [36]
Rnd 29: (sc in next 4 st, dec) repeat 6 times [30]

Fasten off and weave in the yarn end. Insert the safety eyes between rounds 16 and 17, with an interspace of 14 stitches. Embroider eyebrows over rounds 11 and 12 using brown yarn. Stuff the head with fiberfill.

SNOUT *(in white yarn)*
Rnd 1: start 6 sc in a magic ring [6]
Rnd 2: inc in all 6 st [12]
Rnd 3: (sc in next st, inc in next st) repeat 6 times [18]
Rnd 4: (sc in next 2 st, inc in next st) repeat 6 times [24]
Rnd 5: (sc in next 3 st, inc in next st) repeat 6 times [30]
Rnd 6: (sc in next 4 st, inc in next st) repeat 6 times [36]

Fasten off, leaving a long tail for sewing. Position the white snout at 17 rounds from the top of the head. Sew it to the head and add stuffing before closing the seam. Embroider the nose and mouth using brown yarn.

EAR *(make 2, in yellow yarn)*
Rnd 1: start 6 sc in a magic ring [6]

Rnd 2: inc in all 6 st [12]

Rnd 3: (sc in next st, inc in next st) repeat 6 times [18]

Rnd 4: (sc in next 2 st, inc in next st) repeat 6 times [24]

Rnd 5 – 8: sc in all 24 st [24]

Fasten off, leaving a long tail for sewing. The ears don't need to be stuffed.

INNER EAR *(make 2, in brown yarn)*

Rnd 1: start a magic ring with ch 2 + 5 hdc + slst in first ch [6]

Fasten off, leaving a long tail for sewing. Flatten the ears and sew the brown inner ear to one side. Sew the ears to the head at 4 rounds from the top.

ARM *(make 2, start in yellow yarn)*

Rnd 1: start 6 sc in a magic ring [6]

Rnd 2: inc in all 6 st [12]

Rnd 3: (sc in next st, inc in next st) repeat 6 times [18]

Rnd 4 – 7: sc in all 18 st [18]

Rnd 8: dec 2 times, sc in next 14 st [16]

Rnd 9 – 16: sc in all 16 st [16]

Rnd 17: sc in next 9 st, *(change to brown yarn)* sc in next st, dec, sc in next 4 st [15]

Rnd 18 – 24: sc in all 15 st [15]

Rnd 25: sc in next 11 st, dec, sc in next 2 st [14]

Rnd 26 – 28: sc in all 14 st [14]

Stuff the yellow part of the arm with fiberfill. Stuff the brown part only lightly. Flatten the opening of the arm, making sure that the decreases of round 8 are on the side, and work the next round through both layers to close.

Rnd 29: sc in all 7 st [7]

Fasten off, leaving a long tail for sewing.

MANE *(with a C-2 / 3 mm crochet hook, in orange yarn)*

Ch 64. Join with a slst to form a ring. Make sure the ring isn't twisted.

Rnd 1: slst in all 64 st [64]

Rnd 2: hdc in next 63 st, slst in next st [64]

Rnd 3: (skip 1 st, 6 dc in next st, skip 1 st, slst in next st)

repeat 16 times [16 arches]

Fasten off, leaving a long tail for sewing. Sew the mane to the head. Start at 3 rounds underneath the white snout and go around the head and behind the ears.

ASSEMBLY

– Sew the head to the body.

– Sew the arms to the body underneath the seam of the head.

– Use brown yarn to work surface slip stitches on the color change on the body. Make sure to start and end at the back of the body.

LEOPOLDO THE PEACOCK

by Pica Pau (Yan Schenkel)

SKILL LEVEL: ✷ ✷ ✷

SIZE: 9.5" / 24 cm tall when made with the indicated yarn.

MATERIALS:

– Light worsted weight yarn in off-white, blue, navy blue, green and yellow (leftover)
– Size D-3 / 3 mm crochet hook
– Safety eyes (10 mm)
– Yarn needle
– Stitch marker
– Fiberfill for stuffing

AMIGURUMI GALLERY

Scan or visit
www.amigurumi.com/909
to share pictures and find inspiration.

EYE PATCH (make 2, in off-white yarn)

Ch 7. Stitches are worked around both sides of the foundation chain.

Rnd 1: start in second ch from hook, inc in this st, sc in next 4 st, 4 sc in next st. Continue on the other side of the foundation chain, sc in next 4 st, inc in next st [16]

Rnd 2: inc in next st, sc in next 6 st, inc in next 2 st, sc in next 6 st, inc in next st [20]

Rnd 3: inc in next 2 st, sc in next 7 st, inc in next 2 st, sc in next 9 st [24]

Slst in next st. Fasten off, leaving a long tail for sewing. Insert the safety eyes in the off-white eyes, on one side of the oval between rounds 1 and 2, but don't close the washers yet.

BEAK (in yellow yarn)

Rnd 1: start 5 sc in a magic ring [5]

Rnd 2: sc in all 5 st [5]

Rnd 3: inc in all 5 st [10]

Rnd 4 – 5: sc in all 10 st [10]

Rnd 6: (sc in next st, inc in next st) repeat 5 times [15]

Rnd 7 – 8: sc in all 15 st [15]

Rnd 9: (sc in next 2 st, inc in next st) repeat 5 times [20]

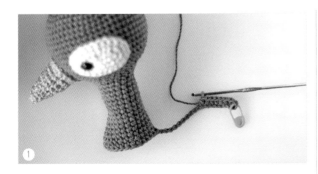

Rnd 10: sc in all 20 st [20]

Fasten off, leaving a long tail for sewing. Stuff the beak with fiberfill.

HEAD AND BODY *(in blue yarn)*

Rnd 1: start 6 sc in a magic ring [6]

Rnd 2: inc in all 6 st [12]

Rnd 3: (sc in next st, inc in next st) repeat 6 times [18]

Rnd 4: (sc in next 2 st, inc in next st) repeat 6 times [24]

Rnd 5: (sc in next 3 st, inc in next st) repeat 6 times [30]

Rnd 6: (sc in next 4 st, inc in next st) repeat 6 times [36]

Rnd 7: (sc in next 5 st, inc in next st) repeat 6 times [42]

Rnd 8: (sc in next 6 st, inc in next st) repeat 6 times [48]

Rnd 9: (sc in next 7 st, inc in next st) repeat 6 times [54]

Rnd 10 – 18: sc in all 54 st [54]

Rnd 19: (sc in next 7 st, dec) repeat 6 times [48]

Rnd 20: (sc in next 6 st, dec) repeat 6 times [42]

Rnd 21: (sc in next 5 st, dec) repeat 6 times [36]

Rnd 22: (sc in next 4 st, dec) repeat 6 times [30]

Rnd 23: (sc in next 3 st, dec) repeat 6 times [24]

Rnd 24: (sc in next 2 st, dec) repeat 6 times [18]

Rnd 25 – 32: sc in all 18 st [18]

Rnd 33: sc in next 8 st, inc in next 2 st, sc in next 8 st [20]

Rnd 34: sc in all 20 st [20]

Rnd 35: sc in next 9 st, inc in next st, sc in next st, inc in next st, sc in next 8 st [22]

Rnd 36: sc in all 22 st [22]

Rnd 37: sc in next 10 st, inc in next st, sc in next 2 st, inc in next st, sc in next 8 st [24]

Rnd 38 – 39: sc in all 24 st [24]

Rnd 40: ch 18 to start the body of the peacock.

Place the stitch marker in the next stitch, this will be the new beginning of the round. Crochet back on the chain, start in second ch from hook, inc in this st, sc in next 16 st (picture 1), continue on the neck, sc in next 24 st, continue on the other side of the chain, sc in next 16 st, 3 sc in next st [61]

Rnd 41: 3 sc in next st, sc in next 27 st, inc in next st, sc in next 3 st, inc in next st, sc in next 28 st [65]

Sew the beak to the head between rounds 15 and 21, Keep the position of the body of the peacock in mind. Add more stuffing before closing the seam.

Insert the safety eyes with the crochet eye patches between rounds 17 and 18. There should be 6 stitches between each safety eye and the beak. Close the washers. Sew the off-white eye patches to the head.

Rnd 42: inc in next 3 st, sc in next 62 st [68]

Rnd 43: sc in all 68 st [68]

Rnd 44: sc in next 34 st, inc in next st, sc in next 4 st, inc in next st, sc in next 28 st [70]

Rnd 45 – 46: sc in all 70 st [70]

Rnd 47: sc in next 4 st, dec, sc in next 27 st, inc in next st, sc in next 6 st, inc in next st, sc in next 27 st, dec [70]

Rnd 48: sc in all 70 st [70]

Stuff the head and neck firmly with fiberfill and continue stuffing as you go.

Rnd 49: sc in next 4 st, dec, sc in next 27 st, inc in next st, sc in next 7 st, inc in next st, sc in next 26 st, dec [70]

Rnd 50: sc in all 70 st [70]

Rnd 51: sc in next 4 st, dec, sc in next 26 st, dec, sc in next 7 st, dec, sc in next 25 st, dec [66]

Rnd 52: sc in next 30 st, dec, sc in next 7 st, dec, sc in next 25 st [64]

Rnd 53: sc in next 4 st, dec, sc in next 23 st, dec, sc in next 7 st, dec, sc in next 22 st, dec [60]

Rnd 54: sc in next 27 st, dec, sc in next 7 st, dec, sc in next 22 st [58]

Rnd 55: sc in next 4 st, dec, sc in next 20 st, dec, sc in next 7 st, dec, sc in next 19 st, dec [54]

Rnd 56 – 57: sc in all 54 st [54]

Rnd 58: (sc in next 8 st, inc in next st) repeat 6 times [60]

Rnd 59: BLO (sc in next 8 st, dec) repeat 6 times [54]

Rnd 60: (sc in next 7 st, dec) repeat 6 times [48]

Rnd 61: (sc in next 6 st, dec) repeat 6 times [42]

Rnd 62: (sc in next 5 st, dec) repeat 6 times [36]

Rnd 63: (sc in next 4 st, dec) repeat 6 times [30]

Rnd 64: (sc in next 3 st, dec) repeat 6 times [24]

Stuff the body with fiberfill up to this point.

Rnd 65: (sc in next 2 st, dec) repeat 6 times [18]

Rnd 66: (sc in next st, dec) repeat 6 times [12]

Rnd 67: dec 6 times [6]

Fasten off, leaving a yarn tail. Using your yarn needle, weave the yarn tail through the front loop of each remaining stitch and pull it tight to close. Weave in the yarn end. Sew a stitch from the bottom of the body to the back (where the back feathers will be located), so that the body doesn't inflate like a ball. This way, the

peacock will sit better.

Optional: You can add a round of slst in the front loops of round 59 of the body.

TAIL

Large tail feather *(make 3, in green yarn)*

Rnd 1: start 6 sc in a magic ring [6]

Rnd 2: inc in all 6 st [12]

Rnd 3: (sc in next st, inc in next st) repeat 6 times [18]

Rnd 4: (sc in next 2 st, inc in next st) repeat 6 times [24]

Rnd 5: (sc in next 3 st, inc in next st) repeat 6 times [30]

Rnd 6 – 11: sc in all 30 st [30]

Rnd 12: (sc in next 3 st, dec) repeat 6 times [24]

Rnd 13 – 16: sc in all 24 st [24]

Rnd 17: (sc in next 2 st, dec) repeat 6 times [18]
Rnd 18 – 21: sc in all 18 st [18]
Rnd 22: (sc in next st, dec) repeat 6 times [12]
Rnd 23 – 26: sc in all 12 st [12]
Rnd 27: (sc in next st, dec) repeat 4 times [8]
Rnd 28 – 30: sc in all 8 st [8]
Rnd 31: dec 4 times [4]
Fasten off, leaving a long tail for sewing. Don't stuff.
Flatten the feathers.

Medium tail feather *(make 2, in green yarn)*
Rnd 1: start 5 sc in a magic ring [5]
Rnd 2: inc in all 5 st [10]
Rnd 3: (sc in next st, inc in next st) repeat 5 times [15]
Rnd 4: (sc in next 2 st, inc in next st) repeat 5 times [20]
Rnd 5: (sc in next 3 st, inc in next st) repeat 5 times [25]
Rnd 6 – 10: sc in all 25 st [25]
Rnd 11: (sc in next 3 st, dec) repeat 5 times [20]
Rnd 12 – 13: sc in all 20 st [20]
Rnd 14: (sc in next 2 st, dec) repeat 5 times [15]
Rnd 15 – 16: sc in all 15 st [15]
Rnd 17: (sc in next st, dec) repeat 5 times [10]
Rnd 18 – 19: sc in all 10 st [10]
Rnd 20: dec 5 times [5]
Fasten off, leaving a long tail for sewing. Don't stuff.
Flatten the feathers.

Tiny tail feather *(make 3 in blue yarn)*
Rnd 1: start 5 sc in a magic ring [5]
Rnd 2: inc in all 5 st [10]
Rnd 3: (sc in next st, inc in next st) repeat 5 times [15]
Rnd 4 – 5: sc in all 15 st [15]
Rnd 6: (sc in next st, dec) repeat 5 times [10]
Rnd 7 – 8: sc in all 10 st [10]
Rnd 9: dec 5 times [5]
Fasten off, leaving a long tail for sewing. Don't stuff.
Flatten the feathers.

Circle *(make 2 in blue and 3 in navy blue yarn)*
Rnd 1: start 5 sc in a magic ring [5]

Rnd 2: inc in all 5 st [10]
Fasten off, leaving a long tail for sewing.

Assembly
– Sew the 3 navy blue circles to the 3 tiny blue feathers.
  Then sew these 3 feathers to the large green tail
  feathers (picture 2).
– Sew the 2 blue circles onto the 2 medium green
  feathers.
– Sew the large feathers onto the peacock's bottom,
  placing the first one in the center and the other 2 on
  each side of the middle one (picture 3). Sew the 2
  medium green feathers on each side of the large ones.
  To keep the feathers from falling, make sure to sew
  almost all the way along their sides (picture 4).

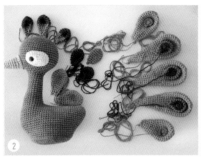  

BACK FEATHERS

Tiny back feather *(make 1 in blue and 2 in navy blue yarn)*
Rnd 1 – 9: repeat the pattern for the tiny tail feather. Fasten off, leaving a long tail for sewing. Don't stuff. Flatten the feathers.

Small back feather *(make 2, in green yarn)*
Rnd 1: start 5 sc in a magic ring [5]
Rnd 2: inc in all 5 st [10]
Rnd 3: (sc in next st, inc in next st) repeat 5 times [15]
Rnd 4: (sc in next 2 st, inc in next st) repeat 5 times [20]
Rnd 5 – 7: sc in all 20 st [20]
Rnd 8: (sc in next 2 st, dec) repeat 5 times [15]
Rnd 9 – 10: sc in all 15 st [15]
Rnd 11: (sc in next st, dec) repeat 5 times [10]
Rnd 12 – 13: sc in all 10 st [10]
Rnd 14: dec 5 times [5]
Fasten off, leaving a long tail for sewing. Don't stuff. Flatten the feathers.

Assembly
Sew the 2 small green back feathers in the center of the peacock's back. Sew the tiny blue and navy blue feathers in front of them.

CREST

Large crest feather *(make 1, start in navy blue yarn)*
Rnd 1: start 5 sc in a magic ring [5]

Rnd 2: inc in all 5 st [10]
Rnd 3: (sc in next st, inc in next st) repeat 5 times [15]
Rnd 4: (sc in next 2 st, inc in next st) repeat 5 times [20]
Rnd 5: sc in all 20 st [20]
Change to blue yarn.
Rnd 6: (sc in next 2 st, dec) repeat 5 times [15]
Rnd 7: (sc in next st, dec) repeat 5 times [10]
Rnd 8 – 10: sc in all 10 st [10]
Rnd 11: dec 5 times [5]
Fasten off, leaving a long tail for sewing. Don't stuff. Flatten the feather.

Small crest feather *(make 2, start in navy blue yarn)*
Rnd 1: start 5 sc in a magic ring [5]
Rnd 2: inc in all 5 st [10]
Rnd 3: (sc in next st, inc in next st) repeat 5 times [15]
Change to blue yarn.
Rnd 4: sc in all 15 st [15]
Rnd 5: (sc in next st, dec) repeat 5 times [10]
Rnd 6 – 7: sc in all 10 st [10]
Rnd 8: dec 5 times [5]
Fasten off, leaving a long tail for sewing. Don't stuff. Flatten the feathers.

Assembly
Sew the large crest feather on top of the head, over the magic ring is. Sew the small crest feathers on either side of the large crest feather.

OATLY THE HORSE

by Crochetbykim
(Kim Bengtsson Friis)

SKILL LEVEL: ✷

SIZE: 9.5" / 24 cm tall when made with the indicated yarn.

MATERIALS

– Worsted weight yarn in beige, light brown, dark brown, white, black, pink (leftover) and light gray (leftover)
– Size G-6/ 4 mm crochet hook
– Safety eyes (12 mm)
– Black satin ribbon (0,5 cm wide, about 8" / 20 cm long)
– Scissors
– Yarn needle
– Stitch marker
– Fiberfill for stuffing

HEAD *(in beige yarn)*

Rnd 1: start 6 sc in a magic ring [6]

Rnd 2: inc in all 6 st [12]

Rnd 3: (sc in next st, inc in next st) repeat 6 times [18]

Rnd 4: (sc in next 2 st, inc in next st) repeat 6 times [24]

Rnd 5: (sc in next 3 st, inc in next st) repeat 6 times [30]

Rnd 6: (sc in next 4 st, inc in next st) repeat 6 times [36]

Rnd 7: (sc in next 5 st, inc in next st) repeat 6 times [42]

Rnd 8: (sc in next 6 st, inc in next st) repeat 6 times [48]

Rnd 9: (sc in next 7 st, inc in next st) repeat 6 times [54]

Rnd 10: (sc in next 8 st, inc in next st) repeat 6 times [60]

Rnd 11 – 21: sc in all 60 st [60]

Stuff the head with fiberfill and continue stuffing as you go. Insert the safety eyes between rounds 15 and 16, with an interspace of 11 stitches.

Rnd 22: (sc in next 8 st, dec) repeat 6 times [54]
Rnd 23: (sc in next 7 st, dec) repeat 6 times [48]
Rnd 24: (sc in next 6 st, dec) repeat 6 times [42]
Rnd 25: (sc in next 5 st, dec) repeat 6 times [36]
Rnd 26: (sc in next 4 st, dec) repeat 6 times [30]
Rnd 27: (sc in next 3 st, dec) repeat 6 times (24]
Rnd 28: (sc in next 2 st, dec) repeat 6 times [18]
Rnd 29: (sc in next st, dec) repeat 6 times [12]
Rnd 30: dec 6 times [6]
Fasten off and weave in the yarn ends.

BODY *(in beige yarn)*
Rnd 1: start 6 sc in a magic ring [6]
Rnd 2: inc in all 6 st [12]
Rnd 3: (sc in next st, inc in next st) repeat 6 times [18]

Rnd 4: (sc in next 2 st, inc in next st) repeat 6 times [24]
Rnd 5: (sc in next 3 st, inc in next st) repeat 6 times [30]
Rnd 6: (sc in next 4 st, inc in next st) repeat 6 times [36]
Rnd 7: (sc in next 5 st, inc in next st) repeat 6 times [42]
Rnd 8: (sc in next 6 st, inc in next st) repeat 6 times [48]
Rnd 9: (sc in next 7 st, inc in next st) repeat 6 times [54]
Rnd 10 – 19: sc in all 54 st [54]
Rnd 20: (sc in next 7 st, dec) repeat 6 times [48]
Rnd 21: sc in all 48 st [48]
Rnd 22: (sc in next 6 st, dec) repeat 6 times [42]
Rnd 23: sc in all 42 st [42]
Rnd 24: (sc in next 5 st, dec) repeat 6 times [36]
Rnd 25: sc in all 36 st [36]
Rnd 26: (sc in next 4 st, dec) repeat 6 times [30]
Stuff the body with fiberfill and continue stuffing as you go.
Rnd 27: sc in all 30 st [30]
Rnd 28: (sc in next 3 st, dec) repeat 6 times [24]
Rnd 29: sc in all 24 st [24]
Fasten off, leaving a long tail for sewing.

MUZZLE *(in white yarn)*
Ch 9. Stitches are worked around both sides of the foundation chain.
Rnd 1: start in second ch from hook, sc in next 7 st, 4 sc in next st. Continue on the other side of the foundation chain, sc in next 6 st, 3 sc in next st [20]
Rnd 2: (inc in next st, sc in next 7 st, inc in next st, sc in next st) repeat 2 times [24]
Rnd 3: (inc in next st, sc in next 9 st, inc in next st, sc in next st) repeat 2 times [28]
Rnd 4: (inc in next st, sc in next 11 st, inc in next st, sc in next st) repeat 2 times [32]
Rnd 5: (inc in next st, sc in next 13 st, inc in next st, sc in next st) repeat 2 times [36]
Rnd 6 – 8: sc in all 36 st [36]
Rnd 9: sc in next 9 st, ch 7, start in second ch from hook, sc in next 6 ch, sc in next 27 st [42 + 7 ch]
Rnd 10: sc in next 14 st, inc in next 2 st, sc in next 32 st [50]

Fasten off, leaving a long tail for sewing. Stuff the muzzle with fiberfill.

ARM *(make 2, start in light brown yarn)*
Rnd 1: start 6 sc in a magic ring [6]
Rnd 2: inc in all 6 st [12]
Rnd 3: (sc in next st, inc in next st) repeat 6 times [18]
Rnd 4: BLO sc in all 18 st [18]
Rnd 5 – 8: sc in all 18 st [18]
Change to white yarn.
Rnd 9 – 10: sc in all 18 st [18]
Stuff the arm with fiberfill and continue stuffing as you go. Change to beige yarn.
Rnd 11: (sc in next 4 st, dec) repeat 3 times [15]
Rnd 12 – 24: sc in all 15 st [15]
Rnd 25: (sc in next 3 st, dec) repeat 3 times [12]
Fasten off, leaving a long tail for sewing.

LEG *(make 2, start in light brown yarn)*
Rnd 1: start 6 sc in a magic ring [6]
Rnd 2: inc in all 6 st [12]
Rnd 3: (sc in next st, inc in next st) repeat 6 times [18]
Rnd 4: (sc in next 2 st, inc in next st) repeat 6 times [24]
Rnd 5: BLO sc in all 24 st [24]
Rnd 6 – 8: sc in all 24 st [24]
Change to white yarn.
Rnd 9 – 10: sc in all 24 st [24]
Stuff the leg with fiberfill and continue stuffing as you go. Change to beige yarn.
Rnd 11: (sc in next 4 st, dec) repeat 4 times [20]
Rnd 12 – 13: sc in all 20 st [20]

Rnd 14: (sc in next 3 st, dec) repeat 4 times [16]
Rnd 15 – 16: sc in all 16 st [16]
Rnd 17: (sc in next 2 st, dec) repeat 4 times [12]
Rnd 18 – 20: sc in all 12 st [12]
Fasten off, leaving a long tail for sewing.

HORSESHOE *(make 2, in light gray yarn)*
Ch 6. Join with a slst to form a ring. Make sure the ring isn't twisted. Crochet the next stitches in the ring (tutorial page 14).
Crochet in the ring: ch 2, 4 tr, 2 dc, 1 tr, 2 dc, 4 tr, ch 2, slst.
Fasten off, leaving a long tail for sewing.

EAR *(make 2, start in beige yarn)*
Rnd 1: start 6 sc in a magic ring [6]
Rnd 2: (sc in next st, inc in next st) repeat 3 times [9]
Rnd 3: (sc in next 2 st, inc in next st) repeat 3 times [12]
Rnd 4: sc in all 12 st [12]
Rnd 5: (sc in next st, inc in next st) repeat 6 times [18]
Rnd 6 – 9: sc in all 18 st [18]
Rnd 10: (sc in next st, dec) repeat 6 times [12]
Rnd 11: sc in all 12 st [12]
Fasten off, leaving a long tail for sewing. The ears don't need to be stuffed.

COLLAR *(in black yarn)*
The head collar consists of 2 pieces: the muzzle band and the head band.

Muzzle band

Ch 36. Join with a slst to form a ring. Make sure the ring isn't twisted.
Rnd 1: hdc in all 36 st [36]
Fasten off, leaving a long tail for sewing.

Head band

Ch 40. Crochet in rows.
Row 1: start in second ch from hook, hdc in all 39 st [39]
Fasten off, leaving a long tail for sewing.

MANE

Use 2 shades of brown to make the mane. Cut 8" / 20 cm yarn strands. You will need about 144 yarn strands of each shade of brown. Use 2 threads at a time, one of each shade. Pull 2 threads of yarn through each loop and make a knot to secure them (pictures 1-3). Work 9 knots on every round and work over 16 rounds in total. Start on round 2 at the front of the head and work towards round 9 at the back. Skip 2 rounds where you'll position the head band and continue working on rounds 12 to 16.

TAIL

Use 2 shades of brown yarn to make the tail. Cut 20" / 50 cm yarn strands. You will need about 25 yarn strands of each shade of brown. Use 2 threads at a time, one of each shade. Pull 2 threads of yarn through each loop and make a knot to secure them. Work 5 knots between rounds 10 and 15 of the body, over 5 stitches per round. Braid the tail and use the satin ribbon to tie a bow at the end.

ASSEMBLY

– Sew the head to the body.
– Sew the muzzle between rounds 17 and 27 of the head.
– Sew the arms to the sides of the body between rounds 28 and 29.
– Sew the legs to the body.
– Pinch the base of the ear and sew it together with a few stitches to hold the shape. Sew the ears to the top of the head, between rounds 9 and 10.
– Sew the collar to the head. Sew the muzzle band around the muzzle. Pin and sew the head band around the head and connect it to the muzzle band on both sides.
– Sew the horseshoes to the legs.
– Embroider nostrils and eyebrows using black yarn.
– Embroider a line under each eye using white yarn.
– Embroider a cross on the tummy using brown yarn.
– Embroider some rouge below the eyes using pink yarn.

CATERINO
THE
WALRUS

by Airali Design (Ilaria Caliri)

SKILL LEVEL: ★ ★

SIZE: 5" / 13 cm tall when made with the indicated yarn.

MATERIALS:

– Sport weight yarn in brown, white and
  navy blue (leftover)
– Size B-1 / 2.5 mm crochet hook
– Safety eyes (5 mm)
– Safety nose (12 mm)
– Black embroidery thread
– Yarn needle
– Stitch marker
– Fiberfill for stuffing

AMIGURUMI GALLERY
Scan or visit
www.amigurumi.com/908
to share pictures and find inspiration.

HEAD AND BODY *(in brown yarn)*

Rnd 1: start 6 sc in a magic ring [6]

Rnd 2: inc in all 6 st [12]

Rnd 3: (sc in next st, inc in next st) repeat 6 times [18]

Rnd 4: (sc in next 2 st, inc in next st) repeat 6 times [24]

Rnd 5: (sc in next 3 st, inc in next st) repeat 6 times [30]

Rnd 6: sc in all 30 st [30]

Rnd 7: (sc in next 4 st, inc in next st) repeat 6 times [36]

Rnd 8 – 11: sc in all 36 st [36]

Rnd 12: (sc in next 5 st, inc in next st) repeat 6 times [42]

Rnd 13 – 18: sc in all 42 st [42]

Rnd 19: (sc in next 6 st, inc in next st) repeat 6 times [48]

Rnd 20: sc in all 48 st [48]

Rnd 21: (sc in next 7 st, inc in next st) repeat 6 times [54]

Rnd 22: sc in all 54 st [54]

Rnd 23: (sc in next 8 st, inc in next st) repeat 6 times [60]

Rnd 24 – 31: sc in all 60 st [60]

Insert the safety eyes between rounds 11 and 12, with an interspace of 8 stitches. Insert the nose between rounds 13 and 14. Stuff with fiberfill and continue stuffing as you go.

Rnd 32: (sc in next 8 st, dec) repeat 6 times [54]

Rnd 33 – 34: sc in all 54 st [54]

Rnd 35: (sc in next 7 st, dec) repeat 6 times [48]

Rnd 36: sc in all 48 st [48]
Rnd 37: (sc in next 6 st, dec) repeat 6 times [42]
Rnd 38: (sc in next 5 st, dec) repeat 6 times [36]
Rnd 39: (sc in next 4 st, dec) repeat 6 times [30]
Rnd 40: (sc in next 3 st, dec) repeat 6 times [24]
Rnd 41: (sc in next 2 st, dec) repeat 6 times [18]
Rnd 42: (sc in next st, dec) repeat 6 times [12]
Rnd 43: dec 6 times [6]
Slst in next st. Fasten off and weave in the yarn ends.

MOUSTACHE *(make 2, in brown yarn)*
Rnd 1: start 6 sc in a magic ring [6]
Rnd 2: inc in all 6 st [12]
Rnd 3 – 4: sc in all 12 st [12]
Slst in next st. Fasten off, leaving a long tail for sewing.
Stuff with fiberfill.

TUSK *(make 2, in white yarn)*
Rnd 1: start 3 sc in a magic ring [3]
Rnd 2: inc in next st, sc in next 2 st [4]
Rnd 3: inc in next st, sc in next 3 st [5]
Rnd 4: inc in next st, sc in next 4 st [6]
Rnd 5: sc in all 6 st [6]
Rnd 6: inc in next st, sc in next 5 st [7]
Slst in next st. Fasten off, leaving a long tail for sewing.
The tusks don't need to be stuffed.

FLIPPER *(make 2, in brown yarn)*
Rnd 1: start 6 sc in a magic ring [6]
Rnd 2: (sc in next 2 st, inc in next st) repeat 2 times [8]
Rnd 3: (sc in next 3 st, inc in next st) repeat 2 times [10]

Rnd 4 – 5: sc in next st, slst in next 5 st, sc in next st, hdc in next 3 st [10]
Rnd 6 – 7: sc in all 10 st [10]
Rnd 8: (sc in next 4 st, inc in next st) repeat 2 times [12]
Rnd 9 – 10: sc in all 12 st [12]
Rnd 11: (sc in next 4 st, dec) repeat 2 times [10]
Rnd 12 – 13: sc in all 10 st [10]
Slst in next st. Fasten off, leaving a long tail for sewing.
Flatten the flippers, they don't need to be stuffed.

TAIL *(in brown yarn)*
Start by making 2 tail fins. Ch 8. Stitches are worked around both sides of the foundation chain.
Rnd 1: start in second ch from hook, sc in next 6 st, 3 sc in next st. Continue on the other side of the foundation chain, sc in next 5 st, inc in next st [16]
Rnd 2 – 3: sc in all 16 st [16]
Rnd 4: (dec, sc in next 6 st) repeat 2 times [14]
Rnd 5: (dec, sc in next 5 st) repeat 2 times [12]
Rnd 6: sc in all 12 st [12]
Rnd 7: (dec, sc in next 4 st) repeat 2 times [10]
Rnd 8: sc in all 10 st [10]
Slst in next st. Fasten off and weave in the yarn end on the first fin. Don't fasten off on the second fin. Hold the fins together, flatten them and place both with the last stitch to the right (pictures 1-2). In the next round, we'll join both tail fins together.
Rnd 9: sc in next 4 st on the first fin, sc in next 9 st on the second fin, skip 1 st on the second fin and skip 1 st on the first fin, sc in next 5 st on the first fin [18] (pictures 3-4)

Rnd 10: inc in next st, (sc in next 3 st, inc in next st) repeat 2 times, sc in next 9 st [21]

Rnd 11: sc in all 21 st [21]

Stuff the fins with fiberfill and continue stuffing the tail as you go.

Rnd 12: sc in next st, inc in next st, (sc in next 4 st, inc in next st) repeat 2 times, sc in next 9 st [24]

Rnd 13: sc in all 24 st [24]

Rnd 14: sc in next 2 st, inc in next st, (sc in next 5 st, inc in next st) repeat 2 times, sc in next 9 st [27]

Rnd 15: sc in all 27 st [27]

Rnd 16: sc in next 3 st, inc in next st, (sc in next 6 st, inc in next st) repeat 2 times, sc in next 9 st [30]

Rnd 17: sc in next 4 st, inc in next st, (sc in next 7 st, inc in next st) repeat 2 times, sc in next 9 st [33]

Rnd 18: sc in next 5 st, inc in next st, (sc in next 8 st, inc in next st) repeat 2 times, sc in next 9 st [36]

Rnd 19: sc in next 6 st, inc in next st, (sc in next 9 st, inc in next st) repeat 2 times, sc in next 9 st [39]

Rnd 20: sc in next 7 st, inc in next st, (sc in next 10 st, inc in next st) repeat 2 times, sc in next 9 st [42]

Rnd 21: sc in next 8 st, inc in next st, (sc in next 11 st, inc in next st) repeat 2 times, sc in next 9 st [45]

Rnd 22: sc in next 9 st, inc in next st, (sc in next 12 st, inc in next st) repeat 2 times, sc in next 9 st [48]

Rnd 23: sc in next 10 st, inc in next st, (sc in next 13 st, inc in next st) repeat 2 times, sc in next 9 st [51]

Rnd 24: sc in next 11 st, inc in next st, (sc in next 14 st, inc in next st) repeat 2 times, sc in next 9 st [54]

Slst in next st. Fasten off, leaving a tail for sewing. Position the tail between rounds 23 and 41 of the body and sew all around. Add a bit more fiberfill before closing the seam. Sew the gap between the fins closed using brown yarn.

HAT *(start in white yarn)*
Rnd 1: start 6 sc in a magic ring [6]
Rnd 2: inc in all 6 st [12]
Rnd 3 – 5: sc in all 12 st [12]
Rnd 6: FLO (sc in next st, inc in next st) repeat 6 times [18]
Rnd 7: sc in all 18 st [18]
Change to navy blue yarn.
Rnd 8: slst in all 18 st [18]
Fasten off and weave in the yarn end. The hat doesn't need to be stuffed.

SCARF *(in white yarn)*
Crochet in rows and work sideways. Ch 22, this chain forms the first tie and is used to knot the scarf at the end.
Row 1: start in second ch from hook, sc in this st, ch 1, turn [1]
Row 2: inc in next st, ch 1, turn [2]
Row 3: sc in next 2 st, ch 1, turn [2]
Row 4: inc in next st, sc in all st until the end of the row, ch 1, turn.
Row 5: sc in all st until the end of the row, ch 1, turn.
Row 6 – 29: repeat rows 4 and 5 alternately, until you reach a width of 15 stitches.
Row 30: dec, sc in all st until the end of the row, ch 1, turn.
Row 31: sc in all st until the end of the row, ch 1, turn.
Row 32 – 55: repeat rows 30 and 31 alternately, until you have only 2 stitches left.
Row 56: skip 1 st, sc in next st [1]

Ch 20, this chain forms the second tie and is used to knot the scarf at the end. Fasten off and weave in the yarn ends. Using navy blue yarn crochet 2 parallel lines of surface slip stitches on the 2 slanting sides of the triangle (one st for each row).

ASSEMBLY
– Sew the flippers between rounds 25 and 26 of the body, with an interspace of 12 stitches. Make sure that the tips of the flippers touch the ground and adjust their position if necessary.
– Sew the moustache between rounds 14 and 17 of the head, under the nose.
– Sew the tusks under the moustache.
– Embroider the anchor on the arm using black embroidery thread.
– Sew the hat on the head with white yarn.
– Put the scarf around the neck and knot the ties together.

— long stitch
• French knot

ANGIE THE ANGLER-FISH

by Sundot Attack
(Jhak Stein)

SKILL LEVEL: ✶ ✶ ✶

SIZE: 4.5" / 11.5 cm when made with the indicated yarn.

MATERIALS:

– Worsted weight yarn in lilac, purple, white and yellow (leftover)
– Size C-2 / 3 mm crochet hook
– Safety eyes (15 mm)
– Yarn needle
– Stitch markers
– Pipe cleaner or aluminum wire (20" / 50 cm long)
– Fiberfill for stuffing

AMIGURUMI GALLERY

Scan or visit
www.amigurumi.com/3006
to share pictures and find inspiration.

MOUTH *(in lilac yarn)*

Rnd 1: start 6 sc in a magic ring [6]

Rnd 2: inc in all 6 st [12]

Rnd 3: (sc in next st, inc in next st) repeat 6 times [18]

Rnd 4: (sc in next 2 st, inc in next st) repeat 6 times [24]

Rnd 5: (sc in next 3 st, inc in next st) repeat 6 times [30]

Rnd 6: (sc in next 4 st, inc in next st) repeat 6 times [36]

Rnd 7: (sc in next 5 st, inc in next st) repeat 6 times [42]

Rnd 8: (sc in next 6 st, inc in next st) repeat 6 times [48]

Rnd 9: (sc in next 7 st, inc in next st) repeat 6 times [54]

Rnd 10: (sc in next 8 st, inc in next st) repeat 6 times [60]

Rnd 11: sc in all 60 st [60]

Fasten off, leaving a long tail for sewing.

LIP LINE *(in purple yarn)*

Pull up a loop of purple yarn in the stitch where you

 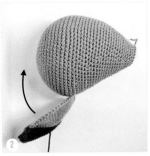  

fastened off the mouth and make a slst. Crochet in rows.

Row 1 – 4: sc in next 24 st, ch 1, turn [24]

Row 5: sc in next 24 st [24]

Fasten off, leaving a long tail for sewing. Mark the 16th stitch of the mouth on the right and the left side, counting from the lip line (picture 1).

HEAD AND BODY *(in lilac yarn)*

Rnd 1: start 6 sc in a magic ring [6]

Rnd 2: inc in all 6 st [12]

Rnd 3: (inc in next st, sc in next st) repeat 6 times [18]

Rnd 4: (inc in next st, sc in next 2 st) repeat 6 times [24]

Rnd 5: (inc in next st, sc in next 3 st) repeat 6 times [30]

Rnd 6: (inc in next st, sc in next 4 st) repeat 6 times [36]

Rnd 7: (inc in next st, sc in next 5 st) repeat 6 times [42]

Rnd 8: (inc in next st, sc in next 6 st) repeat 6 times [48]

Rnd 9: (inc in next st, sc in next 7 st) repeat 6 times [54]

Rnd 10: (inc in next st, sc in next 8 st) repeat 6 times [60]

Rnd 11: sc in all 60 st [60]

Rnd 12: (inc in next st, sc in next 5 st) repeat 6 times, (inc in next st, sc in next 3 st) repeat 6 times [72]

Rnd 13 – 18: sc in all 72 st [72]

Rnd 19: sc in next 20 st, place the mouth (with the lip line on top) in front of the head near the bottom and connect them by inserting your hook in the left stitch marker (A in picture 1) from the mouth and the next stitch of the head. Sc in next 6 st or until you get to the right stitch marker (B in picture 1). Continue on the body and sc in next 46 st [72]

Rnd 20: (dec, sc in next 10 st) repeat 6 times [66]

Rnd 21: sc in next 5 st, (dec, sc in next 4 st) repeat 6 times, sc in next 25 st [60]

Rnd 22 – 24: sc in all 60 st [60]

Stuff the body with fiberfill and continue stuffing as you go.

Rnd 25: sc in next 4 st, (dec, sc in next 3 st) repeat 6 times, sc in next 26 st [54]

Rnd 26 – 27: sc in all 54 st [54]

Rnd 28: (dec, sc in next 7 st) repeat 6 times [48]

Rnd 29 – 30: sc in all 48 st [48]

Rnd 31: (dec, sc in next 6 st) repeat 6 times [42]

Rnd 32: sc in all 42 st [42]

Rnd 33: (dec, sc in next 5 st) repeat 6 times [36]

Rnd 34: sc in all 36 st [36]

Rnd 35: (dec, sc in next 4 st) repeat 6 times [30]

Rnd 36 – 37: sc in all 30 st [30]

Rnd 38: (dec, sc in next 3 st) repeat 6 times [24]

Rnd 39 – 40: sc in all 24 st [24]

Rnd 41: (dec, sc in next 2 st) repeat 6 times [18]

Rnd 42: sc in all 18 st [18]

Fasten off, leaving a long tail for sewing (picture 2). Fold and sew row 5 of the lip line to row 1 of the lip line on the right side of your work to create a voluptuous lip (picture 3). Weave in the yarn ends.

TEETH *(use 2 strands of white yarn)*

Crochet in rows.

Row 1: (ch 5, start in second ch from hook, slst in this st, sc in next st, hdc in next st, dc in next st, ch 6, start in second ch from hook, slst in this st, sc in next st, hdc in next st, dc in next 2 st,

ch 5, start in second ch from hook, slst in this st, sc in next st, hdc in next st, dc in next st) repeat 2 times [6 teeth]

Fasten off, leaving a long tail for sewing. Sew the teeth to the wrong side of the lip line (picture 4). Sew the remaining stitches of the mouth to the head using the lilac yarn tail (picture 5).

TAIL FIN (in purple yarn)

Pull up a loop of purple yarn in the stitch where you fastened off the body and make a slst.

Rnd 1: sc in all 18 st [18]

Rnd 2: (inc in next st, sc in next 2 st) repeat 6 times [24]

Rnd 3: sc in all 24 st [24]

Rnd 4: (inc in next st, sc in next 3 st) repeat 6 times [30]

Rnd 5 – 6: sc in all 30 st [30]

Fold the tail fin lengthwise and stuff the tail with fiberfill. Make a few sc stitches to get to the corner if needed.

Crochet the next round through both sides to close.

Rnd 7: ch 4, 2 tr in next st, tr in next st, dc in next 2 st, hdc in next 2 st, sc in next 3 st, hdc in next 2 st, dc in next 2 st, tr in next st, 2 tr in next st, ch 4, slst in same st. Fasten off and weave in the yarn end. Embroider 5 lines on both sides of the tail fin using lilac yarn (picture 6).

EYEBALL (make 2, in white yarn)

Rnd 1: start 8 sc in magic ring [8]

When you pull the yarn tail to tighten the magic ring, make sure you leave a hole large enough to fit the post of the safety eye later.

Rnd 2: inc in all 8 st [16]

Rnd 3: (dec, sc in next 2 st) repeat 4 times [12]

Fasten off, leaving a long tail for sewing. Insert the safety eye in the center of the magic ring. Pull the yarn tail to tighten the ring around the post.

EYELID (make 2, in purple yarn)

Ch 11. Crochet in rows.

Row 1: start in second ch from hook, sc in next 10 st, ch 1, turn [10]

Row 2: skip 1 st, sc in next st, hdc in next st, sc in next 4 st, hdc in next st, sc in next st [8]

Fasten off, leaving a long tail for sewing. Sew the eyes to rounds 8 to 11 of the head, with an interspace of 8 stitches (picture 7). Sew the straight side of the eye lids to the eyes, covering a third of the eyeballs.

DORSAL FIN (in purple yarn)

Ch 32, join with a slst to form a ring. Make sure the ring isn't twisted. Work in joined rounds.

Rnd 1 – 2: sc in next 32 st, slst in first st, ch 1 [32]

Rnd 3: (inc in next st, sc in next 7 st) repeat 4 times [36]

Flatten the dorsal fin. The dorsal fin doesn't need to be stuffed. Work the next round through both layers to close.

Rnd 4: ch 4, 2 tr in next st, dc in next 2 st, hdc in next st, slst in next st, (ch 4, 2 tr in the same st where the slst is made, dc in next 2 st, hdc in next st, slst in next st) repeat 2 times, ch 4, 2 tr in the same st where the slst is made, dc in next 3 st, hdc in next st, slst in next st [4 spikes]

Fasten off, leaving a long tail for sewing. Embroider 4 lines on both sides of the dorsal fin using lilac yarn. Sew the dorsal fin on top of the body, between rounds 23 and 36 (picture 8).

SIDE FIN *(make 2, start in lilac yarn)*
Leave a long starting yarn tail.
Ch 12, join with a slst to form a ring. Make sure the ring isn't twisted. Work in joined rounds.

Rnd 1: sc in next 12 st, slst in first st, ch 1 [12]
Change to purple yarn.
Rnd 2 – 3: sc in next 12 st, slst in first st, ch 1 [12]
Rnd 4: (inc in next st, sc in next st) repeat 6 times, slst in first st, ch 1 [18]
Rnd 5 – 6: sc in next 18 st, slst in first st, ch 1 [18]
Flatten the side fin. The side fin doesn't need to be stuffed. Work the next round through both layers to close.

Rnd 7: sc in next 2 st, hdc in next 2 st, dc in next 2 st, 2 tr in next 2 st, ch 4, slst in same st [11 + 4 ch]
Fasten off and weave in the yarn ends. Use the starting lilac yarn tail yarn to embroider 4 lines on both sides of the side fin. Sew the side fins on both sides of the body, between rounds 21 and 24.

LUMINESCENT ESCA *(start in yellow yarn)*
Rnd 1: start 6 sc in a magic ring [6]
Rnd 2: inc in all 6 st [12]
Rnd 3: (inc in next st, sc in next st) repeat 6 times [18]
Rnd 4 – 6: sc in all 18 st [18]
Rnd 7: (dec, sc in next st) repeat 6 times [12]
Rnd 8: sc in all 12 st [12]
Rnd 9: (dec, sc in next st) repeat 4 times [8]
Change to lilac yarn. Stuff the yellow part with fiberfill.
Rnd 10: sc in all 8 st [8]
Rnd 11: (dec, sc in next 2 st) repeat 2 times [6]
Rnd 12 – 41: sc in all 6 st [6]
Rnd 42: (inc in next st, sc in next st) repeat 3 times [9]
Rnd 43 – 44: sc in all 9 st [9]
Fasten off, leaving a long tail for sewing.

The rod doesn't need to be stuffed. Take a long wire with a length of 20 in / 50 cm (twice the length of the bulb and rod + a few more inches/cm at the end as the wire will be inserted into the head). Fold the wire in half. Fold the ends and secure them with a piece of sticky tape or wrap them with yarn to cover them up. Insert the wire in the rod. Insert the other end of the wire through the top of the head between rounds 16 and 17, centered between the eyes. Sew the luminescent esca to the head and bend it to your liking.

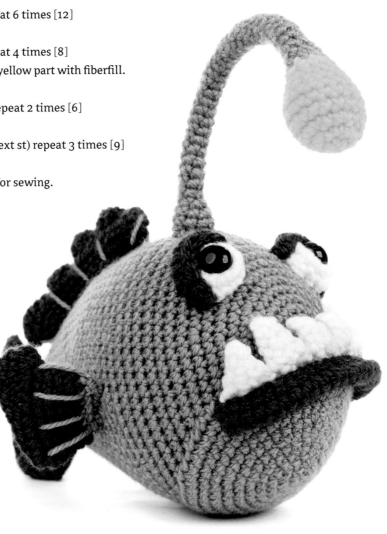

PERRY THE OTTER

by Irene Strange

SKILL LEVEL: ★

SIZE: 8" / 20 cm tall when made with the indicated yarn.

MATERIALS:

– Fingering weight yarn in dark blue, cream, brown (leftover), light blue and pink
– Size C-2 / 3 mm crochet hook
– Safety eyes (10 mm)
– Stitch marker
– Yarn needle
– Fiberfill for stuffing

AMIGURUMI GALLERY

Scan or visit
www.amigurumi.com/3011
to share pictures and find inspiration.

NOSE *(in brown yarn)*

Rnd 1: start 6 sc in a magic ring [6]

Rnd 2: (3 sc in next st, sc in next st) repeat 3 times [12]

Rnd 3: (sc in next st, 3 sc in next st, sc in next 2 st) repeat 3 times [18]

Fasten off, leaving a long tail for sewing.

HEAD *(in dark blue yarn)*

Rnd 1: start 6 sc in a magic ring [6]

Rnd 2: inc in all 6 st [12]

Rnd 3: (sc in next 3 st, inc in next 3 st) repeat 2 times [18]

Rnd 4: sc in next 3 st, (inc in next st, sc in next st) repeat 3 times, sc in next 3 st, (inc in next st, sc in next st) repeat 3 times [24]

Rnd 5: sc in next 3 st, (sc in next 2 st, inc in next st) repeat 3 times, sc in next 3 st, (sc in next 2 st, inc in next st) repeat 3 times [30]

Rnd 6: sc in next 3 st, (sc in next 3 st, inc in next st) repeat 3 times, sc in next 3 st, (sc in next 3 st, inc in next st) repeat 3 times [36]

Rnd 7: sc in next 6 st, (sc in next 2 st, inc in next st) repeat 3 times, sc in next 9 st, (sc in next 2 st, inc in next st) repeat 3 times, sc in next 3 st [42]

Rnd 8 – 17: sc in all 42 st [42]

Rnd 18: sc in next 9 st, (dec, sc in next 2 st) repeat 3 times, sc in next 9 st, (dec, sc in next 2 st) repeat 3 times [36]

Rnd 19: sc in next 9 st, (sc in next st, dec) repeat 3 times, sc in next 9 st, (sc in next st, dec) repeat 3 times [30]

Rnd 20: (sc in next 9 st, dec 3 times) repeat 2 times [24]
Slst in next st. Fasten off, leaving a long tail for sewing.

CHEEK *(make 2, in cream yarn)*
Rnd 1: start 6 sc in a magic ring [6]
Rnd 2: inc in all 6 st [12]
Rnd 3: (sc in next st, inc in next st) repeat 6 times [18]
Rnd 4: sc in all 18 st [18]
Fasten off, leaving a long tail for sewing.

TAIL AND BODY *(in dark blue yarn)*
Rnd 1: start 6 sc in a magic ring [6]
Rnd 2: sc in all 6 st [6]
Rnd 3: inc in next st, sc in next 5 st [7]

Rnd 4: sc in all 7 st [7]
Rnd 5: inc in next st, sc in next 6 st [8]
Rnd 6: sc in all 8 st [8]
Rnd 7: (inc in next st, sc in next 3 st) repeat 2 times [10]
Rnd 8: sc in all 10 st [10]
Rnd 9: (inc in next st, sc in next 4 st) repeat 2 times [12]
Rnd 10: sc in all 12 st [12]
Rnd 11: (inc in next st, sc in next 5 st) repeat 2 times [14]
Rnd 12: sc in all 14 st [14]
Rnd 13: (inc in next st, sc in next 6 st) repeat 2 times [16]
Rnd 14 – 15: sc in all 16 st [16]
Rnd 16: (inc in next st, sc in next 7 st) repeat 2 times [18]
Rnd 17 – 19: sc in all 18 st [18]
Rnd 20: inc in next 6 st, sc in next 12 st [24]
Rnd 21: (inc in next st, sc in next st) repeat 6 times, sc in next 12 st [30]
Rnd 22: (sc in next 4 st, inc in next st) repeat 6 times [36]
Rnd 23: (sc in next 5 st, inc in next st) repeat 6 times [42]
Rnd 24: (sc in next 6 st, inc in next st) repeat 6 times [48]
Rnd 25 – 30: sc in all 48 st [48]
Rnd 31: (dec, sc in next st) repeat 6 times, sc in next 3 st, (sc in next st, dec) repeat 6 times, sc in next 9 st [36]
Rnd 32 – 49: sc in all 36 st [36]
Rnd 50: dec 6 times, sc in next 4 st, dec 6 times, sc in next 8 st [24]
Rnd 51: sc in all 24 st [24]
Rnd 52: slst in all 24 st [24]
Fasten off and weave in the yarn end.

ARM *(make 2, in dark blue yarn)*
Rnd 1: start 6 sc in a magic ring [6]
Rnd 2: inc in all 6 st [12]
Rnd 3 – 8: sc in all 12 st [12]
In the next round we start making the upper arm.
Rnd 9: ch 9, skip next 9 st, sc in next 3 st [9 ch + 3]
Rnd 10 – 13: sc in all 12 st [12]
Fasten off, leaving a long tail for sewing and shaping.

LEG *(make 2, in dark blue yarn)*
Rnd 1: start 6 sc in a magic ring [6]

Rnd 2: inc in all 6 st [12]

Rnd 3 – 8: sc in all 12 st [12]

Fasten off, leaving a long tail for sewing.

EAR *(make 2, in dark blue yarn)*

Rnd 1: start 5 sc in a magic ring [5]

Rnd 2: inc in all 5 st [10]

Rnd 3 – 5: sc in all 10 st [10]

Fasten off, leaving a long tail for sewing.

TUMMY *(in cream yarn)*

Rnd 1: start 6 sc in a magic ring [6]

Rnd 2: inc in all 6 st [12]

Rnd 3: (sc in next 3 st, inc in next 3 st) repeat 2 times [18]

Rnd 4: sc in next 3 st, (inc in next st, sc in next st) repeat 3 times, sc in next 3 st, (inc in next st, sc in next st) repeat 3 times [24]

Rnd 5: sc in next 3 st, (sc in next 2 st, inc in next st) repeat 3 times, sc in next 3 st, (sc in next 2 st, inc in next st) repeat 3 times [30]

Rnd 6: sc in all 30 st [30]

Fasten off, leaving a long tail for sewing.

SHELL *(make 2 halves, one in pink/light blue and one in cream yarn)*

Rnd 1: start 6 sc in a magic ring [6]

Rnd 2: (3 sc in next st, sc in next st) repeat 3 times [12]

Rnd 3: (sc in next st, 3 sc in next st, sc in next 2 st) repeat 3 times [18]

Rnd 4: (sc in next 2 st, 3 sc in next st, sc in next 3 st) repeat 3 times [24]

Rnd 5: (sc in next 3 st, 3 sc in next st, sc in next 4 st) repeat 3 times [30]

Rnd 6 – 7: sc in all 30 st [30]

Fasten off, leaving a long tail for sewing and shaping.

ASSEMBLY

– Insert the safety eyes between rounds 13-14, with an interspace of 12 stitches.
– Stuff the head and body with fiberfill and sew them together, going under the slst round of the body and the front posts of the stitches of the head (picture 1).
– Sew the cheeks between rounds 13 and 17. Add a bit of stuffing before closing the seam (picture 2).
– Sew the ears to the top of the head along the center line, between rounds 5 and 9.
– Sew the nose above the cheeks, lining it up to the tops of the cheeks (picture 3).
– Sew the tummy to the front of the body (picture 4).
– Stuff the legs and sew them between rounds 23 and 27 of the body, with an interspace of 6 stitches.
– Stuff the arms and sew them between rounds 43 and 47 of the body. Using some spare dark blue yarn, stitch down the tops of the arms over the bottoms so that the arm is folded (pictures 5-7).
– Embroider the mouth, freckles and claws using brown yarn. You can work the claws as French knots or gradually build them up in layers of stitches (picture 8): work 3 short horizontal stitches over the foot, then work 2 short vertical stitches over the previous stitches, then 1 short horizontal stitch over the last few stitches, weave the yarn back into the foot and secure the end.
– To make the shell, sew the 2 halves together through the front posts of the corresponding stitches. Add a bit of stuffing just before closing the seam. Use the yarn tail to shape the shell into 3 segments by pulling the yarn from the center of the shell over the outer edge to the other side twice. Pull the yarn tail tight each time to create the shell ridges. Wrap the remaining tail around the narrow point of the shell and pull tight to shape the end. Weave in the ends.

WILBUR THE PENGUIN

by Patchwork Moose (Kate E. Hancock)

SKILL LEVEL: ✶ ✶
SIZE: 6" / 15 cm tall when made with the indicated yarn.
MATERIALS:
– Light worsted weight yarn in black, orange and white
– Size E-4 / 3.5 mm crochet hook
– Safety eyes (20 mm)
– Stitch marker
– Yarn needle
– Fiberfill for stuffing

AMIGURUMI GALLERY
Scan or visit
www.amigurumi.com/304
to share pictures and find inspiration.

HEAD *(in black yarn)*
Rnd 1: start 6 sc in a magic ring [6]
Rnd 2: inc in all 6 st [12]
Rnd 3: (sc in next st, inc in next st) repeat 6 times [18]
Rnd 4: (sc in next 2 st, inc in next st) repeat 6 times [24]
Rnd 5: (sc in next 3 st, inc in next st) repeat 6 times [30]
Rnd 6: sc in all 30 st [30]
Rnd 7: (sc in next 4 st, inc in next st) repeat 6 times [36]
Rnd 8: sc in all 36 st [36]
Rnd 9: (sc in next 5 st, inc in next st) repeat 6 times [42]
Rnd 10 – 12: sc in all 42 st [42]
Rnd 13: (sc in next 5 st, dec) repeat 6 times [36]

Rnd 14: (sc in next 4 st, dec) repeat 6 times [30]
Rnd 15: (sc in next 3 st, dec) repeat 6 times [24]
Rnd 16: (sc in next 2 st, dec) repeat 6 times [18]
Fasten off, leaving a long tail for sewing. Stuff the head firmly with fiberfill.

EYE PATCHES *(make 2, in white yarn)*
Mark the second sc you make on round 1 with a stitch marker. This will show you where to place the eyes later.
Rnd 1: start 6 sc in a magic ring [6]
Rnd 2: (sc in next st, inc in next st) repeat 3 times [9]
Rnd 3: (sc in next st, inc in next 2 st) repeat 3 times [15]
Rnd 4: (sc in next 2 st, inc in next 2 st, sc in next st) repeat 3 times [21]
Fasten off, leaving a long tail for sewing.

RIGHT EYELID *(in white yarn)*
Ch 7. Crochet in rows.
Row 1: start in second ch from hook, sc in this st, hdc in

next st, dc in next st, hdc in next st, sc in next st, slst in next st [6]

Fasten off, leaving a long tail for sewing.

LEFT EYELID *(in white yarn)*

Ch 7. Crochet in rows.

Row 1: start in second ch from hook, slst in this st, sc in next st, hdc in next st, dc in next st, hdc in next st, sc in next st [6]

Fasten off, leaving a long tail for sewing.

BEAK *(in orange yarn)*

Rnd 1: start 6 sc in a magic ring [6]

Rnd 2: (sc in next st, inc in next 2 st) repeat 2 times [10]

Rnd 3 – 4: sc in all 10 st [10]

Fasten off, leaving a long tail for sewing.

BODY *(in black yarn)*

Rnd 1: start 6 sc in a magic ring [6]

Rnd 2: inc in all 6 st [12]

Rnd 3: (sc in next st, inc in next st) repeat 6 times [18]

Rnd 4: (sc in next 2 st, inc in next st) repeat 6 times [24]

Rnd 5: (sc in next 3 st, inc in next st) repeat 6 times [30]

Rnd 6: (sc in next 4 st, inc in next st) repeat 6 times [36]

Rnd 7: (sc in next 5 st, inc in next st) repeat 6 times [42]

Rnd 8 – 12: sc in all 42 st [42]

Rnd 13: (sc in next 5 st, dec) repeat 6 times [36]

Rnd 14: sc in all 36 st [36]

Rnd 15: (sc in next 4 st, dec) repeat 6 times [30]

Rnd 16: sc in all 30 st [30]

Rnd 17: (sc in next 3 st, dec) repeat 6 times [24]

Rnd 18: sc in all 24 st [24]

Rnd 19: (sc in next 2 st, dec) repeat 6 times [18]

Rnd 20: sc in all 18 st [18]

Fasten off and weave in the yarn ends. Stuff the body firmly with fiberfill.

WING *(make 2, in black yarn)*

Rnd 1: start 6 sc in a magic ring [6]

Rnd 2: sc in all 6 st [6]

Rnd 3: inc in all 6 st [12]

Rnd 4 – 5: dec 2 times, sc in next 3 st, inc in next 2 st, sc in next 3 st [12]

Rnd 6: sc in all 12 st [12]

Rnd 7: sc in next 4 st, inc in next 6 st, sc in next 2 st [18]

Rnd 8 – 17: sc in all 18 st [18]

Rnd 18: (sc in next st, dec) repeat 6 times [12]

Fasten off, leaving a long tail for sewing. The wings don't need to be stuffed.

TAIL *(in black yarn)*

Rnd 1: start 6 sc in a magic ring [6]

Rnd 2: sc in all 6 st [6]

Rnd 3: inc in all 6 st [12]

Rnd 4: sc in all 12 st [12]

Rnd 5: (sc in next st, inc in next st) repeat 6 times [18]

Rnd 6: sc in all 18 st [18]

Fasten off, leaving a long tail for sewing. Stuff the tail with fiberfill.

BELLY PATCH *(in white yarn)*
Rnd 1: start 6 sc in a magic ring [6]
Rnd 2: inc in all 6 st [12]
Rnd 3: (sc in next st, inc in next st) repeat 6 times [18]
Rnd 4: (sc in next 2 st, inc in next st) repeat 6 times [24]
Rnd 5: (sc in next 3 st, inc in next st) repeat 6 times [30]
Rnd 6: (sc in next 4 st, inc in next st) repeat 6 times [36]
Fasten off, leaving a long tail for sewing.

FOOT *(make 2, in orange yarn)*
The feet are worked from toe to heel. Ch 6. Stitches are worked around both sides of the foundation chain.
Rnd 1: start in second ch from hook, 3 sc in this st, sc in next 3 st, 3 sc in next st. Continue on the other side of the foundation chain, sc in next 3 st [12]
Rnd 2: (inc in next st, sc in next st, inc in next st, sc in next 3 st) repeat 2 times [16]
Rnd 3: (sc in next st, inc in next st, sc in next st, inc in next st, sc in next 4 st) repeat 2 times [20]
Rnd 4 – 5: sc in all 20 st [20]
Rnd 6: (sc in next 2 st, dec) repeat 5 times [15]
Rnd 7 – 8: sc in all 15 st [15]
Stuff the foot with fiberfill and continue stuffing as you go.
Rnd 9: (sc in next st, dec) repeat 5 times [10]
Rnd 10 – 11: sc in all 10 st [10]
Fasten off, leaving a long tail for sewing. Flatten the foot and sew the heel closed. Leave a long yarn tail.

Shaping the toes *(in orange yarn)*
Use a yarn needle and orange yarn to create 3 toes. Make your first stitch a third of the way across the foot (3 stitches from the end), bringing your needle into the foot from the front and bringing it back out again through the back. Sew again in the same place, looping the yarn horizontally around the side of the foot. Pull the yarn tightly and repeat. Then sew again in the same place, but loop the yarn vertically, around the top of the foot, to create the first toe. Pull the thread tightly and repeat. Now make a horizontal stitch across the middle third of the foot and

repeat these 2 stitches on the last third of the foot (at 5 stitches from your first stitch), so that you are making a toe on the opposite side of the first one. Sew around the horizontal middle stitch a couple of times, pulling the yarn tightly as you go, to finish the middle toe (picture 1). Fasten off and weave in the yarn end.

ASSEMBLY
– Insert the safety eyes in round 1 of the eye patches, in the marked stitches. This will put the eye slightly closer to one corner of the triangular eye patch. This corner will be positioned closest to the center of the head (where the beak will be). Position the eye patches on the head with the back of the eye posts between rounds 10 and 11 of the head, with an inter-space of 9 stitches. Sew the eye patches on. Sew the eyelids on, making sure that the round side of the eyelids curves around the eyes.
– Stuff the beak and push it into an oval shape. Align the top of the beak to round 11 of the head and sew it on.
– Sew the body to the head along the neck edges.
– Sew the wings to the sides of the body, at the neckline, with the curved side facing backwards.
– Position the belly patch with the bottom edge on round 6 of the body and sew it on.
– Push the tail into an oval shape and sew it to the back.
– Sit your penguin on a flat surface and sew the feet to the front of the body, placing them so that the toes slightly face out and your penguin can sit up by itself.

MAMA AND BABY KANGA-ROO

by DIY Fluffies
(Mariska Vos-Bolman)

SKILL LEVEL: ★

SIZE: Mama: 10" / 25 cm tall, **Baby:** 3"/8 cm tall when made with the indicated yarn.

MATERIALS:
− Sport weight yarn in brown (3 balls), beige, black (leftover)
− Size B-1 / 2.5 mm crochet hook
− Safety eyes (11 mm for Mama and 6 mm for Baby)
− Yarn needle
− Pins
− Stitch markers
− Fiberfill for stuffing

AMIGURUMI GALLERY

Scan or visit
www.amigurumi.com/3406
to share pictures and find inspiration.

MAMA KANGAROO

HEAD AND BODY *(in brown yarn)*

Rnd 1: start 6 sc in a magic ring [6]
Rnd 2: inc in all 6 st [12]
Rnd 3: (sc in next st, inc in next st) repeat 6 times [18]
Rnd 4: (sc in next 2 st, inc in next st) repeat 6 times [24]
Rnd 5: (sc in next 3 st, inc in next st) repeat 6 times [30]
Rnd 6: sc in all 30 st [30]
Rnd 7: (sc in next 4 st, inc in next st) repeat 6 times [36]
Rnd 8: sc in all 36 st [36]
Rnd 9: (sc in next 5 st, inc in next st) repeat 6 times [42]
Rnd 10: sc in all 42 st [42]
Rnd 11: (sc in next 6 st, inc in next st) repeat 6 times [48]
Rnd 12: sc in all 48 st [48]
Rnd 13: (sc in next 7 st, inc in next st) repeat 6 times [54]

Rnd 14 – 20: sc in all 54 st [54]

Insert the safety eyes between rounds 14 and 15, with an interspace of 16 stitches.

Rnd 21: (sc in next 7 st, dec) repeat 6 times [48]

Rnd 22: sc in all 48 st [48]

Rnd 23: (sc in next 6 st, dec) repeat 6 times [42]

Rnd 24: sc in all 42 st [42]

Rnd 25: (sc in next 5 st, dec) repeat 6 times [36]

Rnd 26: (sc in next 4 st, dec) repeat 6 times [30]

Rnd 27: sc in all 30 st [30]

Rnd 28: (sc in next 3 st, dec) repeat 6 times [24]

Rnd 29 – 30: sc in all 24 st [24]

Rnd 31: (sc in next 3 st, inc in next st) repeat 6 times [30]

Rnd 32: sc in all 30 st [30]

Rnd 33: (sc in next 4 st, inc in next st) repeat 6 times [36]

Rnd 34 – 35: sc in all 36 st [36]

Rnd 36: (sc in next 5 st, inc in next st) repeat 6 times [42]

Rnd 37 – 38: sc in all 42 st [42]

Rnd 39: (sc in next 6 st, inc in next st) repeat 6 times [48]

Rnd 40 – 41: sc in all 48 st [48]

Stuff the head with fiberfill and continue stuffing as you go.

Rnd 42: (sc in next 7 st, inc in next st) repeat 6 times [54]

Rnd 43 – 49: sc in all 54 st [54]

Rnd 50: (sc in next 7 st, dec) repeat 6 times [48]

Rnd 51: sc in all 48 st [48]

Rnd 52: (sc in next 6 st, dec) repeat 6 times [42]

Rnd 53: sc in all 42 st [42]

Rnd 54: (sc in next 5 st, dec) repeat 6 times [36]

Rnd 55: (sc in next 4 st, dec) repeat 6 times [30]

Rnd 56: (sc in next 3 st, dec) repeat 6 times [24]

Rnd 57: (sc in next 2 st, dec) repeat 6 times [18]

Rnd 58: (sc in next st, dec) repeat 6 times [12]

Rnd 59: dec 6 times [6]

Fasten off, leaving a yarn tail. Using your yarn needle, weave the yarn tail through the front loop of each remaining stitch and pull it tight to close. Weave in the yarn end.

SNOUT *(in brown yarn)*

Rnd 1: start 6 sc in a magic ring [6]

Rnd 2: inc in all 6 st [12]

Rnd 3: sc in all 12 st [12]

Rnd 4: (sc in next st, inc in next st) repeat 6 times [18]

Rnd 5: (sc in next 2 st, inc in next st) repeat 6 times [24]

Rnd 6: sc in all 24 st [24]

Rnd 7: (sc in next 3 st, inc in next st) repeat 6 times [30]

Rnd 8: sc in all 30 st [30]

Rnd 9: (sc in next 4 st, inc in next st) repeat 6 times [36]

Rnd 10 – 11: sc in all 36 st [36]

Rnd 12: (sc in next 5 st, inc in next st) repeat 6 times [42]

Rnd 13: sc in all 42 st [42]

Rnd 14: (sc in next 6 st, inc in next st) repeat 6 times [48] Slst in next st. Fasten off, leaving a long tail for sewing. Stuff the snout with fiberfill and sew it between the eyes, between rounds 9 and 28.

NOSE *(in black yarn)*
Rnd 1: start 6 sc in a magic ring [6]
Rnd 2: (sc in next st, inc in next st) repeat 3 times [9]
Rnd 3: sc in all 9 st [9]
Slst in next st. Fasten off, leaving a long tail for sewing. Sew the nose on top of the snout, over rounds 1 to 3.

OUTER EAR *(make 2, in brown yarn)*
Rnd 1: start 6 sc in a magic ring [6]
Rnd 2: inc in all 6 st [12]

Rnd 3: sc in all 12 st [12]
Rnd 4: (sc in next st, inc in next st) repeat 6 times [18]
Rnd 5: sc in all 18 st [18]
Rnd 6: (sc in next 2 st, inc in next st) repeat 6 times [24]
Rnd 7 – 10: sc in all 24 st [24]
Rnd 11: (sc in next 6 st, dec) repeat 3 times [21]
Rnd 12: sc in all 21 st [21]
Rnd 13: (sc in next 5 st, dec) repeat 3 times [18]
Rnd 14 – 15: sc in all 18 st [18]
Slst in next st. Fasten off, leaving a long tail for sewing. The ears don't need to be stuffed. Flatten the outer ear.

INNER EAR *(make 2, in beige yarn)*
Rnd 1: start 6 sc in a magic ring [6]
Rnd 2: inc in all 6 st [12]
Rnd 3: (sc in next st, inc in next st) repeat 2 times, hdc in next st, hdc + dc + hdc in next st, hdc in next st, inc in next st, (sc in next st, inc in next st) repeat 2 times [19]
Slst in next st. Fasten off, leaving a long tail for sewing. Sew the inner ear to the outer ear between rounds 5 and 15. Sew the ears to the sides of the head, between rounds 4 and 10.

BELLY *(in beige yarn)*
Ch 2. Crochet in rows.
Row 1: start in second ch from hook, 3 sc in this st, ch 1, turn [3]
Row 2: inc in all 3 st, ch 1, turn [6]
Row 3: sc in next st, inc in next st, sc in next 2 st, inc in next st, sc in next st, ch 1, turn [8]
Row 4: sc in next 2 st, inc in next st, sc in next 2 st, inc in next st, sc in next 2 st, ch 1, turn [10]
Row 5: sc in next 2 st, inc in next st, sc in next 4 st, inc in next st, sc in next 2 st, ch 1, turn [12]
Row 6: sc in next 3 st, inc in next st, sc in next 4 st, inc in next st, sc in next 3 st, ch 1, turn [14]
Row 7: sc in all 14 st, ch 1, turn [14]
Row 8: sc in next 3 st, inc in next st, sc in next 6 st, inc in next st, sc in next 3 st, ch 1, turn [16]

Row 9 – 14: sc in all 16 st, ch 1, turn [16]
Row 15: sc in next 3 st, dec, sc in next 6 st, dec, sc in next 3 st, ch 1, turn [14]
Row 16: sc in all 14 st, ch 1, turn [14]
Row 17: sc in next 3 st, dec, sc in next 4 st, dec, sc in next 3 st, ch 1, turn [12]
Row 18: sc in all 12 st, ch 1, turn [12]
Row 19: sc in next 2 st, dec, sc in next 4 st, dec, sc in next 2 st, ch 1, turn [10]
Row 20 – 22: sc in all 10 st, ch 1, turn [10]
Row 23: sc in next st, dec, sc in next 4 st, dec, sc in next st, ch 1, turn [8]
Row 24: sc in all 8 st, ch 1, turn [8]
Row 25: dec, sc in next 4 st, dec, ch 1, turn [6]
Row 26: dec, sc in next 2 st, dec, ch 1, turn [4]
Row 27: dec 2 times, turn [2]
Row 28: skip first st, slst in next st [1]
Fasten off, leaving a long tail for sewing. Sew the belly to the body, between rounds 31 and 57.

POUCH *(in beige yarn)*
Ch 2. Crochet in rows.
Row 1: start in second ch from hook, 3 sc in this st, ch 1, turn [3]
Row 2: inc in all 3 st, ch 1, turn [6]
Row 3: sc in next st, inc in next st, sc in next 2 st, inc in next st, sc in next st, ch 1, turn [8]
Row 4: sc in next 2 st, inc in next st, sc in next 2 st, inc in next st, sc in next 2 st, ch 1, turn [10]
Row 5: sc in next 2 st, inc in next st, sc in next 4 st, inc in next st, sc in next 2 st, ch 1, turn [12]
Row 6: sc in next 3 st, inc in next st, sc in next 4 st, inc in next st, sc in next 3 st, ch 1, turn [14]
Row 7: sc in next 3 st, inc in next st, sc in next 6 st, inc in next st, sc in next 3 st, ch 1, turn [16]
Row 8: sc in next 4 st, inc in next st, sc in next 6 st, inc in next st, sc in next 4 st, ch 1, turn [18]
Row 9: sc in all 18 st, ch 1, turn [18]
Row 10: sc in next 4 st, inc in next st, sc in next 8 st, inc in next st, sc in next 4 st, ch 1, turn [20]

Row 11 – 15: sc in all 20 st [20]
Slst in next st. Fasten off, leaving a long tail for sewing. Sew the pouch over the bottom half of the belly. Leave the top side open.

ARM *(make 2, in brown yarn)*
Rnd 1: start 6 sc in a magic ring [6]
Rnd 2: inc in all 6 st [12]
Rnd 3 – 5: sc in all 12 st [12]
Rnd 6: (sc in next 2 st, dec) repeat 3 times [9]
Rnd 7 – 13: sc in all 9 st [9]
Stuff the arm with fiberfill.
Rnd 14: (sc in next st, dec) repeat 3 times [6]
Fasten off, leaving a long tail for sewing. Using your yarn needle, weave the yarn tail through the front loop of each remaining stitch and pull it tight to close. Sew the arms to the sides of the body, on rounds 34 and 35.

FOOT *(make 2, in brown yarn)*
Rnd 1: start 6 sc in a magic ring [6]
Rnd 2: inc in all 6 st [12]
Rnd 3: (sc in next st, inc in next st) repeat 6 times [18]
Rnd 4 – 7: sc in all 18 st [18]
Rnd 8: (sc in next 4 st, dec) repeat 3 times [15]
Rnd 9 – 15: sc in all 15 st [15]
Stuff the foot with fiberfill and continue stuffing as you go.
Rnd 16: (sc in next 3 st, dec) repeat 3 times [12]
Rnd 17: dec 6 times [6]
Fasten off, leaving a yarn tail. Using your yarn needle, weave the yarn tail through the front loop of each remaining stitch and pull it tight to close. Weave in the yarn end.

LEG *(make 2, in brown yarn)*
Rnd 1: start 6 sc in a magic ring [6]
Rnd 2: inc in all 6 st [12]
Rnd 3: (sc in next st, inc in next st) repeat 6 times [18]
Rnd 4: (sc in next 2 st, inc in next st) repeat 6 times [24]

Rnd 5 – 6: sc in all 24 st [24]
Rnd 7: (sc in next 3 st, inc in next st) repeat 6 times [30]
Rnd 8: sc in all 30 st [30]
Rnd 9: (sc in next 4 st, inc in next st) repeat 6 times [36]
Rnd 10 – 11: sc in all 36 st [36]
Rnd 12: (sc in next 4 st, dec) repeat 6 times [30]
Rnd 13: (sc in next 3 st, dec) repeat 6 times [24]
Rnd 14: sc in all 24 st [24]
Rnd 15: (sc in next 2 st, dec) repeat 6 times [18]
Rnd 16: (sc in next st, dec) repeat 6 times [12]
Slst in next st. Fasten off, leaving a long tail for sewing.
Stuff the legs with fiberfill and sew them to the feet.
You can use the same yarn tail or a new end of yarn to
sew the legs to the body between rounds 41 and 53.

TAIL *(in brown yarn)*
Rnd 1: start 4 sc in a magic ring [4]
Rnd 2: inc in all 4 st [8]
Rnd 3 – 4: sc in all 8 st [8]
Rnd 5: sc in next 7 st, inc in next st [9]
Rnd 6 – 7: sc in all 9 st [9]
Rnd 8: sc in next 8 st, inc in next st [10]
Rnd 9 – 10: sc in all 10 st [10]
Rnd 11: sc in next 9 st, inc in next st [11]
Rnd 12 – 13: sc in all 11 st [11]
Rnd 14: sc in next 10 st, inc in next st [12]
Rnd 15: sc in all 12 st [12]
Rnd 16: sc in next 11 st, inc in next st [13]
Rnd 17: sc in all 13 st [13]
Rnd 18: sc in next 12 st, inc in next st [14]
Rnd 19: sc in all 14 st [14]
Rnd 20: (sc in next 6 st, inc in next st) repeat 2 times [16]
Rnd 21: sc in all 16 st [16]
Rnd 22: (sc in next 7 st, inc in next st) repeat 2 times [18]
Rnd 23: (sc in next 2 st, inc in next st) repeat 6 times [24]
Rnd 24 – 25: sc in all 24 st [24]
Rnd 26: (sc in next 3 st, inc in next st) repeat 6 times [30]
Rnd 27: sc in all 30 st [30]
Slst in next st. Fasten off, leaving a long tail for sewing.
Stuff the tail with fiberfill. Sew the tail to the back,
between rounds 3 and 15.

BABY KANGAROO

HEAD *(in brown yarn)*
Rnd 1: start 6 sc in a magic ring [6]
Rnd 2: inc in all 6 st [12]
Rnd 3: (sc in next st, inc in next st) repeat 6 times [18]
Rnd 4: sc in all 18 st [18]
Rnd 5: (sc in next 5 st, inc in next st) repeat 3 times [21]
Rnd 6 – 8: sc in all 21 st [21]
Insert the safety eyes between rounds 5 and 6, with an
interspace of 5 stitches.
Rnd 9: (sc in next 5 st, dec) repeat 3 times [18]
Stuff the head with fiberfill and continue stuffing as

you go.

Rnd 10: (sc in next st, dec) repeat 6 times [12]

Rnd 11: dec 6 times [6]

Fasten off, leaving a yarn tail. Using your yarn needle, weave the yarn tail through the front loop of each remaining stitch and pull it tight to close. Weave in the yarn end.

SNOUT *(in brown yarn)*

Rnd 1: start 4 sc in a magic ring [4]

Rnd 2: (sc in next st, inc in next st) repeat 2 times [6]

Rnd 3: sc in all 6 st [6]

Rnd 4: (sc in next st, inc in next st) repeat 3 times [9]

Rnd 5: (sc in next 2 st, inc in next st) repeat 3 times [12]

Slst in next st. Fasten off, leaving a long tail for sewing. Embroider a nose on the snout with black yarn. Stuff the snout with fiberfill and sew it between the eyes, between rounds 4 and 9.

EAR *(make 2, in brown yarn)*

Rnd 1: start 4 sc in a magic ring [4]

Rnd 2: inc in all 4 st [8]

Rnd 3 – 6: sc in in all 8 st [8]

Slst in next st. Fasten off, leaving a long tail for sewing. Pinch the ears and sew them to the sides of the head, on round 3.

BODY *(make 2, in brown yarn)*

Start by making 2 legs.

Rnd 1: start 6 sc in a magic ring [6]

Rnd 2 – 3: sc in all 6 st [6]

Slst in next st. Fasten off and weave in the yarn end on the first leg. Don't fasten off on the second leg. Mark the first stitch of round 3 on the first leg with a stitch marker. Mark the fourth stitch of round 3 on the second leg.

Joining the legs

In the next round, we'll join both legs together.

Rnd 4: sc in next 3 st, continue in the marked stitch on the first leg, sc in next 6 st, continue in the marked stitch on the second leg, sc in next 3 st [12]

Rnd 5: (sc in next 2 st, inc in next st) repeat 4 times [16]

Rnd 6: sc in all 16 st [16]

Rnd 7: (sc in next 2 st, dec) repeat 4 times [12]

Rnd 8: sc in all 12 st [12]

Rnd 9: (sc in next st, dec) repeat 4 times [8]

Slst in next st. Fasten off, leaving a long tail for sewing. Stuff the body with fiberfill and sew it to the head.

ARM *(make 2, in brown yarn)*

Rnd 1: start 6 sc in a magic ring [6]

Rnd 2 – 4: sc in all 6 st [6]

Slst in next st. Fasten off, leaving a long tail for sewing. Stuff the arms with fiberfill and sew them to the sides of the body, on round 5.

HEDLEY THE HEDGEHOG

by Moji-Moji Design (Janine Holmes)

SKILL LEVEL: ★ ★ ★

SIZE: 10" / 25 cm tall when made with the indicated yarn.

MATERIALS:

– Light worsted weight yarn in beige, brown, cream, blue and black (leftover)
– Chunky yarn in multi-tone light/dark browns (This example was made with *Wendy - Celtic Tweed effect Chunky, shade 2768*)
– Size D-3 / 3.25 mm crochet hook
– Safety eyes (9 mm)
– Yarn needle
– Brown pencil crayon
– Stitch marker
– Fiberfill for stuffing

AMIGURUMI GALLERY
Scan or visit
www.amigurumi.com/309 to share
pictures and find inspiration.

HEAD *(start in black yarn)*

Rnd 1: start 6 sc in a magic ring [6]

Rnd 2: (sc in next st, inc in next st) repeat 3 times [9]
Change to brown yarn.

Rnd 3: sc in all 9 st [9]

Rnd 4: (sc in next 2 st, inc in next st) repeat 3 times [12]

Rnd 5: (sc in next 3 st, inc in next st) repeat 3 times [15]

Rnd 6: (sc in next 4 st, inc in next st) repeat 3 times [18]

Rnd 7: (sc in next 5 st, inc in next st) repeat 3 times [21]

Rnd 8: (sc in next 6 st, inc in next st) repeat 3 times [24]

Rnd 9: (sc in next 7 st, inc in next st) repeat 3 times [27] Change to beige yarn.
Rnd 10: (sc in next 8 st, inc in next st) repeat 3 times [30]
Rnd 11: (sc in next 4 st, inc in next st) repeat 6 times [36]
Rnd 12: (sc in next 5 st, inc in next st) repeat 6 times [42]
Rnd 13: (sc in next 6 st, inc in next st) repeat 6 times [48]
Rnd 14 – 20: sc in all 48 st [48]
Insert the safety eyes between rounds 11 and 12, with an interspace of 11 stitches.
Rnd 21: (sc in next 6 st, dec) repeat 6 times [42]
Rnd 22: (sc in next 5 st, dec) repeat 6 times [36]
Rnd 23: (sc in next 4 st, dec) repeat 6 times [30]
Rnd 24: (sc in next 3 st, dec) repeat 6 times [24]
Rnd 25: (sc in next 2 st, dec) repeat 6 times [18]
Stuff the head with fiberfill.
Rnd 26: (sc in next st, dec) repeat 6 times [12]
Rnd 27: dec 6 times [6]
Fasten off, leaving a yarn tail. Using your yarn needle, weave the yarn tail through the front loop of each remaining stitch and pull it tight to close. Weave in the yarn end.
Embroider a vertical running stitch below the nose for the mouth, using black yarn. Give the eyes a light shade using a brown pencil crayon, building up the color, using the flat side of the crayon point (picture 1).

BODY *(in beige yarn)*
Rnd 1: start 6 sc in a magic ring [6]

Rnd 2: inc in all 6 st [12]
Rnd 3: (sc in next st, inc in next st) repeat 6 times [18]
Rnd 4: (sc in next 2 st, inc in next st) repeat 6 times [24]
Rnd 5: (sc in next 3 st, inc in next st) repeat 6 times [30]
Rnd 6: (sc in next 4 st, inc in next st) repeat 6 times [36]
Rnd 7: (sc in next 5 st, inc in next st) repeat 6 times [42]
Rnd 8: (sc in next 6 st, inc in next st) repeat 6 times [48]
Rnd 9: (sc in next 7 st, inc in next st) repeat 6 times [54]
Rnd 10: (sc in next 8 st, inc in next st) repeat 6 times [60]
Rnd 11 – 17: sc in all 60 st [60]
Rnd 18: (sc in next 18 st, dec) repeat 3 times [57]
Rnd 19 – 20: sc in all 57 st [57]
Rnd 21: (sc in next 17 st, dec) repeat 3 times [54]
Rnd 22 – 23: sc in all 54 st [54]
Rnd 24: (sc in next 16 st, dec) repeat 3 times [51]
Rnd 25: sc in all 51 st [51]
Rnd 26: (sc in next 15 st, dec) repeat 3 times [48]
Rnd 27: sc in all 48 st [48]
Rnd 28: (sc in next 14 st, dec) repeat 3 times [45]
Rnd 29: sc in all 45 st [45]
Rnd 30: (sc in next 13 st, dec) repeat 3 times [42]
Rnd 31: (sc in next 12 st, dec) repeat 3 times [39]
Rnd 32: (sc in next 11 st, dec) repeat 3 times [36]
Fasten off, leaving a long tail for sewing. Stuff the body with fiberfill. Sew the body to the head between rounds 13-22.

HEAD SPINES *(in chunky multi-tone light/dark brown yarn)*
The tutorial on the loop stitch can be found on page 15. Pull the loops out to approximately 1.5" / 4 cm long.
Rnd 1: start 6 sc in a magic ring [6]
Rnd 2: loop 2 in all 6 st [12]
Rnd 3: (loop 1 in next st, loop 2 in next st) repeat 6 times [18]
Rnd 4: (loop 1 in next 2 st, loop 2 in next st) repeat 6 times [24]
Rnd 5: (loop 1 in next 3 st, loop 2 in next st) repeat 6 times [30]
Rnd 6: (loop 1 in next 4 st, loop 2 in next st) repeat 6 times [36]

Rnd 7: (loop 1 in next 5 st, loop 2 in next st) repeat 6 times [42]

Rnd 8: (loop 1 in next 6 st, loop 2 in next st) repeat 6 times [48]

Rnd 9: loop 1 in all 48 st [48]

Rnd 10: (loop 1 in next 6 st, dec) repeat 6 times [42]

Rnd 11: loop 1 in all 42 st [42]

Fasten off, leaving a long tail for sewing. Sew the piece to the top and back of the head.

BODY SPINES (in chunky multi-tone light/dark brown yarn)

Rnd 1: start 6 sc in a magic ring [6]

Rnd 2: loop 2 in all 6 st [12]

Rnd 3: (loop 1 in next st, loop 2 in next st) repeat 6 times [18]

Rnd 4: (loop 1 in next 2 st, loop 2 in next st) repeat 6 times [24]

Rnd 5: (loop 1 in next 3 st, loop 2 in next st) repeat 6 times [30]

Rnd 6: (loop 1 in next 4 st, loop 2 in next st) repeat 6 times [36]

Rnd 7: (loop 1 in next 5 st, loop 2 in next st) repeat 6 times [42]

Rnd 8: (loop 1 in next 6 st, loop 2 in next st) repeat 6 times [48]

Rnd 9: (loop 1 in next 7 st, loop 2 in next st) repeat 6 times [54]

Rnd 10: (loop 1 in next 8 st, loop 2 in next st) repeat 6 times [60]

Rnd 11 – 19: loop 1 in all 60 st [60]

Fasten off, leaving a long tail for sewing. Sew the piece to the back and underside of the body.

EAR (make 2, in brown yarn)

Rnd 1: start 6 sc in a magic ring [6]

Rnd 2: inc in all 6 st [12]

Rnd 3 – 4: sc in all 12 st [12]

Rnd 5: dec 6 times [6]

Fasten off, leaving a long tail for sewing. The ears don't need to be stuffed. Pinch the base of the ear and sew it together with a few stitches to hold the shape. Sew the ears to the sides of the head at the place where the spines start, with an interspace of 18 stitches.

TUMMY PATCH *(in cream yarn)*
Ch 9. Crochet in rows.
Row 1: start in second ch from hook, sc in next 8 st, ch 1, turn [8]
Row 2: sc in all 8 st, ch 1, turn [8]
Row 3: inc in next st, sc in next 6 st, inc in next st, ch 1, turn [10]
Row 4 – 5: sc in all 10 st, ch 1, turn [10]
Row 6: inc in next st, sc in next 8 st, inc in next st, ch 1, turn [12]
Row 7 – 8: sc in all 12 st, ch 1, turn [12]
Row 9: inc in next st, sc in next 10 st, inc in next st, ch 1, turn [14]
Row 10 – 13: sc in all 14 st, ch 1, turn [14]
Row 14: dec, sc in next 10 st, dec, ch 1, turn [12]
Row 15: dec, sc in next 8 st, dec, ch 1, turn [10]
Row 16: dec, sc in next 6 st, dec, ch 1, turn [8]
Row 17: dec, sc in next 4 st, dec [6]
Fasten off, leaving a long tail for sewing. Sew the edges of the patch to the front of the body, with the straight edge at the neck and the curved edge at the bottom.

ARM *(make 2, in brown yarn)*
Rnd 1: start 6 sc in a magic ring [6]
Rnd 2: inc in all 6 st [12]
Rnd 3: (sc in next st, inc in next st) repeat 6 times [18]
Rnd 4 – 6: sc in all 18 st [18]
Rnd 7: (sc in next st, dec) repeat 6 times [12]
Rnd 8: dec 6 times [6]
Rnd 9: inc in all 6 st [12]
Rnd 10 – 21: sc in all 12 st [12]
Fasten off, leaving a long tail for sewing. Stuff the arm with fiberfill. Sew the top of the arm closed. Embroi-der 3 long running stitches through the hand to flatten

it and create 4 fingers, using a strand of black yarn (picture 2). Sew the top of the arms to the sides of the body at the neck crease. Sew the underside of the arms to the body in the position you prefer.

FOOT *(make 2, in brown yarn)*
Rnd 1: start 6 sc in a magic ring [6]
Rnd 2: (sc in next st, inc in next st) repeat 3 times [9]
Rnd 3: (sc in next 2 st, inc in next st) repeat 3 times [12]
Rnd 4: (sc in next 3 st, inc in next st) repeat 3 times [15]
Rnd 5: (sc in next 4 st, inc in next st) repeat 3 times [18]
Rnd 6 – 8: sc in all 18 st [18]
Continue working on the toes.

First toe
Rnd 1: sc in next 6 st, skip next 12 st (creating a smaller round) [6]
Rnd 2 – 3: sc in all 6 st [6]
Stuff the foot and toe with fiberfill. Fasten off, leaving a yarn tail. Using your yarn needle, weave the yarn tail through the front loop of each remaining stitch and pull it tight to close. Weave in the yarn end.

Second toe
Leave a long starting yarn tail. Pull up a loop of brown yarn in the stitch immediately to the left of the first toe.
Rnd 1: ch 1 (this doesn't count as a st), sc in the same st where you pulled up the yarn, sc in next 2 st,

skip 6 st, sc in next 3 st (creating a smaller round) [6]
Rnd 2 – 3: sc in all 6 st [6]
Fasten off, leaving a yarn tail. Stuff the toe with fiberfill. Using your yarn needle, weave the yarn tail through the front loop of each remaining stitch and pull it tight to close. Weave in the yarn end.

Third toe
Leave a long starting yarn tail. Pull up a loop of brown yarn in the stitch immediately to the left of the second toe.
Rnd 1: ch 1 (this doesn't count as a st), sc in same st where you pulled up the yarn, sc in next 5 st [6]
Rnd 2 – 3: sc in all 6 st [6]
Fasten off, leaving a yarn tail. Stuff the toe with fiberfill. Using your yarn needle, weave the yarn tail through the front loop of each remaining stitch and pull it tight to close. Weave in the yarn end.
Sew up any gaps between the toes. Sew the feet to the lower front of the body.

SCARF *(in blue yarn)*
Ch 7. Crochet in rows.
Row 1: start in second ch from hook, sc in next 6 st, ch 1, turn [6]
Row 2: sc in all 6 st, ch 1, turn [6]
Repeat row 2 until the scarf measures approximately 23.5" / 60 cm, omitting the ch 1, turn at the end of the final row. Fasten off and weave in the yarn ends. Tie the scarf around the neck with a knot made to the side.

OTTO THE TURTLE
by Kamlin Patterns

SKILL LEVEL: ✱ ✱
SIZE: 11.5" / 30 cm tall when seated and made with the indicated yarn.
MATERIALS:
– Worsted weight yarn in green, red, brown and white
– Size G-6 / 4 mm crochet hook
– Safety eyes (20 mm)
– Black, white and brown embroidery thread
– 2 buttons for the legs
– A piece of white felt
– Yarn needle
– Pins
– Stitch marker
– Fiberfill for stuffing

EYELID *(make 2, in green yarn)*
Rnd 1: start 7 sc in a magic ring, ch 1, turn [7]
Continue crocheting in rows. When you pull the yarn tail to tighten the magic ring, make sure you leave a hole large enough to fit the post of the safety eye in later.
Row 2: inc in next st, sc in next 5 st, inc in next st, ch 1, turn [9]
Row 3 – 5: sc in all 9 st, ch 1, turn [9]
Fasten off, leaving a long tail for sewing. Cut an oval shape from the white felt and make a hole in the center. Insert the safety eye into the hole and the magic ring of the eyelid.

Rnd 11: sc in next 18 st, 2 hdc in next 3 st, sc in next 16 st, 2 hdc in next 3 st, sc in next 18 st [64]

Rnd 12: sc in next 18 st, 2 hdc in next 6 st, sc in next 16 st, 2 hdc in next 6 st, sc in next 18 st [76]

Rnd 13: sc in next 18 st, dec, sc in next 8 st, dec, sc in next 16 st, dec, sc in next 8 st, dec, sc in next 18 st [72]

Rnd 14 – 25: sc in all 72 st [72]

Rnd 26: (sc in next 10 st, dec) repeat 6 times [66]

Rnd 27: (sc in next 9 st, dec) repeat 6 times [60]

Rnd 28: (sc in next 8 st, dec) repeat 6 times [54]

Rnd 29: (sc in next 7 st, dec) repeat 6 times [48]

Rnd 30: (sc in next 6 st, dec) repeat 6 times [42]

Rnd 31: (sc in next 5 st, dec) repeat 6 times [36]

Rnd 32: (sc in next 4 st, dec) repeat 6 times [30]

Rnd 33: (sc in next 3 st, dec) repeat 6 times [24]

Insert the safety eyes with the felt pieces in round 10, where you created the 3 hdc. Stuff the head with fiberfill and continue stuffing as you go.

Rnd 34: (sc in next 2 st, dec in next st) repeat 6 times [18]

Rnd 35: (sc in next st, dec in next st) repeat 6 times [12]

Rnd 36: dec 6 times [6]

Rnd 37: dec 3 times [3]

Fasten off, leaving a long tail for sewing. Sew the corners of the eyelids to the head.

BODY *(in green yarn)*

Rnd 1: start 12 sc in a magic ring [12]

Rnd 2: (sc in next st, inc in next st) repeat 6 times [18]

Rnd 3: (sc in next 2 st, inc in next st) repeat 6 times [24]

Rnd 4: (sc in next 3 st, inc in next st) repeat 6 times [30]

Rnd 5: (sc in next 4 st, inc in next st) repeat 6 times [36]

Rnd 6: (sc in next 5 st, inc in next st) repeat 6 times [42]

Rnd 7: (sc in next 6 st, inc in next st) repeat 6 times [48]

Rnd 8: (sc in next 7 st, inc in next st) repeat 6 times [54]

Rnd 9: (sc in next 8 st, inc in next st) repeat 6 times [60]

Rnd 10: (sc in next 9 st, inc in next st) repeat 6 times [66]

Rnd 11: (sc in next 10 st, inc in next st) repeat 6 times [72]

Rnd 12: (sc in next 11 st, inc in next st) repeat 6 times [78]

Rnd 13 – 22: sc in all 78 st [78]

Rnd 23: (sc in next 11 st, dec) repeat 6 times [72]

HEAD *(in green yarn)*

Rnd 1: start 6 sc in a magic ring [6]

Rnd 2: inc in all 6 st [12]

Rnd 3: (sc in next st, inc in next st) repeat 6 times [18]

Rnd 4: (sc in next 2 st, inc in next st) repeat 6 times [24]

Rnd 5: (sc in next 3 st, inc in next st) repeat 6 times [30]

Rnd 6: (sc in next 4 st, inc in next st) repeat 6 times [36]

Rnd 7: (sc in next 5 st, inc in next st) repeat 6 times [42]

Rnd 8: (sc in next 6 st, inc in next st) repeat 6 times [48]

Rnd 9: (sc in next 7 st, inc in next st) repeat 6 times [54]

Rnd 10: sc in next 18 st, 3 hdc in next st, sc in next 16 st, 3 hdc in next st, sc in next 18 st [58]

Rnd 24 – 25: sc in all 72 st [72]
Rnd 26: (sc in next 10 st, dec) repeat 6 times [66]
Rnd 27 – 28: sc in all 66 st [66]
Rnd 29: (sc in next 9 st, dec) repeat 6 times [60]
Rnd 30 – 31: sc in all 60 st [60]
Rnd 32: (sc in next 8 st, dec) repeat 6 times [54]
Rnd 33: sc in all 54 st [54]
Rnd 34: (sc in next 7 st, dec) repeat 6 times [48]
Rnd 35: sc in all 48 st [48]
Rnd 36: (sc in next 6 st, dec) repeat 6 times [42]
Rnd 37: sc in all 42 st [42]
Rnd 38: (sc in next 5 st, dec) repeat 6 times [36]
Rnd 39: sc in all 36 st [36]
Rnd 40: (sc in next 4 st, dec) repeat 6 times [30]
Rnd 41: sc in all 30 st [30]
Rnd 42: (sc in next 3 st, dec) repeat 6 times [24]
Rnd 43 – 44: sc in all 24 st [24]
Fasten off, leaving a long tail for sewing. Stuff the body with fiberfill and sew it to the head.

ARM *(make 2, in green yarn)*
Start by making 3 fingers for each hand.

Finger *(make 3 for each hand)*
Rnd 1: start 6 sc in a magic ring [6]
Rnd 2: inc in all 6 st [12]
Rnd 3 – 6: sc in all 12 st [12]
Fasten off and weave in the yarn ends on 2 fingers. Don't fasten off on the third finger. In the next round we'll join the fingers together.

Hand and arm
Rnd 7: sc in next 6 st on the third finger, continue on the second finger, sc in next 6 st, continue on the first finger, sc in next 12 st, continue on the second fingers, sc in next 6 st, continue on the third finger, sc in next 6 st [36]
Rnd 8: sc in all 36 st [36]
Rnd 9: (sc in next 4 st, dec) repeat 6 times [30]
Rnd 10: sc in all 30 st [30]

Rnd 11: (sc in next 3 st, dec) repeat 6 times [24]
Rnd 12: (sc in next 2 st, dec) repeat 6 times [18]
Rnd 13 – 35: sc in all 18 st [18]
Fasten off, leaving a long tail for sewing. Sew the holes between the fingers closed with the leftover yarn tails. Stuff the hand and arm with fiberfill and sew them to the sides of the body.

SHOE

Upper part *(make 2, in red yarn)*
Ch 17. Stitches are worked around both sides of the foundation chain.

Rnd 1: start in third ch from hook, sc in next 14 st, 3 sc in next st. Continue on the other side of the foundation chain, sc in next 13 st, inc in next st [32]
Rnd 2: (sc in next 15 st, 3 sc in next st) repeat 2 times [36]
Rnd 3: inc in next st, sc in next 13 st, inc in next 5 st, sc in next 13 st, inc in next 4 st [46]
Rnd 4: sc in next st, inc in next st, sc in next 13 st, inc in next st, sc in next 8 st, inc in next st, sc in next 13 st, inc in next st, sc in next 7 st [50]
Rnd 5: sc in all 50 st [50]
Rnd 6: inc in next st, sc in next 15 st, inc in next 13 st, sc in next 15 st, inc in next 6 st [70]
Rnd 7 – 14: sc in all 70 st [70]
Fasten off and weave in the yarn end.

Sole *(make 2, in white yarn)*
Ch 17. Stitches are worked around both sides of the foundation chain.
Rnd 1: start in third ch from hook, sc in next 14 st, 3 sc in next st. Continue on the other side of the foundation chain. sc in next 13 st, inc in next st, slst in first st [32]
Rnd 2: (sc in next 15 st, 3 sc in next st) repeat 2 times [36]
Rnd 3: inc in next st, sc in next 13 st, inc in next 5 st, sc in next 13 st, inc in next 4 st [46]
Rnd 4: sc in next st, inc in next st, sc in next 13 st, inc in next st, sc in next 8 st, inc in next st, sc in next 13 st, inc in next st, sc in next 7 st [50]
Rnd 5: sc in all 50 st [50]
Rnd 6: inc in next st, sc in next 15 st, inc in next 13 st, sc in next 15 st, inc in next 6 st [70]
Rnd 7 – 8: sc in all 70 st [70]
Place the upper part of the shoe on top of the lower part and work the next round through both parts to join. Stuff with fiberfill before closing the seam.
Rnd 9: sc in all 70 st [70]
Fasten off and weave in the yarn end.

LEG *(make 2, in green yarn)*
Leave a long starting yarn tail. Ch 31. Join with a slst to form a ring. Make sure the ring isn't twisted.

Rnd 1 – 16: sc in all 30 st [30]
Rnd 17: (sc in next 3 st, dec) repeat 6 times [24]
Rnd 18: (sc in next 2 st, dec) repeat 6 times [18]
Rnd 19: (sc in next st, dec) repeat 6 times [12]
Rnd 20: dec 6 times [6]
Rnd 21: dec 3 times [3]
Fasten off and weave in the yarn end. Stuff the leg with fiberfill and sew the open part to the shoe.

BACK SHELL *(in brown yarn)*
Ch 12. Stitches are worked around both sides of the foundation chain.
Rnd 1: start in third ch from hook, sc in next 9 st, 3 sc in next st. Continue on the other side of the foundation chain, sc in next 8 st, inc in next st [22]
Rnd 2: inc in next st, sc in next 8 st, inc in next 3 st,

sc in next 8 st, inc in next 2 st [28]

Rnd 3: inc in next 2 st, sc in next 8 st, inc in next 6 st, sc in next 8 st, inc in next 4 st [40]

Rnd 4 – 5: sc in all 40 st [40]

Rnd 6: sc in next 2 st, (inc in next 2 st, sc in next 8 st) repeat 3 times, inc in next 2 st, sc in next 6 st [48]

Rnd 7: (inc in next 5 st, sc in next 10 st, inc in next 5 st, sc in next 4 st) repeat 2 times [68]

Rnd 8 – 10: sc in all 68 st [68]

Rnd 11: (sc in next 3 st, inc in next st) repeat 17 times [85]

Rnd 12 – 21: sc in all 85 st [85]

Rnd 22: (sc in next st, inc in next st) repeat 42 times, sc in next st [127]

Rnd 23: sc in all 127 st [127]

Fasten off, leaving a long tail for sewing. Stuff the shell with fiberfill and sew it to the body.

FRONT SHELL *(in brown yarn)*

Ch 12. Stitches are worked around both sides of the foundation chain.

Rnd 1: start in third ch from hook, sc in next 9 st, 3 sc in next st. Continue on the other side of the foundation chain, sc in next 8 st, inc in next st [22]

Rnd 2: inc in next st, sc in next 8 st, inc in next 3 st, sc in next 8 st, inc in next 2 st [28]

Rnd 3: inc in next 2 st, sc in next 8 st, inc in next 6 st, sc in next 8 st, inc in next 4 st [40]

Rnd 4 – 5: sc in all 40 st [40]

Rnd 6: sc in next 2 st, (inc in next 2 st, sc in next 8 st) repeat 3 times, inc in next 2 st, sc in next 6 st [48]

Rnd 7: (inc in next 5 st, sc in next 10 st, inc in next 5 st, sc in next 4 st) repeat 2 times [68]

Rnd 8 – 10: sc in all 68 st [68]

Fasten off, leaving a long tail for sewing. Sew the front shell to the body.

ASSEMBLY

– Using pins, decide on the placement of the legs. If you would like to make the legs movable, you can use

strong sewing thread and buttons. Sew the top center of each leg to the body at one point only. Go back and forth through the button, the leg and the body, pulling the thread tightly each time.

– Embroider the nose, the mouth and the stripes on the front shell using black embroidery thread. Embroider the stripes on the back shell using brown embroidery thread. Embroider the shoe embellishments and the shoe laces using white embroidery thread.

LIL QUACK THE DUCK

by Little Muggles (Amy Lin)

HEAD (in white yarn)

Rnd 1: start 6 sc in a magic ring [6]

Rnd 2: inc in all 6 st [12]

Rnd 3: (sc in next st, inc in next st) repeat 6 times [18]

Rnd 4: (sc in next 2 st, inc in next st) repeat 6 times [24]

Rnd 5: sc in all 24 st [24]

Rnd 6: (sc in next 3 st, inc in next st) repeat 6 times [30]

Rnd 7: (sc in next 4 st, inc in next st) repeat 6 times [36]

Rnd 8: (sc in next 5 st, inc in next st) repeat 6 times [42]

Rnd 9: (sc in next 6 st, inc in next st) repeat 6 times [48]

Rnd 10 – 11: sc in all 48 st [48]

Rnd 12: (sc in next 7 st, inc in next st) repeat 6 times [54]

Rnd 13 – 14: sc in all 54 st [54]

Rnd 15: (sc in next 7 st, dec) repeat 6 times [48]

Rnd 16: sc in all 48 st [48]

Rnd 17: (sc in next 6 st, dec) repeat 6 times [42]

Rnd 18: (sc in next 5 st, dec) repeat 6 times [36]

Rnd 19: (sc in next 4 st, dec) repeat 6 times [30]

Insert the safety eyes between rounds 11 and 12 with an interspace of 8 stitches. Stuff the head with fiberfill and continue stuffing as you go.

Rnd 20: (sc in next 3 st, dec) repeat 6 times [24]

Rnd 21: (sc in next 2 st, dec) repeat 6 times [18]

Fasten off, leaving a long tail for sewing.

DUCK BILL (in orange yarn)

Ch 6. Stitches are worked around both sides of the

SKILL LEVEL: ★

SIZE: 7" / 17 cm tall when made with the indicated yarn.

MATERIALS:

– Worsted weight yarn in white, blue and orange

– Size G-6 / 4 mm crochet hook

– Safety eyes (9 mm)

– Stitch marker

– Yarn needle

– Fiberfill for stuffing

AMIGURUMI GALLERY

Scan or visit
www.amigurumi.com/109
to share pictures and find inspiration.

foundation chain.

Rnd 1: start in second ch from hook, sc in next 4 st, inc in next st. Continue on the other side of the foundation chain, sc in next 4 st, inc in next st [12]

Rnd 2 – 3: sc in all 12 st [12]

Fasten off, leaving a long tail for sewing. Stuff the bill lightly with fiberfill. Sew the duck bill to the head over rounds 13-15.

HAT *(start in blue yarn)*

Rnd 1: start 6 sc in a magic ring [6]

Rnd 2: inc in all 6 st [12]

Rnd 3: (sc in next st, inc in next st) repeat 6 times [18]

Rnd 4: sc in all 18 st [18]

Rnd 5: (sc in next 2 st, inc in next st) repeat 6 times [24]

Rnd 6: sc in all 24 st [24]

Rnd 7: (sc in next 3 st, inc in next st) repeat 6 times [30]

Rnd 8: sc in all 30 st [30]

Rnd 9: (sc in next 4 st, inc in next st) repeat 6 times [36]

Rnd 10: sc in all 36 st [36]

Change to white yarn.

Rnd 11: sc in all 36 st [36]

Fasten off and weave in the yarn ends. Take the hat and push the top part in with your finger. Flip it upside down to make a cute little sailor hat. The brim will show the white edging.

BODY *(in white yarn)*

Rnd 1: start 6 sc in a magic ring [6]

Rnd 2: inc in all 6 st [12]

Rnd 3: (sc in next st, inc in next st) repeat 6 times [18]

Rnd 4: (sc in next 2 st, inc in next st) repeat 6 times [24]

Rnd 5: (sc in next 3 st, inc in next st) repeat 6 times [30]

Rnd 6: sc in all 30 st [30]

Rnd 7: (sc in next 4 st, inc in next st) repeat 6 times [36]

Rnd 8: (sc in next 5 st, inc in next st) repeat 6 times [42]

Rnd 9 – 10: sc in all 42 st [42]

Rnd 11: (sc in next 6 st, inc in next st) repeat 6 times [48]

Rnd 12: sc in all 48 st [48]

Rnd 13: (sc in next 6 st, dec) repeat 6 times [42]

Rnd 14: sc in all 42 st [42]

Stuff the body with fiberfill and continue stuffing as you go.

Rnd 15: (sc in next 5 st, dec) repeat 6 times [36]

Rnd 16: (sc in next 4 st, dec) repeat 6 times [30]

Rnd 17: (sc in next 3 st, dec) repeat 6 times [24]

Rnd 18: (sc in next 2 st, dec) repeat 6 times [18]

Rnd 19 – 20: sc in all 18 st [18]

Fasten off, leaving a long tail for sewing. Sew the head to the body.

SAILOR SHAWL

Main body *(start in blue yarn)*

Ch 14. Crochet in rows.

Row 1: start in second ch from hook, sc in next 13 st, ch 1, turn [13]

Row 2 – 4: sc in all 13 st, ch 1, turn [13]

Change to white yarn.

Row 5: sc in all 13 st [13]

Fasten off and weave in the yarn ends.

Arm *(make 2, in blue yarn)*
Ch 19. Crochet in rows.
Row 1: start in second ch from hook, sc in next 18 st, ch 1, turn [18]
Row 2: sc in next 6 st [6] Leave the remaining stitches unworked.
Fasten off and weave in the yarn ends. Sew the arms of the shawl to the main body of the shawl (the side with the shorter row faces out) (picture 1).

WING *(make 2, in white yarn)*
Rnd 1: start 6 sc in a magic ring
Rnd 2: inc in all 6 st [12]
Rnd 3: (sc in next st, inc in next st) repeat 6 times [18]
Rnd 4: sc in all 18 st [18]
Rnd 5: (sc in next st, dec) repeat 6 times [12]
Rnd 6: (sc in next st, dec) repeat 4 times [8]
Fasten off, leaving a long tail for sewing. Sew the wings to the sides of the body at 3 rounds below the neck.

FOOT *(make 2, in orange yarn)*
Ch 5. Stitches are worked around both sides of the foundation chain.
Rnd 1: start in second ch from hook, sc in next 3 st, inc in next st. Continue on the other side of the foundation chain, sc in next 3 st, inc in next st [10]
Rnd 2: (sc in next st, inc in next st, sc in next 2 st, inc in next st) repeat 2 times [14]
Rnd 3: sc in next st, inc in next st, sc in next 4 st, inc in next st, sc in next 2 st, inc in next st, sc in next

3 st, inc in next st [18]
Rnd 4: (sc in next 3 st, inc in next st) repeat 3 times, sc in next 5 st, inc in next st [22]
Rnd 5: sc in all 22 st [22]
Rnd 6: sc in next 9 st, dec, (sc in next st, dec) repeat 2 times, sc in next 5 st [19]
Rnd 7: sc in next 7 st, dec, (sc in next st, dec) repeat 2 times, sc in next 4 st [16]
Rnd 8: sc in next 6 st, dec, (sc in next st, dec) repeat 2 times, sc in next 2 st [13]
Rnd 9: sc in next 7 st, (dec, sc in next st) repeat 2 times [11]
Rnd 10: (sc in next 2 st, dec) repeat 2 times, sc in next 3 st [9]
Rnd 11: sc in all 9 st [9]
Fasten off, leaving a long tail for sewing. Sew the feet to the body. Tie the shawl around the neck.

REGGIE THE MOUSE

by Kristi Tullus

SKILL LEVEL: ✶ ✶

SIZE: 10" / 25 cm tall when made with the indicated yarn.

MATERIALS:

– Light worsted weight yarn in gray, orange and pink (leftover)
– Size C-2 / 2.75 mm crochet hook
– Safety eyes (9 mm)
– Button (12 mm)
– Yarn needle
– Stitch marker
– Fiberfill for stuffing

AMIGURUMI GALLERY

Scan or visit
www.amigurumi.com/907
to share pictures and find inspiration.

HEAD *(in gray yarn)*

Rnd 1: start 6 sc in a magic ring [6]

Rnd 2: inc in all 6 st [12]

Rnd 3: (sc in next st, inc in next st) repeat 6 times [18]

Rnd 4: (inc in next st, sc in next 2 st) repeat 6 times [24]

Rnd 5: (sc in next 3 st, inc in next st) repeat 6 times [30]

Rnd 6: sc in next st, inc in next st, (sc in next 4 st, inc in next st) repeat 5 times, sc in next 3 st [36]

Rnd 7: (sc in next 5 st, inc in next st) repeat 6 times [42]

Rnd 8: sc in next 2 st, inc in next st, (sc in next 6 st, inc in next st) repeat 5 times, sc in next 4 st [48]

Rnd 9: (sc in next 7 st, inc in next st) repeat 6 times [54]

Rnd 10 – 18: sc in all 54 st [54]

Rnd 19: (sc in next 7 st, dec) repeat 6 times [48]

Rnd 20: sc in next 9 st, dec, (sc in next 2 st, dec) repeat 6 times, sc in next 11 st, dec [40]

Mark the 16th stitch of round 21 as a guide to place the eyes later.

Rnd 21: sc in next 4 st, dec, sc in next 8 st, dec, sc in next 6 st, dec, sc in next 9 st, dec, sc in next 5 st [36]

Rnd 22: sc in next 9 st, dec, (sc in next 5 st, dec) repeat 2 times, sc in next 11 st [33]

Rnd 23: sc in next 3 st, dec, sc in next 23 st, dec, sc in next 3 st [31]

Rnd 24: dec, sc in next 13 st, dec, sc in next 14 st [29]

Insert the safety eyes to either side of the stitch

marker, between rounds 21 and 22, with an interspace of 11 stitches. Stuff the head with fiberfill and continue stuffing as you go.

Rnd 25: sc in next 7 st, dec, sc in next 9 st, dec, sc in next 9 st [27]

Rnd 26: sc in next 9 st, dec, sc in next 4 st, dec, sc in next 10 st [25]

Rnd 27: sc in next 11 st, dec, sc in next 10 st, dec [23]

Rnd 28: sc in next 6 st, dec, sc in next 8 st, dec, sc in next 5 st [21]

Rnd 29: sc in next 8 st, dec, sc in next 2 st, dec, sc in next 7 st [19]

Rnd 30: sc in next 4 st, dec, sc in next 9 st, dec, sc in next 2 st [17]

Rnd 31: dec, sc in next 6 st, dec, sc in next 7 st [15]

Rnd 32: sc in next 4 st, dec, sc in next 3 st, dec, sc in next 4 st [13]

Rnd 33: dec 6 times, sc in next st [7]

Fasten off, leaving a yarn tail. Using your yarn needle, weave the yarn tail through the front loop of each

remaining stitch and pull it tight to close. Weave in the yarn end.

NOSE *(in pink yarn)*
Rnd 1: start 6 sc in a magic ring [6]
Rnd 2: (inc in next st, sc in next st) repeat 3 times [9]
Rnd 3: sc in next 7 st, dec [8]
Fasten off, leaving a long tail for sewing. Stuff the nose firmly with fiberfill. Sew the nose to the head.

BODY *(in gray yarn)*
Rnd 1: start 6 sc in a magic ring [6]
Rnd 2: inc in all 6 st [12]
Rnd 3: (sc in next st, inc in next st) repeat 6 times [18]
Rnd 4: (inc in next st, sc in next 2 st) repeat 6 times [24]
Rnd 5: (sc in next 2 st, inc in next st) repeat 8 times [32]
Rnd 6: sc in next 5 st, inc in next st, sc in next 15 st, inc in next st, sc in next 10 st [34]
Rnd 7 – 12: sc in all 34 st [34]
Rnd 13: (dec, sc in next 15 st) repeat 2 times [32]
Rnd 14: sc in next 8 st, dec, sc in next 14 st, dec, sc in next 6 st [30]
Rnd 15: sc in next 4 st, dec, sc in next 13 st, dec, sc in next 9 st [28]
Stuff the body with fiberfill and continue stuffing as you go.
Rnd 16: sc in all 28 st [28]
Rnd 17: sc in next 5 st, dec, (sc in next 7 st, dec) repeat 2 times, sc in next 3 st [25]
Rnd 18: (sc in next 6 st, dec) repeat 3 times, sc in next st [22]
Rnd 19: (sc in next 3 st, dec) repeat 4 times, sc in next 2 st [18]
Rnd 20: sc in all 18 st [18]
Fasten off, leaving a long tail for sewing. Sew the head to the body between rounds 13 and 17 of the head.

ARM *(make 2, in gray yarn)*
Rnd 1: start 6 sc in a magic ring [6]
Rnd 2: inc in all 6 st [12]

Rnd 3: (sc in next 2 st, inc in next st) repeat 4 times [16]

Rnd 4 – 6: sc in all 16 st [16]

Rnd 7: (dec, sc in next 2 st) repeat 4 times [12]

Rnd 8: (sc in next 2 st, dec) repeat 3 times [9]

Stuff the arm with fiberfill and continue stuffing as you go. Stuff the upper part of the arm only lightly.

Rnd 9: sc in all 9 st [9]

Rnd 10: sc in next 4 st, dec, sc in next 3 st [8]

Rnd 11 – 20: sc in all 8 st [8]

Flatten the opening of the arm and work the next round through both layers to close.

Rnd 21: sc in next 4 st [4]

Fasten off, leaving a long tail for sewing. Sew the arms to the sides of the body, one row below the head.

LEG *(make 2, in gray yarn)*

Rnd 1: start 6 sc in a magic ring [6]

Rnd 2: inc in all 6 st [12]

Rnd 3: (sc in next st, inc in next st) repeat 6 times [18]

Rnd 4: (sc in next 3 st, inc in next st) repeat 4 times, sc in next 2 st [22]

Rnd 5 – 8: sc in all 22 st [22]

Rnd 9: (sc in next 5 st, dec) repeat 3 times, sc in next st [19]

Rnd 10: sc in next 2 st, dec, sc in next 9 st, dec, sc in next 4 st [17]

Rnd 11: sc in next 4 st, dec, sc in next 3 st, dec, sc in next 6 st [15]

Rnd 12 – 13: sc in all 15 st [15]

Stuff the feet firmly with fiberfill. Continue crocheting in rows.

Row 14: sc in next 7 st, ch 1, turn [7] Leave the remaining stitches unworked

Row 15: skip next 2 st, sc in next 10 st, ch 1, turn [10]

Row 16: skip next 2 st, sc in next 8 st, ch 1, turn [8]

Row 17: skip next 2 st, sc in next 6 st, ch 1, turn [6]

Row 18: skip next 2 st, sc in next st, dec, sc in next st [3] (picture 1)

Move the stitch marker to the last stitch, this will be the new end of the round. Continue crocheting in rounds.

Rnd 19: work 4 sc down the row-ends, 3 sc across the

skipped stitches from row 14, 4 sc up the other side
of row-ends and 3 sc back across the top [14] (pictures
2-3)

Rnd 20: sc in next 12 st, dec [13]
Stuff the leg lightly with fiberfill and continue stuffing
as you go.

Rnd 21: sc in next 5 st, dec, sc in next 6 st [12]

Rnd 22 – 23: sc in all 12 st [12]

Rnd 24: dec, sc in next 10 st [11]

Rnd 25 – 26: sc in all 11 st [11]

Rnd 27: dec, sc in next 9 st [10]

Rnd 28 – 37: sc in all 10 st [10]

Rnd 38: (sc in next st, dec) repeat 3 times,
sc in next st [7]
Fasten off, leaving a long tail for sewing.
Sew the legs just above round 5, slightly to the
front of the body, with an interspace of 6 stitches.

TAIL (in gray yarn)

Rnd 1: start 6 sc in a magic ring [6]

Rnd 2 – 31: sc in all 6 st [6]
Fasten off, leaving a long tail for sewing. The tail
doesn't need to be stuffed. Sew the tail to the lower
back, just above round 5.

EAR (make 2, in gray yarn)

Rnd 1: start 6 sc in a magic ring [6]

Rnd 2: inc in all 6 st [12]

Rnd 3: (sc in next st, inc in next st) repeat 6 times [18]

Rnd 4: (sc in next 3 st, inc in next st) repeat 4 times,
sc in next 2 st [22]

Rnd 5: sc in next 2 st, inc in next st, (sc in next 4 st,

inc in next st) repeat 3 times, sc in next 4 st [26]

Rnd 6: (sc in next 5 st, inc in next st) repeat 4 times, sc in next 2 st [30]

Rnd 7 – 8: sc in all 30 st [30]

Rnd 9: (sc in next 3 st, dec) repeat 6 times [24]

Rnd 10: (dec, sc in next 2 st) repeat 6 times [18]

Rnd 11: (sc in next st, dec 4 times) repeat 2 times [10]

Fasten off, leaving a long tail for sewing. The ears don't need to be stuffed. Flatten the ears and sew them to round 13 of the head, with an interspace of 14 to 16 stitches.

VEST (in orange yarn)

Ch 12. Crochet in rows.

Row 1: start in third ch from hook, hdc in all 10 st, ch 2, turn [10]

Row 2 – 4: BLO hdc in next 10 st, ch 2, turn [10]

Row 5 – 6: BLO hdc in next 4 st, ch 2, turn [4]

Row 7: BLO hdc in next 4 st, ch 6, ch 2, turn [4 + 6 ch]

Row 8: (skip the 2 turning ch) BLO hdc in next 6 ch, hdc in next 4 st, ch 2, turn [10]

Row 9 – 14: BLO hdc in next 10 st, ch 2, turn [10]

Row 15 – 16: BLO hdc in next 4 st, ch 2, turn [4]

Row 17: BLO hdc in next 4 st, ch 6, ch 2, turn [4 + 6 ch]

Row 18: (skip the 2 turning ch) BLO hdc in next 6 ch, hdc in next 4 st, ch 2, turn [10]

Row 19 – 21: BLO hdc in next 10 st, ch 2, turn [10]

Row 22: sc in next 4 st, ch 5, skip next st, sc in next 5 st [9 + 5 ch]

Fasten off. Fold the sides to the center and make a few stitches to the top corners, creating shoulder seams (pictures 4-5). Put the vest on and sew the button opposite the buttonhole (picture 6). Weave in the yarn ends.

Designers who contributed to this book

ELISA'S CROCHET — United States — For Elisa, crocheting is a way to translate memories, ideas and emotions into something she can share with those she cares about.
▷ www.amigurumi.com/shop/Elisas-crochet/

CROCHETBYKIM — Sweden — Kim made her very first amigurumis as Christmas gifts, and it ended up becoming her favorite hobby. She works as a 911 dispatcher and is very pleased to combine this intense work with the creative outlet that crocheting is.
▷ www.amigurumi.com/shop/Crochetbykim/

LITTLE MUGGLES — United States — Amy finds crocheting to be super fun and thoroughly relaxing. After discovering the amazing world of amigurumi, she started designing her own dolls, learning something new with each one she creates.
▷ www.amigurumi.com/shop/Little-Muggles/

IRENE STRANGE — United Kingdom — Irina is a graphic designer and amigurumi-maker with a ball of yarn and a few crochet hooks as permanent handbag residents. What was first a quick fix birthday gift fast became her crochet obsession.
▷ www.amigurumi.com/shop/Irene-Strange/

LEMON YARN CREATIONS — Portugal — Andreia enjoys creating characters with funny stories, mostly inspired by nature and her love of pop culture. Amigurumi are her way of bringing happiness to the world.
▷ www.amigurumi.com/shop/Lemon-Yarn-Creations/

DIY FLUFFIES — The Netherlands — When Mariska's sons leave for school and her husband goes off to work, she gets behind the sewing machine and picks up her crochet hook. With her boundless imagination, she makes the coolest patterns for stuffies!
▷ www.amigurumi.com/shop/DIY-Fluffies/

SUNDOT ATTACK — Australia — An avid animal lover, Jhak uses her designs to spread love, appreciation and respect for these cute critters. Crochet is more than a hobby to her, it has the power to heal, inspire and connect, and create new things that reach all the way to your (limitless) imagination!
▷ www.amigurumi.com/shop/Sundot-Attack/

KAMLIN PATTERNS – The Czech Republic – Katka can create almost anything using her crochet hook and a ball of yarn. She inspired hundreds of people to pick up a crochet hook and create a handmade toy.
▷ www.amigurumi.com/shop/Kamlin-Patterns/

PEPIKA – Bosnia-Herzegovina – Sanda is a graphic designer and in her spare time she loves to play with yarn and hook. She looks for cute shapes in nature and transforms them into amigurumis. Her daughter Mia is her main inspiration!
▷ www.amigurumi.com/shop/Pepika/

AIRALI DESIGN – Italy – Ilaria spends several hours of the day with a crochet hook and yarn in her hands. Amigurumi are her first and greatest love. After giving it a try, it's impossible to resist making these funny characters.
▷ www.amigurumi.com/shop/Airali-handmade/

ZIPZIPDREAMS – Turkey / Hungary – Edina lives in Turkey, far away from her home country Hungary. Thanks to amigurumi she met crochet friends from all around the world who share her passion and join her in the amigurumi happiness.
▷ www.amigurumi.com/shop/zipzipdreams/

MOJI-MOJI DESIGN – United Kingdom – Janine has been passionate about textiles of all kinds ever since she can remember. Knitting and crochet are now her full-time occupations. She has more wool in her stash than she could ever possibly use.
▷ www.amigurumi.com/shop/Moji-Moji-Design/

PICA PAU – Argentina – Yan first began combining her drawings with crochet while waiting to pick up her son from school. Years later she has illustrated a children's book, designed for stop-motion animations and written several crochet books.
▷ www.amigurumi.com/shop/Pica-Pau/

LISA JESTES DESIGNS – United States – Lisa loves to crochet. She feels it's a joy to start with a simple ball of yarn and to make it into a cute plush toy.
▷ www.amigurumi.com/shop/Lisa-Jestes/

LITTLEAQUAGIRL – Australia – Erinna is a scientist by day and a crochet lover by night. She loves soft colors and 'kawaii' characters. Her amigurumi score high on the scale of cuteness.
▷ www.amigurumi.com/shop/LittleAquaGirl/

PATCHWORK MOOSE – United Kingdom – Kate makes the cutest little crochet creatures to brighten up your day. Amigurumi has drawn her into crochet. She saw these adorable little creatures and knew she had to learn to make them herself.
▷ www.amigurumi.com/shop/Patchwork-Moose/

AMALOU DESIGNS – Germany – Marielle loves trying something new, from using a piece of felt or fabric in her crochet amigurumi to trying new techniques like needle felting. The smile of a child holding her creation is her greatest motivation!
▷ www.amigurumi.com/shop/AmalouDesigns/

KRISTI TULLUS – Estonia – In her search for the ultimate personalized gift for a newborn, Kristi discovered amigurumi. Through her designs she wants to inspire others to (re)discover crochet.
▷ www.amigurumi.com/shop/Kristi-Tullus/

YOUNIQUE CRAFTS – United States – Noah always loved every kind of art, from doodling in a sketch book to writing original music. But crocheting offers him something different from every other art form: it gives him the ability to create an inanimate object and yet give it a character and personality that reflects himself.
▷ www.amigurumi.com/shop/YOUnique-crafts/

A MORNING CUP OF JO CREATIONS – United States – Josephine treasures the journey, enjoys the little things in life, and embraces the ability to connect and inspire through her amigurumi.
▷ www.amigurumi.com/shop/A-Morning-Cup-of-Jo-Creations/

Our gratitude goes towards all other designers who joined us in the Zoomigurumi series:
Ana Yogui – Susan Morishita – Tilda & Filur – Lilleliis – Pii_Chii – Footloosefriend – Sarsel – AmiAmore – Auroragurumi – Jessica Boyer – Emi Kanesada – Sweet 'n Cute Creations – Bluephone Studios – Woolytoons – IlDikko – Los Sospechosos – Christel Krukkert – One and Two Company – Theresa's Crochet Shop – Elfin Thread – An Jiyoun – Critterbeans – Smartapple Creations – Hello Yellow Yarn – Sabrina Somers – Lilian Miller – Maja Hansen – Lex In Stitches – YarnWave – RNata

Descabdello

Jessica Liu

Annamária Majláth

Vira Velmozhna

Hannah Lucas

Katerina Savchuk

Sonja Meier

Adrienn Wéber

Irene Morazzoni

Katrien Sprangers

Angie Vega

Sonja Meier

Marjan van der Leer

Wendie Van Roy

Julie Jacquemin

Carolina Otero

We've had the honor of being part of your creative journey these past 10 years.
We love discovering what you make with the patterns from our Zoomigurumi books!

Scan or visit **www.amigurumi.com/3800/**
to share pictures of the creations you made with
patterns from this book or find inspiration in
characters made by others.

ZOOMIGURUMI

The first volume in the popular Zoomigurumi series brings together a delightful collection of 15 cute and cuddly amigurumi animal patterns. With Johnny the monkey, Wasabi the bunny, Roary the tiger and many others.

ISBN 978-949164-300-2

ZOOMIGURUMI 2

This second collection of projects provides all the inspiration you need to keep you crocheting! With Otto the turtle, Humphrey the elephant, Manfred the mouse and many others.

ISBN 978-949164-302-6

ZOOMIGURUMI 3

Just when you thought amigurumi couldn't get any cuter, along comes Zoomigurumi 3! This volume features new amigurumi animal patterns from 12 top designers. Includes Henry the hippo, Wilbur the penguin, Orion the turtle …

ISBN 978-949164-303-3

ZOOMIGURUMI 4

You'll fall head over heels with the animals in this fourth Zoomigurumi book! With Hector the horse, Orwell the orangutan, Doris the dolphin and many others.

ISBN 978-949164-306-4

ZOOMIGURUMI 5

The fifth edition in the Zoomigurumi series contains the sweetest new projects by the Zoomigurumi designers. You'll find Scout the puppy, Alicia the alpaca, Caterino the Walrus …

ISBN 978-949164-309-5

ZOOMIGURUMI 6

Fans know the sixth book in the series assembles 15 amazing new projects. With Mortimer the mammoth, Carlos the hummingbird, Manu and Brigitte the dachshunds, Alvin the hedgehog and many more.

ISBN 978-949164-314-9

ZOOMIGURUMI 7

This book in the Zoomigurumi series follows the trail of 15 adorable amigurumi. Come along with Monty the moose, Hamish the hamster, Cheryl the chicken and many more.

ISBN 978-949164-321-7

ZOOMIGURUMI 8

You can never have enough amigurumi friends! This collection of projects provides all the inspiration you need to keep you crocheting! Meet Sammy the seal, Pablo the parrot or Milo the hummingbird!

ISBN 978-949164-328-6

ZOOMIGURUMI 9

The 15 adorable animals in this collection will bring you lots of fresh inspiration and will make a big splash in your yarn stash. You'll discover Hilda the highland cow, Toco the toucan, Angie the anglerfish and lots of others!

ISBN 978-949164-334-7

ZOOMIGURUMI 10

Just when you thought you'd rest your crochet hook and yarn for a second, along comes Zoomigurumi 10! Meet Bao the giraffe, Ruff the squirrel, Max the mouse and many more!

ISBN 978-949164-338-5